Medieval Culture and the Mexican American Borderlands

NUMBER SIX:

RIO GRANDE / RÍO BRAVO

BORDERLANDS CULTURE AND TRADITIONS

NORMA E. CANTÚ, GENERAL EDITOR

Medieval Culture and the Mexican American Borderlands

MILO KEARNEY and
MANUEL MEDRANO

Texas A&M University Press
College Station

First edition

The paper used in this book meets the minimum requirements of the American National Standard for Permanence of Paper for Printed Library Materials, Z39.48–1984. Binding materials have been chosen for durability.
∞

Library of Congress Cataloging-in-Publication Data

Kearney, Milo.
Medieval culture and the Mexican American borderlands / Milo Kearney and Manuel Medrano.—1st ed.
p. cm. — (Rio Grande/ Río Bravo ; no. 6)
Includes bibliographical references and index.
ISBN 1-58544-132-5 (cloth : alk. paper)
1. Mexican-American Border Region—Civilization. 2. United States—Relations—Mexico. 3. Mexico—Relations—United States. 4. United States—Civilization—English influences. 5. Mexico—Civilization—Spanish influences. 6. England—Civilization—1066–1485. 7. Spain—Civilization—711–1516. 8. Middle Ages. 9. England—Relations—Spain. 10. Spain—Relations—England. I. Medrano, Manuel, 1949– II. Title. III. Series.

F787 .K435 2001
972′.1—dc21 2001002736

This book is dedicated to our wives, our joy,
Vivian Kearney and Chavela Medrano;
to our children, our pride,
Kathleen and Danny Anzak,
Sean and Lisa Kearney, and
Noe, Estevan, and Daniel Medrano;
and to Jesus Christ,
our whole hope and only strength.

CONTENTS

ACKNOWLEDGMENTS

The research for this book was facilitated by a grant from the University of Texas at Brownsville. We would like to thank Professor Fred Cazel of the University of Connecticut, Professor David Vassberg of the University of Texas–Pan American, Professor Donald Chipman of the University of North Texas, the late Professor Américo Paredes of the University of Texas at Austin, our colleagues at the University of Texas at Brownsville, including Professors Harriet Denise Joseph, Will Stephenson, Mimosa Stephenson, Tony Knopp, Jim Sullivan, George Green, Cipriano Cardenas, Lidia Díaz, Tony Zavaleta, and Joe Zavaletta, as well as librarians Tom LaFleur, Doug Ferrier, John Hawthorne, Yolanda Gonzalez, and Luisa Serna, staff members Isabel de la Torre and Carmen Gonzalez, and work-study students Diana Rosales and Janie Balboa for their encouragement, suggestions, and help.

Thanks go also to several students in Milo Kearney's graduate seminar on this topic at the University of Texas at Brownsville for their ideas and suggestions made in discussions and in research projects in a number of fields: Rosa Higareda (folklore), Matthew John (architecture), Patricia John (food and food preparation), James Keillor (law), Elias Rodriguez (Christianity), Laura Sikes (government), William Velto (witchcraft), and Christopher Wilson (ranching).

We are also grateful to Milo Kearney's son, Sean, son-in-law, Danny Anzak, and daughter-in-law, Lisa, for helping us with (sometimes very nocturnal) computer problems, to his daughter, Kathleen Anzak, for aiding with photocopying chores and for locating materials in the libraries of the University of Texas at Austin, and most of all to his loving and beloved wife, Vivian, for her cheerful research assistance, editorial diligence, and insightful suggestions.

Medieval Culture and the Mexican American Borderlands

INTRODUCTION

This book is based on three interlinking theses. First, it asserts that the culture of the Mexican-American Borderlands, the zone of mixed Anglo and Hispanic culture extending north from the U.S.–Mexican border to a shifting northern limit, cannot be fully understood without knowledge of its medieval underpinnings in both Castile and in England. Indeed, pre-Castilian Spain and pre-English Britain lie below these undergirdings in supportive roles. Second, it attempts to demonstrate that certain parallels in the medieval evolution of Hispanic and Anglo societies make the two cultures much more closely related than is often remembered (a commonality that went beyond the participation of Castile and England in general medieval culture and in many ways set their two histories apart from those of other European societies). This is true despite the many differences that have added to the richness of border culture. Third, the book shows how, despite the similarities, the origins of Anglo-Hispanic mutual tensions and misunderstandings also trace back to the Middle Ages (before Bartolomé de las Casas and the origin of the "Black Legend"). In exploring these three theses, this study will emphasize the premodern European sources of various Borderlands cultural phenomena rather than elaborating on the Borderlands itself.

A better understanding of the Borderlands' medieval roots might draw its Hispanic and Anglo societies closer together. Many studies have dwelt on the early modern and modern periods of Anglo-Hispanic conflict and their divergent paths. A look at the earlier period in which the two groups had more in common, along with an understanding of how problems first arose between them, might help to boost mutual understanding. This is not to argue that the intervening centuries and the non-European influences have been unimportant in shaping the nature of Anglos and Hispanics and their interrelationship in the Borderlands. It merely affirms that no matter how far away one gets from an early setting, and however much it may have been forgotten, a reminder of that past can always serve in the role of self-knowledge. Borderlanders seem to feel instinctively that this is the case. A local thirst for such knowledge is suggested by regular inclusion of a feature entitled "Root Search" in the *Vista* magazine of Freedom newspapers in the U.S. Southwest, which gives the historical background on Hispanic names. Also expressing this interest is Nash Candelaria's novel *Memories of the Alhambra* (1977), with its Mexican American protagonist who travels to Spain in search of his most distant genealogy.

The significance of the medieval roots of American society has been the subject of some controversy. One school of thought stresses the medieval basis of Western civilization in general and of the cultures of the United States and Mexico in particular. Most notably, Lynn White's seminal article "Legacy of the Middle Ages in the American Wild West" makes this case for the United States as does Luis Weckmann's *La herencia medieval de México* for Mexico. Another school of thought questions the pertinence of the Middle Ages to American society. Owen Ulph argues that, although such an approach can be meaningful, medieval European influences on America are no more significant than those transmitted from other times and places. Even if true, this notion should not diminish the importance of the heritage from any one of various sources. If the medieval roots are important for an understanding of the United States and Mexico, how much more vital must they be for the Borderlands, where Mexican and American societies overlap. This study addresses a lack of focus on the specifically medieval developments that helped to shape Mexican-American border culture.

Although this book is not primarily a linguistic study, we should note that the Borderlands' two dominant languages, English and Spanish, represent perhaps the most obvious of the medieval influences on the

Mexican-American Borderlands. Speech is a powerful conveyor of social heritage, influencing each participant in a direction that may or may not coincide with genetic ancestry. All Borderlanders of whatever race, immersed as they are in an English and Spanish linguistic milieu, function in a culture that traces in part back to the societies in which those languages were first formed. Just as a psychiatrist may investigate a person's early childhood to clarify current issues in that patient's life, so the study of a society's linguistic ancestors may clarify some of its most basic current characteristics. Similar arguments can be made for the pertinence of the medieval past to other aspects of Borderlands culture.

Studies of the roots of Mexican-American Borderlands society have tended to emphasize one particular ethnic heritage or another. The nineteenth century view was often influenced by the aforementioned "Black Legend," which deprecated Hispanic influence and accused it of encouraging fanaticism, superstition, corruption, laziness, authoritarianism, and cowardliness. Hispanics retaliated by describing Anglos as materialistic, irreligious, and unconcerned with beauty. In the early twentieth century, Herbert Eugene Bolton, professor at the University of California at Berkeley from 1911 to 1953, emphasized the positive features of the Spanish roots of the culture of the U.S. Southwest. He noted that Castilian influence is stronger in the U.S.-Mexican border region than it is in interior Mexico, since *el norte* was less populated with Indians when Spanish settlers arrived. In contrast, Walter Prescott Webb of the University of Texas at Austin praised the Anglo contribution to the U.S. Southwest as more conducive to work, material progress, organization, and freedom than the Hispanic heritage. Since World War II, Carey McWilliams (*North from Mexico,* 1948), David Weber (*The Spanish Frontier in North America,* 1992), and Rodolfo Acuña (*Occupied America,* 1972) have focused attention on the Mexican and Indian roots of the region. In addition, David Montejano of the University of Texas at Austin in his 1987 book *Anglos and Mexicans in the Making of Texas, 1836–1986* traces the history of Anglo prejudices against Hispanics.

With differences between the two groups so frequently stressed, Borderlands residents with a Hispanic ancestral heritage have often been viewed as being distinct in culture from those with an Anglo blood line. Such a perspective was once supported by a sharply defined, ghetto-like demarcation of social boundaries in the region. The tendency of new immigrants, whether from Minnesota or Guanajuato, to move in homogenous social circles fed the pattern. However, Borderlanders are gradually integrating Hispanic and Anglo ethnic groups into a new bilingual and bicultural entity that transcends its two components. Increasingly, individual members of Borderlands society, whatever their family background, are becoming cultural descendants of both the Castilian conquistador and the Anglo-Saxon seafarer (as well as of the Indian brave, the Mexican ranchero, and the American pioneer farmer). Once again, language usage offers a case in point. Item 12, Section 8 of the Constitution of the State of New Mexico, adopted on January 21, 1911, specifies that the legislature provide for training of bilingual English-Spanish teachers to qualify them to teach Spanish-speaking students. Many Spanish words were adopted into English in the nineteenth century, in part through the border area. The assimilation of English with Spanish speech and of Hispanic with Anglo traits in the mixed culture termed *pochismo* has brought contrasting values and characteristics into play within families and even within individuals. *Pachuco* slang, invented by gangs in El Paso in the 1930s and subsequently spreading west to Arizona and Los Angeles, likewise mingles anglicisms with Mexican influences and invents new terms on a Spanish base. The resulting tug-of-war between the two languages is most clearly manifested in "code switching" or "flip-flop," in which the speaker constantly changes back and forth between a Spanish and English vocabulary. Code-switching puns include the reading of "Y 2 K" as ¿Y tu qué?, and Hygeia Milk's advertisement "Es mooey bueno." Residents with Anglo family names are as comfortable with *pochismo* as their Hispanic-surnamed neighbors. Therefore, the medieval Hispanic and Anglo heritages of the Borderlands deserve equal attention.

An understanding of the Borderlands' medieval roots requires a review of where, when, and how each element first arose in the Old World. This study will accordingly investigate the early formation of Hispanic and Anglo traditions in premodern Europe; the surprising parallels, important differences, and complex interactions between them; and the elements they passed down to Mexican-American border culture. It will not deal with the mainstream Indian and Mexican heritage of border culture, with the postmedieval European heritage, or the Borderlands per se, important though they are, since those interesting matters have been examined elsewhere. Instead, six main aspects of the medieval heritage will be treated: (1) linguistic and cultural contributions; (2) political and legal developments (mainly from the High Middle Ages); (3) economic influences and social-class outlooks (mainly from the Late Middle Ages); (4) religious approaches; (5) modes of creativity; and (6) the development of Anglo-Hispanic conflict. A link runs through these six considerations. Warfare between linguistic groups progressed differently in Castile from the way war occurred in England, resulting in contrasting political and legal developments, which in turn underlay separate economic paths. The variance in economies in turn molded separate social class structures. Finally, all of the above factors shaped religious distinctiveness, creative expression, and the rise of conflict between the two groups.

With regard to chronology, the book respects four sub-periods: antiquity (through the fifth century); the Dark Ages or Early Middle Ages (sixth to eleventh century), in which most of the linguistic contributions were made; the High Middle Ages (eleventh through thirteenth centuries); and the Late Middle Ages (fourteenth and fifteenth centuries). While antiquity is prior to the medieval period, its influence lingered on through the Middle Ages, forming an important part of its culture and, hence, its legacy to the Borderlands. The political and legal foundations will concentrate on the High Middle Ages, whereas the economic and social-class developments involve a focus on the Late Middle Ages. The chapters on religion and creativity again make a survey of antiquity, Dark Ages, High Middle Ages, and Late Middle Ages. Finally, the chapter on the development of Anglo-Hispanic hostilities will deal partly with the High Middle Ages but will concentrate on the Late Middle Ages.

The ways in which this early material helps in an understanding of modern border culture will be investigated throughout the work. Some of the medieval influences considered are shared with virtually the whole world today (some only with the rest of Western society and some merely with the Hispanic or Anglo worlds), while others are unique to the Borderlands. However, those traits unique to either the Hispanic or Anglo worlds respectively overlap exactly in the Mexican-American Borderlands, going far to create its unique flavor. Some of these influences are merely quaint, while others are profound. Whatever their nature, all of these cultural relics call for a look back at the medieval heritage and will be considered. Thus may we better understand who we are and from whom we have come.

ONE

Linguistic and Cultural Influences

Language is a central, defining aspect of the bilingual Spanish-and-English Mexican-American Borderlands culture. While Borderlanders are a blend of four major ethnic strains (Mexican Indian, American Indian, Spanish, and English) and various minor ones, in the words and names they use they are overwhelmingly early European in origin. The languages they speak were largely developed in the Iberian Peninsula and the British Isles before 1500. First, we will survey the influence of early linguistic groups (mainly from ancient times and the Dark Ages) on customs, speech, and names that have been passed on to the Borderlands. Next, we will examine the impact of high and late medieval society on customs, speech, sayings, and names. Finally, consideration will be given to the culture of childhood and its role in transmitting concerns from early times.

The impact of words on society is controversial. Some linguists argue that people are rarely aware of the etymology of the words they use. Few people think of *breakfast* as breaking the night's fast, but only as the first meal of the day. Other linguists maintain that, on the contrary, language symbols play a major role in shaping thought, so that any attempt to know ourselves should involve an investigation of the roots and implications of vocabulary. One outlook, for instance, is engendered by the English word *stepmother,* with its concept of being a step removed in relationship, and another by its Spanish equivalent *madrastra,* a word also used for a brother. Marshall McLuhan has argued that each new technology looks back as in a rearview mirror at earlier times, using updated older words. Thus we use the term *car,* once applied by the Celts to their horse-drawn, two-wheeled chariots, to denote the self-propelled gasoline-fueled vehicle. The application of names of past objects to new inventions helps to provide a continuum of shared perceptions so that a society will not feel abruptly transplanted from its accustomed frame of reference. Many examples of such medieval word survivals will be quoted from the modern Borderlands language.

The Impact of Early Linguistic Groups on Customs, Speech, and Names

Hispanic and Anglo societies have more in common than is sometimes remembered, for their two linguistic heritages were shaped by almost the same linguistic groups: Basques, Hamites, Semites, Celts, Greco-Romans, Germanic folk, and French. Much of this heritage was laid down in ancient times and the Dark Ages. In looking at the linguistic and cultural heritage of each of these folk groups, we will first describe each group involved and then briefly mention its influence on the customs, speech, and names of the Borderlands.

The Linguistic Groups

The earliest Homo sapiens in both the Iberian Peninsula and the British Isles lived by means of hunting and gathering, shaping stone tools and weapons, and dwelling in caves when they were available. According to one theory, these early hunters in both Spain and Britain may have been the ancestors of the Basques. All other known language groups of these two regions except for Basque can be dated as coming into the area later, apparently restricting the Basques gradually to their present homeland in and around the western Pyrenees. The Basque language, which is documented by references dating from the Roman period, is not related to the surrounding Indo-European languages or to any other known tongue.

Much of the Basque influence on the Borderlands has come from the latter-day Basque descendants of these early peoples. Modern Basque sheepherding settlements were established in the twentieth century in California, Nevada, and Colorado.

The second group of modern people who inhabited Spain and Britain are sometimes referred to as the Iberians. They were farmers of wheat, barley, and millet, allowing them to create a much denser population distribution and a more advanced culture than the Basque hunters and gatherers achieved. Their languages may have been related to the Berber tongues native to the Maghreb region of northwestern Africa, where these folk originated. The Iberians are believed to have spread from the Maghreb to Spain before 4000 B.C. in search of new areas to farm. They settled along river banks, the name *Iberian* deriving from the later Celtic word *aber,* meaning *river.* From Spain, they expanded over the Atlantic coast of Europe into the British Isles. The Iberians brought advances in the mining of copper, gold, and silver. Metals and furs were traded by sea from port towns such as those at Niebla and Huelva. Under this trading impetus three scripts were developed in Spain by the first millennium B.C., each with twenty-eight signs, carved on lead sheets, stone monuments, and receptacles. The main walled trading town, called Tartessos by the Greeks, was located on an island in a river delta (probably the Guadalquivir) in southwestern Spain. The Iberians also established trade in Britain.

In the second and first millennia B.C., Celtic peoples from north-central Europe invaded the Iberian Peninsula and the British Isles. The word Celt means people of the "kilt" or covering. They are also known as Gauls, a name they left on Wales in Britain and on Galicia in northwestern Spain. The need for tin to make bronze (90 percent copper, 10 percent tin) made the tin mines of Galicia in Spain and of Cornwall in Britain particularly attractive targets for conquest. The first wave of invaders in the second millennium B.C. made use of their bronze weapons to conquer the British Isles. At the end of that millennium, a second wave using iron weapons invaded Spain across the eastern Pyrenees and later Britain. The Celts were mainly pastoral, herding cattle and pigs in addition to farming. Their isolated pastoral lifestyle gave them a strong individuality, and their thirst for mead (a fermented honey drink) and beer reinforced their reputation for emotional arguing and brawling, as well as for singing and poetry.

Leaving aside the distinct origins of modern Spanish (a romance language) and English (a Germanic language), subsequent divergence between the two during the Middle Ages affecting linguistic traditions and customs developed, in part, from the far greater influence of Semitic cultures in Spain than in Britain. Three branches of the Semitic peoples shared in influencing Hispanic culture: the Phoenicians, the Jews, and the Arabs. Through much of the history of Spain, these three Semitic peoples cooperated closely with each other. Phoenicians appeared in Spain and Britain as traders early in the first millennium B.C. Phoenicians from Tyre established Gadir (Punic, or Phoenician, for "fortress"), the present Cádiz, as their main trading town in Spain in ca. 1100 B.C. From Iberia, the Phoenicians obtained copper, gold, silver, pelts, tuna, and esparto grass for making rope. The Phoenicians traded with the so-called Tin Islands, apparently the Scilly Islands off the coast of tin-rich Cornwall. In the eighth century B.C., the Punic colony of Carthage in Tunisia assumed the leadership of Punic interests in the West. Carthaginian general Hamilcar Barca and his son Hannibal led a successful effort to conquer much of the Spanish hinterland in the third century B.C.

Between the seventh and the third centuries B.C., Spain was drawn into the classical Greco-Roman world, as Greek merchants traded and founded towns in northeastern Spain and traded along the Atlantic coast up to Britain. Greek influences continued to have an impact on Spain through contact with the often Greek-speaking Romans, later through the occupation of the region around Murcia by Justinian's Greek-speaking forces in the sixth century A.D., and later yet through the use of Greek for scientific terms.

At about the beginning of the first century Rome eventually absorbed both Spain and Britain into its rule. The stone-lined amphitheater at Mérida has a British counterpart in the simple, grassy amphitheater known as King Cole's Kitchen built in Camelodunum/Colchester. Bath in Britain still has remains of Roman baths, as an impressive aqueduct still towers over Segovia in Spain. However, the Celtic tongue continued to predominate in Britain, in contrast to the extensive Latinization of the speech of the Iberian Peninsula. While Spaniards acquired Latin rights *(Ius Latii)* from Vespasian in A.D. 75, full Roman citizenship came to both Spaniards and Britons simultaneously in A.D. 212, when Caracalla granted this status to all parts of the Empire.

With the decline of the Western Roman Empire, Germanic tribes settled in both Spain and the British Isles. Vandals and some Suevi (Schwaben) entered Spain in 409. Both tribes established short-lived kingdoms in the Iberian Peninsula—the Vandals in southern Spain (henceforth called Vandalucia or Andalucia), and the Suevi in Galicia. Jutes (Geats or Goths), Angles, and Saxons invaded England in the second half of the fifth century. Meanwhile, after the collapse of the Western Roman Empire in 476 left Spain with no clear master, Visigothic King Euric conquered the Iberian Peninsula. The early sixth century in Britain witnessed one last major attempt by the Celts to maintain their control of Britain. The Germanic invaders consolidated their conquests of both Spain and England in the second half of the sixth century. In 554 Atanagildo founded a new Visigothic dynasty centered at Toledo, while at the end of the sixth century, Ethelbert of Kent emerged as the first *bretwald* (high king) of England. Spain and England, strengthened by these conquests, were the two most powerful regions of Latin Christendom not included in the Carolingian Empire.

With the exception of the Phoenicians and the Greeks, all of the previously mentioned ethnic groups settled in both Spain and Britain. In the eighth through the eleventh centuries, two new groups of people invaded, one of which (the Moors) settled only in Spain, and the other (the Vikings) only in England. While there was never a Moorish migration to England, a few Islamic touches did appear there. The statement that "There is no god but Allah" was woven in Arabic script into a robe sent along with other presents from Caliph Harun al-Rashid of Baghdad to Charlemagne and subsequently used to cover the disinterred corpse of St. Cuthbert in 1104. The same statement was also stamped on the gold coins of King Offa of Mercia in 774, in imitation of Muslim gold coins. Conversely, Norsemen occupied both Lisbon and Seville in 844, but the Moors defeated the Vikings outside Seville. Abd al-Rahman II sent the poet al-Gazal as an ambassador to the land of the Vikings, but sporadic Viking raids continued. In the 860s, Haesten, a problem for Alfred the Great, terrorized Spain's Mediterranean coast as well. In 1008 Norman Vikings attacked Galicia, destroying Compostela and seventeen other towns, while Olaf Haroldsson of Norway raided Spain's Atlantic coast. However, the Vikings never tried to conquer Spain, anymore than the Moors invaded England.

The result of these one-sided invasions was a slight diminishing of the similarities between Hispanic and Anglo societies. This distancing was limited by the fact that the Moors who settled in Spain and the Vikings who came to England were mainly warriors who accommodated themselves to the local culture by taking local wives and concubines, minimizing the ethnic and cultural break. Just as early English, called Anglo-Saxon or Old English, continued to be the language of England, an early form of Spanish remained the dominant language throughout Spain. In both countries, a small area of native resistance survived (Covadonga in Spain and the Isle of Athelney in England) from which reconquest efforts developed. In the second half of the eleventh century, the last serious efforts of both Moors and Vikings to control the two regions were defeated. However, fringe Viking rule lingered for centuries (in the Orkney Isles), just as Moorish rule lingered marginally for four more centuries (in Granada).

The next ethno-linguistic group to exert an impact, the French, played a major role in both Castile and England, drawing their societies closer again. In the eleventh century, French society was experiencing a rapid population growth and economic upswing. French influence in both kingdoms initially came through peaceful immigration. Many French clergymen, pilgrims, townsmen, and crusading knights who visited Spain eventually settled there. Some of the northern Spanish towns came to have a majority of French immigrants, and in the late eleventh and early twelfth centuries most of the bishops in Castile were French. French crusaders came to help the Castilians push the *Reconquista* south. French influence first entered England under King Edward the Confessor (1042–66), who had been raised by his mother's family in Normandy and throughout his life had tried to surround himself with Frenchmen. After the Norman Conquest of England by William the Conqueror in 1066, French became the language of the upper class, of secular dealings of the clergy, of the courts, schools, and public business in that land. Only with the loss of most of the French territory of the English kings, and then with the anti-French mood of the Hundred Years War, did the English tongue, greatly modified by its contact with French, regain prestige in the last three centuries of the Middle Ages.

Jews played a significant role in both Spain and England, reaching a peak of influence in the High Middle Ages. However, the Jewish imprint was more profound on Spain, where Jews were present in far greater numbers and economically more important than in England. The Sephardic Jews (*Sapharad* being the Hebrew word for Spain) may have first put in an appearance in Iberia in the first millennium B.C. as trading partners and allies of the Phoenicians. They became important there in the diaspora of the second century A.D. Jews first entered England after the Norman Conquest in the late eleventh century. Under Edward I most of the Jews in England were expelled in 1290, but in Spain the massive expulsion of the Jews occurred much later, under Ferdinand and Isabella in 1492. It is notably the *converso* element in Borderland Hispanic society (descendants of Sephardic Jews forced into Christian conversion), especially that element interested in claiming a Jewish identity, that focuses most on its Castilian as opposed to its Mexican roots. Such Borderlanders of *converso* descent devote special attention to the religious oppression that drove their ancestors to deny their Jewish heritage. For this reason, somewhat more attention will be given here to the Jewish contribution and its difficulties with the Spanish church.

In Visigothic times, the Spanish Christian clergy clashed with the Jews. The Christian world was feeling beleaguered when in 611–17 Persia briefly captured Antioch, Jerusalem, and Egypt. Since the Nestorian and Monophysite heresies favored by the Semitic and Hamitic regions of the Middle East had played their role in the loss of the Holy Land to Christendom, this power shift spurred a Spanish push for doctrinal conformity. San Isidro of Seville, San Ildefonso, and San Julián of Toledo tried to persuade the Jews that Jesus was the promised Messiah. A discussion within the Jewish community on this issue did cause some members of the Jewish community to convert to Christianity during the Middle Ages. However, Judaism had taken a new doctrinal direction when, in the wake of the Roman destruction of the Temple at Jerusalem, Rabbi Jochanan ben Zakkai had led the Council of Jabnah in announcing that sacrifice for sin was no longer necessary but, rather, that people could achieve atonement by good behavior. Given this doctrine, those Jews who were inclined to view Jesus as the promised Messiah sometimes came to an Ebionite interpretation, which acknowledged Jesus as an earthly Messiah but not as God or redeemer. This was a similar view to that of Arianism, which had just been suppressed by the Spanish church in the sixth century. Frustrated, the church took extreme measures, decreeing in 633 that *conversos* (converts to Christianity) who apostatized back to Judaism were to be sold into slavery and their goods confiscated.

Spanish Christendom was thrown into a greater panic when in 635–40 the Arab Caliph Umar took Syria, Jerusalem, and Egypt. In 638 the Sixth Council of Toledo declared that the Jews were to be expelled from Spain, an ineffectual edict that mainly created alarm. Recesvinto, king from 649 to 672, gave orders for Jewish children in his realm to be taken from their parents and raised in monasteries. At the end of the seventh century, while the Arabs were steadily conquering their way across North Africa, King

Egica (687–702) forbade Jews to own land or to do business with Christians. As a result, when the Moors invaded Spain, many Jews hailed them as liberators, supplying provisions, acting as guides, and providing a division of soldiers. When Toledo prepared to resist under the leadership of its Archbishop, a Jew opened a town gate to the Moors. Jewish merchants prospered under Moorish rule, making an especially lucrative business of importing slaves. Resentment against the Jews resurfaced after the Christian reconquest of southern Spain. In the Black Death, Jews were charged with having poisoned wells. In the 1390s, in the reign of Enrique III, the majority of Spanish Jews were forcibly converted to Christianity under the threat of death. Those who escaped conversion were expelled from Spain a century later, in 1492. These "Sephardic" Jews scattered around the entire Mediterranean Basin, where they have maintained their fifteenth-century Spanish Ladino tongue down to the present. While the openly professing Jews were thereby eliminated from Spanish society, many of the *conversos* secretly remained Jewish believers.

Anti-Semitic hysteria in England experienced its initial outburst in 1144, when the death of twelve-year-old William of Norwich was blamed on the Jews. Their essential role as moneylenders provided some protection for a while, since Christians were forbidden from charging interest. However, in the thirteenth century Italian banker-merchants took over much of the Jewish role in money-lending by hiding their interest surcharges in money exchange rates. In 1290 Edward I won popular applause by expelling the Jews from England in exchange for a huge special tax granted to him by Parliament. Only a few converted Jews remained.

Gypsies were the final premodern ethno-linguistic group to exert an impact on Mexican-American border culture. Romany, the Gypsy tongue, belongs to the Indic family of languages, along with Sanskrit and Hindi. Tamerlane's attacks at the end of the fourteenth century may have induced masses of these people to make their way into the Balkans, from where they spread across all of Europe. Europeans, knowing that they had come in from the eastern Mediterranean, thought of them as Egyptians and called them *gitanos* in Castile and "gypsies" in England. According to one source, they entered England sometime between 1430 and 1440. They crossed the Pyrenees into Spain in 1435. Not sharing the Judeo-Christian code of ethics with the Europeans, the Gypsies created controversy wherever they spread. An English folk song tells a story of a man whose wife runs away to live with the gypsies, and refuses to return home. In Castile, the Gypsies won favor by procuring fine horses for their patrons and by presenting themselves as victims of the Muslims. They were thus permitted to settle in the region, most famously in caves outside the Muslim city of Granada. Although not of great importance in shaping the development of Spanish language and culture, traces of the customs and language of the Spanish *gitanos,* as well as of the English Gypsies, found their way to the Borderlands of the New World.

The Impact of Early Linguistic Groups on Customs

Many specific customs found in the Borderlands—some distinctly indicative of it and others widely shared—can be traced back to premodern Spain and England. The Iberians' mining technology, augmented by that of the Phoenicians and Romans and applied through the Middle Ages in the Asturian and Galician mines, was eventually transmitted to the Borderlands. The Phoenician method of winnowing wheat by blasts of air was applied to placer deposits to remove the gold dust from the sand. The Middle Eastern device for grinding grain was likewise applied to the so-called *arrastre* for pulverizing ore. Pairs or quads of drag-stones were attached to a vertical stone pole braced by timbers. As a horse or donkey turned the pole, the stones were dragged around a walled circular lava floor over watered ore. A drain with a screen let out the resulting pulp. This technique, along with Spanish placer methods, was transmitted in the 1849 gold rush to California by Mexicans and Chileans.

Spanish mining expertise, together with the role of Mexican miners in the California gold rush, has given American English such mining terms as *placer* and *bonanza.* When James Marshall first found gold at Sutter's Mill in January 1848, he shouted the Spanish word "*¡Chispa!*" (sparkle). News of the gold discovery reached the East Coast, and that August the *New York Herald* published a letter about the discovery. Soon 80,000 Yankees suffering from "gold fever" arrived in California. Few knew mining techniques, but they learned quickly from Mexicans (and Australians) who were already schooled in the use of the washing pan, the cradle, the sluice box, and more sophisticated devices for extracting precious metals from sand and gravel. The Spanish-American system was the foundation of the rules and customs adopted. No industry had a greater impact on the Borderlands than mining. Farming attracted many, but mining attracted far more, drawing thousands of settlers to California and then scattering them throughout the West. During the Great Depression of the 1930s the Phoenician winnowing method was resuscitated in the attempt to squeeze more ore from the old California mines.

Ritual fertility dances once performed to the accompaniment of the *castañeta* and tambourine in the Punic temples of Tanit in Gades (Cádiz) became the foundation for the Andalusian flamenco music and dances still performed on the Border. It is said that the term *flamenco* (Flemish) was added in the early sixteenth century, when King Philip the Handsome of Castile justified watching these dances to his super-jealous wife, Juana la Loca, by claiming that the sound of the castanets reminded him of the clacking of the wooden shoes in the Flemish folk dances. The traditional narrative of these performances is still the temptress beguiling a lover.

Even though Celtic dominance in Britain ended with the start of the Middle Ages, the Germanic Anglo-Saxons absorbed some Celtic influences, not only at the time of the conquest but also transmitted through later, ongoing interaction of Anglos with the indigenous Celtic peoples of the British Isles. Our system of Roman numerals, however, comes from the Celts via the Romans. Pre-Roman writing systems (including Hebrew and Greek) used the same symbols for letters and numbers. The so-called Arabic numerals employed in the Hispanic and Anglo traditions are based on the Arabic system, with the symbols for the numbers only slightly reworked as follow:

1 = ١, 2 = ٢, 3 = ٣, 4 = ٤, 5 = ٥, 6 = ٦, 7 = ٧, 8 = ٨, 9 = ٩, 10 = ١٠

When the Romans adopted an alphabet, they chose a variation of the Greek writing system. However, they borrowed their way of writing numbers from the Celtic system called Ogham, consisting of twenty-five stick-like letter-numbers inscribed on the edges of rocks.

Roman influence in the Borderlands has come in a variety of forms. *Machismo* was a part of Roman military orientation conveyed to its daughter "Latin" cultures, including Spain. Reinforced by the Moorish presence and then by the warrior ethic of the *Reconquista,* traditional male predominance came to Border culture more from its Hispanic than from its Anglo strain.

One ongoing Anglo-Saxon custom is that of execution by hanging. Used for border lynchings in the nineteenth and early twentieth centuries, this practice stems from the early German use of hanging for sacrifices to Odin. The secularization of the custom is evidenced in the first half of the eleventh century in both England and Spain. The Mediterranean peoples had employed hanging by a rope only for suicide, while the Justinian Code specified a form of hanging without a rope, where the head would be suspended in a fork of a tree and held in place by a board nailed behind the head.

The eight hundred years of Moorish presence in Spain left a major imprint on Spanish culture, so that a strong Spanish Moorish heritage has been passed to Mexican Americans through Castilians and Mexicans. Moorish techniques of farming and farming products were carried by the Spaniards to the American Southwest. A variety of citrus trees including oranges, limes, and lemons were introduced. Fruit trees such as pears, pomegranates, cherries, apples, peaches, and figs, as well as strawberries were also planted by the Spanish. The mission grape became the "seed" for the vineyards and wineries of California as well as for the raisin culture there. In the early 1800s the Spanish introduced a cotton seed that would later be used extensively in the Deep South. Techniques of irrigation, including the digging and construction of both hand-drawn and water-wheel wells, were also passed from the Moors to the Borderlanders, enabling farmers to draw water with plant-rich sediment directly from streams to fields. Principal canals *(madres acequias)* came off both sides of the rivers at intervals of eight to ten miles, distributing water to the intervening farms via smaller ditches.

Islamic influence can also be traced in the shaping of Hispanic (including Mexican American) hospitality and in the transmittal of games. The well-known phrase *mi casa es su casa* is a translation of the Arabic *al-beyt beytak.* Moorish custom is seen in the retention of some popular superstitions and in a variety of blessings and curses, including standing a broom upside down to end the visit of a guest who has stayed too long. While the custom of the siesta brought by the Moors to Spain has been overridden in the Borderlands by the Anglo tradition of working straight through the day, the Moorish contribution to games continues here as elsewhere. Chess was introduced to Spain from the Muslim world by 1008. It was modified in Europe, the vizier being replaced with the queen and the elephant with the bishop. It spread rapidly to England, whose King John played it as a boy and being a bad loser once bashed his opponent over the head with the playing board. The Moors also introduced playing cards, in the fourteenth century. The cards and the associated gambling became so popular in the late fifteenth century that the English Parliament in 1463 tried to protect the sales of English card manufacturers by prohibiting the import of foreign cards. In 1497 English apprentices were forbidden to play cards except at Christmas and in their masters' houses, in an attempt to keep them at work and at peace.

Part of the problem of racial discrimination in the Borderlands can be traced from Moorish Spain via colonial Mexico into the Borderlands, where it was strongly reinforced by an Anglo racism developed mainly in postmedieval times. In the ninth through eleventh centuries, a flourishing trade funneled slaves, including many captive Englishmen, to markets in Moorish Spain. Spanish Muslims paid less for a black slave *(abd)* than for a white one *(mamluk)*. The *mamluk* was more expensive, as many mamluks could be ransomed for a high sum or exchanged for a Muslim captive. As a result, while mamluks were generally made household servants, abds were assigned to the hard-labor jobs and other assignments of lower social standing. This distinction led to a lesser esteem of blacks in al-Andalus as undependable, stupid, and ignorant. The fourteenth-century historian Ibn Khaldun threw doubt on the human identity of blacks, comparing them to animals. These social institutions of the Spanish Moors, supported by their unwritten Islamic law, the sunna, had an impact on the medieval Castilian laws regarding slaves. As a result, this discrimination was transmitted to the Spanish Christians, who in the fourteenth century were showing the same distinction between their own light-skinned and dark-skinned slaves. They, too, then deprecated the blacks, likewise comparing them to animals. Dark-skinned individuals are depicted with scorn in Alfonso X's *Cantigas de Santa Marìa* and elsewhere. Felipe II's race-based caste system, which has left a heightened awareness of color differences in Border society with its sometimes unhealthy sensitivity to the differences between the *güero* (blond) and the *prieto* (dark-complexioned), thus had roots in Moorish Spain. However, Hispanic racism was strongly counteracted in the sixteenth century by church rulings defining blacks (and Indians) as human, in contrast to the English legal definition of blacks as chattel. In the Borderlands, this discrimination was greatly intensified by the demeaning view of blacks that grew out of the slavery system in the antebellum U.S. South.

The Border has had ongoing problems with discrimination against blacks by both Hispanics and Anglos. The issue was brought to the surface most notably in periods when black troops were stationed along the Border. After tensions generated by the arrival of black Union troops in the Brownsville area in the Civil War, black soldiers were attacked by Mexican Americans in the Rio Grande Valley in 1875, and black soldiers were insulted in the streets of El Paso in 1899. In the early twentieth century, violence erupted along the Borderlands. During the Brownsville Raid of 1906 tensions between the townsmen and black soldiers stationed at Fort Brown led to the death of one townsman and the wounding of another. Ten years later, an anti-black fracas broke out in Del Rio, followed in 1918 by a shoot-out between black soldiers and residents in Nogales. Charges of discrimination against blacks by Borderlanders were still heard at the end of the twentieth century. While the Moorish influence came into the Borderlands transmitted especially by Hispanics, the Borderland Anglos have embraced this element so enthusiastically that it has become a hallmark of the U.S. Southwest in general.

Scandinavians settled in the northern English Midlands in a strip of high country in Nottinghamshire, Derbyshire, and Cheshire to the south and Lancashire and Yorkshire to the north, continuing a Norse-speaking tradition through much of the Middle Ages and exerting a special long-term influence. In the period between 1675 and 1725, emigrants to America from this area settled the Delaware Valley, from where their culture spread into the Middle West. In the twentieth century, the earlier east-to-west migration, which had first brought Appalachian-based Anglo culture to the Borderlands, was replaced by a north-to-south migration bringing midwesterners into the border region.

A French impact on the Mexican-American Borderlands came through both the Hispanic and Anglo traditions. The shape we give our letters is one example. The French introduced to both Spain and England the Carolingian minuscule, the simplified handwriting of the court of Charlemagne that used lowercase letters in addition to the ancient Roman capitals. Taken as the standard for printing in the fifteenth century, this style of writing laid the basis for modern Western letters. The full-blown chivalric system of courtly love (although many of its features originating in Moorish love verse coming into France via Moorish Spain) developed fully in France and from there entered both Castile and England. The romanticism expressed in serenades under a girl's window and in love poetry, with such metaphors as love's wounding arrow, trace back in some measure to the French impact.

It was mainly the Christianized Spanish Jews (the *conversos*) who transmitted Jewish influences to the later Mexican-American Borderlands culture. Conscious awareness among descendants—and self-presumed descendants—of the late medieval *conversos* is an outstanding example of medieval heritage understood by Borderland residents. It is also a clear example of an effort to maintain that heritage. Many Mexican American Borderlanders of Hispanic Jewish heritage, with an identity long suppressed by the effects of the Inquisition, are presently rediscovering or reasserting their Hebrew roots in a resurrection of interest in Hebrew studies and attendance at synagogues. Ongoing Ladino customs include grandmothers making little pillows for their grandchildren within three or four days of their birth. It is still considered stylish even by some non-Jewish residents of the Borderlands to wear the Magen David (literally Shield of David), which was worn on the shields of King David's warriors and formed out of letters of the Paleo-Hebrew script of King David's day ▼†▲, not the modern Hebrew letters דוד, combined in the stylized form of the star symbol ✡. The song "Kol Nidre" ("All My Vows"), by the Jewish poet Shlomo ibn Gabirol (Avicebron), a protégé of Vizier Shmuel ibn Nagdela of Granada in the eleventh century, is still traditionally sung in synagogues on Yom Kippur. This song asks God to cancel all vows extracted by force because the Jews in eleventh-century Spain were suffering under forced conversion to Islam.

One of the more curious claims of medieval Jewish influence on the Borderlands concerns a theory regarding the cost codes used by local Jewish businesses before the introduction of electronic bar codes in merchandising. This practice may well have stemmed from the use of the Hebrew alphabet to stand for both letters and numbers, in the manner of the cabalistic code for writing הוה׳ אלה׳נו הוה׳ (ADONAI ELOHENU ADONAI [Lord God Lord]) on the back of a mezuzah or doorpost amulet. The elaboration of cabalistic numerology reached a height of development in late medieval Spain. In this particular practice, each letter is replaced by the letter following it in the Hebrew alphabet. The above Hebrew phrase would thus read כוזו במוכסז כוזו, meaningless in Hebrew unless the code is understood. It is posited that this system influenced the use of a similar code in marking the wholesale cost of items in Jewish stores (in addition to the retail price shown in Arabic numerals), so that a store owner would know at a glance how much discount might be acceptable. This system was applied not by the *conversos* but by the eastern European Ashkenazi Jews who pioneered in developing Border business in the late nineteenth and early twentieth centuries. Some of these Jewish immigrants came via the northeastern United States, where they had already developed inside code names using Yiddish. El Paso's Given Brothers, Levine's Department Stores of Texas, and Zale Corporation of Texas all used this system.

Like the Scandanavian, French, and Jewish peoples, Gypsies also continue as a cultural force in the Borderlands, some of them still earning a living as fortune tellers. The practice seems as ubiquitous as human gullibility. In the 1970s the Brownsville business of one gypsy fortune teller, styled Madame Palm, was closed by the courts when she was accused of failing to fulfill a promise to cure a woman of cancer. One Gypsy contribution which was carried into the Mexican-American Borderlands in the colonial period was the *cante jondo* (deep song, associated with flamenco music). This type of singing weaves together an amazing variety of musical sources, even including the Muslim muezzin's call to prayer.

The Impact of Early Linguistic Groups on Speech

Many of the groups and cultural forces we have defined in ancient and medieval Europe have helped to shape certain speech patterns in the Borderlands. The most basic Iberian heritage of the Mexican-American Borderlands is the rolled double *rr* of Spanish, which comes from the pre-Roman speech of the Iberian Peninsula and which imposed itself on the pronunciation of Latin in Roman Spain. *Páramo* (a desert tableland) is the most common word in Spanish surviving from a pre-Roman, non-Basque word. Some general observations regarding the Celtic influence relating Spanish and English and the impact this conveys to the Borderlands might also be considered. We still refer to the Celtic sky god Lug in English expressions and words such as *you big lug, luggage,* and *to lug something around.* The Celtic word *vates,* occurring also in Latin, is perpetuated in the Spanish word *vate* for a "bard, seer or poet." Some of the Spanish words derived from Celtic are anchored in a military emphasis, including *brío* (vigor), *caballo* (horse), and *lanza* (lance). Other words refer to their trading activity, including *camino* (road), *carro* (cart), and *cambiar* (to exchange). Still other

Celtic-based Spanish words include *ola* (wave), as a reminder of how well Celts took to the sea as sailors; *gato* (cat), connected with Celtic superstitions; and *pieza* (piece) and *roca* (rock), memorials of Celtic skill in working rocks into megaliths. Perhaps the most widely used, and in some ways most stereotypical, Spanish word of Celtic heritage, a word often associated with the crooning and ready brawling of border bars (Hispanic and Anglo), is *cerveza,* the word for *beer,* which derives from a Celtic word. But some Celtic words have come down as part of English, having been reworked into French and then reintroduced in that form after the Norman Conquest. Examples include *battle, car, cargo, carpenter, gravel, truant,* and *valet.*

The Phoenician or Punic tongue contributed a few words to the Spanish and English languages. One suggested derivation of the name of España or Spain, thus *Hispanic,* is from the Punic word *span* or *spania* meaning hidden or remote, as in lying in the far west. The Hispanics, who spread so extensively across the Western Hemisphere, are appropriately described in the etymological meaning of the term, the peoples of the West. (It might be noted in comparison that the presumed derivation of the Germanic word *Anglo* from the Old English *angel* meaning *fish-hook* likewise pointed the Anglos etymologically to and, hence, across the sea.)

The tremendous impact of Greco-Roman society on Western civilization naturally affects the Mexican-American Borderlands as well. Aside from Greek-based scientific nomenclature, other Greek-based words in Spanish include *arete* (earring) from the Greek ἀρετή (virtue), and various masculine nouns ending in *a,* including *problema, tema,* and *idioma.* Most Greek-based Spanish terms were derived through the medium of Latin, including *tumba* (tomb) from τύμβη, *masa* (flour) from μᾶζα, *carta* (letter) from χάρτης, *golpe* (blow) from κόαφος, and *iglesia* (church) from ἐκκλσσία. English shared with Spanish the Greek base for such words as *bodega* (apothecary) from ἀποθήκη, *Cristo* (Christ) from Χριστος, *ritmo* (rhythm) from ρυθμόζ, *zodíaco* (zodiac) from ζωδιακός, and *cristal* (crystal) from κρύσταλλος.

The cults of the pagan gods of life and death are still reflected in the often contrasting names for some of the days of the week, which are rendered here in Spanish for their Latin form and in English as a replacement Germanic form. The sun god is remembered in the English *Sunday,* having given way to *domingo* for the Lord's day in Spanish; *Tuesday* (Tiu's Day) and *mardi* (Mar's Day), as well as *miercoles* (Mercury's Day) and Wednesday (Woden's Day) commemorate gods of differing cultures. However, both *lunes* and *Monday* still refer to the moon, *jueves* (Jove's Day) and *Thursday* (Thor's Day) to gods of lightning (although Woden is also associated with lightning), and *viernes* (Venus's Day) and Friday (Freya's Day) to goddesses of love. *Sabato* is said to indicate the Sabbath, and *Saturday* to refer to Saturn's Day.

One of the most obvious Roman influences on the Mexican-American Borderlands coming via both Spain and Britain is the impact of the Latin language. Iberia was thoroughly Latinized in speech and in many of its customs during its six hundred years of Roman occupation, laying the principal foundation for the later emergence of Spanish as a Romance language. The following words are only a few of the examples of the Latin basis for most Spanish words: *comer* (to eat) from *comedere; corazón* (heart) from *cor; cojo* (lame) from *coxus; cuyo* (whose) from *cuius; hablar* (to talk) from *fabulare; hermoso* (beautiful) from *formosus; miedo* (fear) from *metus; medir* (to measure) from *metire; murciélago* (bat) from *mus caecus; barrer* (to sweep) from *verrere; decir* (to say) from *dicere;* and *pedir* (to request) from *petere.* Latin impacted English speech and tradition in three distinct ways and periods. Although the Romans occupied England for four hundred years prior to the onset of the Middle Ages, they left some but relatively little enduring effect on Celtic language, and not until the fifth century did the Germanic tribes whose tongue is the true source of English arrive. During the Middle Ages, Old English absorbed some Latin vocabulary through its use by church and university. Far more significant, however, was Latin's impact coming by way of the Romance language of French after the Norman Conquest. Examples of Latin words taken into English in the Middle Ages include *allegory, legal, mechanical, nervous, prosody, pulpit, rosary, scripture, secular, testify, testimony,* and *ulcer.*

But the more direct Germanic influence on Mexican-American border culture came mainly through the Anglo-Saxons. The modern English language is mostly Anglo-Saxon, or Old English, in origin. The original meanings of words have sometimes been generally forgotten, as in the case of the word *fee,* which originally referred to cattle (in which fines were sometimes paid) and is thus related to the modern German word for cattle, *Vieh.* The word *henchman* for a follower comes from the Old English *hengest man* (horseman), from the days when a ruler's guard was mounted. However, the Germanic impact on Spain, via the Visigoths, was not insignificant, and a number of Germanic influences came to the Borderlands via the Hispanic route as well. Since Germanic rule represented a great setback in cultural level for Spain after the centuries of Roman rule, few German-based words in Spanish have to do with the world of the intellect. Spanish usage still makes reference to *godo* (for *Goth, Gothic*) as something primitive, and a *niño gótico* is a retarded child. *Godo* is also applied as a derogatory term for the Anglo in Border Spanish. Not all Spanish words with a Germanic derivation come from the Visigoths. Germanic influence also came to Spanish from German soldiers in the Roman legions and from the general German impact on the late Roman Empire. Some Germanic-based Spanish words concern warfare, including *bandera* (flag), *botín* (booty), and *guerra* (war). Other examples are *albergue* (shelter), *falda* (skirt), *ropa* (clothing), *arrancar* (tear away), *bramar* (to roar), *desmayar* (to faint), and *listo* (ready, quick).

Many Spanish and English words derive from Arabic, especially those referring to architecture, arts and crafts, astronomy, botany, chemistry, farming, mathematics, medicine, and sailing. There are over 4,000 Arabic-based words in Spanish. These include farming terms like *acequia* (irrigation line) from *al-saqiya, noria* (a draw well, and a name used for the town of Norias in South Texas) from *al-na'ura, tarea* (task) from *tariha,* and *zanahoria* (carrot) from *isfannariya*. They include terms of urban settlement and government: *alcalde* (mayor) comes from *al-qadi, aldea* (village) from *al-day'a,* and *barrio* (district) from *barri*. Spanish vocabulary that derived from the impact of Moorish architecture include *albañil* (bricklayer) from *al-banna, azulejo* (tile) from *al-zulayj, albañal* (drain) from *al-balla'a, alfombra* (carpet) from *al-khumra,* and *almohada* (cushion) from *al-mukhadda*. There are also terms for leisure pursuits, including *ajedrez* (chess) from *al-shitranj* and *taza* (cup) from *tassa*. Muslim Córdoba's fame for producing leather goods gave rise to the English words *cordoban leather* and *cordwainer*.

Arabic-derived words found in both Spanish and English include *alcachofa*/artichoke (from *al-kharshufa*), *alcohol* (from *al-kuhl*), *algodón*/cotton (from *al-qutn*), *azafrán*/saffron (from *al-za'faran*), *azúcar*/sugar (from *sukkar*), *jarabe*/syrup (from *sharab*), and *jarra*/jar (from *jarra*). Math terms with an Arabic base include *cero*/zero, *cifra*/cipher, *cenit*/zenith, and *nadir*. Arabic-influenced idioms and idiomatic expressions still found in Borderland speech include *blanquillo* (little white one) as an additional word for an egg; *buen provecho* (good use) for *bon appétit;* and *Que Dios te bendiga* (God bless you) as an expression of leave-taking. Many Spanish sayings are drawn from the Koran or reworked from other Arabic sources. Islamic influence has been seen as lying behind the quiet and accepting strain in Hispanic (including in Mexican American) society as expressed in such phrases as *ojalá (may it be so* from *wa xa Allah* or *wish to Allah), olé* (from *wallah* or O Allah), *si Dios quiere* (If God wills), and *estaba de Dios que iba a pasar* (it was God's will), all directly translated or transliterated from Arab phrases.

The Scandinavian influence on Mexican-American border culture has come from its English-speaking settlers. Because the Danish Vikings who settled in England gradually blended into the closely related Anglo-Saxon inhabitants, a Danish imprint was left on the English language. Many words spoken with an *sh* sound (written as *sc*) under Danish influence came to be spoken with a hard *k*, including *bask, scare, scrub, skull,* and *sky.* The *y* sound in other English words was influenced to shift to a *g* or *k,* as in *egg, get, give,* and *kid.* The word *plow,* among others, derives from Danish. The Scandinavian-influenced dialect of the northern English Midlanders was the foundation for the equally direct, literal, and plain-spoken speech of American midwesterners who moved into the Borderlands at that time. That dialect passed on not only its pronunciation but many grammatical forms. Typical words passed on include *bamboozled, blather, brat, budge, by golly, by gum, to chuck, chock-full, cuddle, crib, dad, dresser, dumb-founded, egg on, elbow grease, flabbergasted, gab, gallivant, good grief, grub, gumption, guzzle, heap, home-coming, kindling, knuckle under, mad, nap, pummel, road, rumpus, scalawag, sick, skimpy, slam, slug, thingamajig, tiff, upsa daisy,* and *wallop.*

Gallicisms adopted into Spanish in the Middle Ages include *jamón* (ham), *jardín* (garden), *lenguaje* (language), *linaje* (lineage), *mensaje* (message), *monje* (monk), *omenaje* (homage), *sergente* (sergeant), and *usaje* (usage). English, despite its Germanic base, was greatly influenced by French vocabulary and by a simplifying of English grammar and morphology, not by adoption of French grammatical and morphological structures but by forcing English to jettison an enormously complex linguistic structure in the name of accommodation in a bilingual society—the English peasantry and middle class, on one side, and the French nobility and bureaucracy, on the other. Although remaining Germanic at its core, English grammatical inflections fell away, and French words swelled the English vocabulary, coincidentally giving English a far greater affinity with Spanish (which was already related to French as a Latin-based Romance language). English words deriving from French were especially numerous in the areas of food (for instance, *appetite, boil, broil, dinner, fruit, napkin, pastry, roast, supper,* and *taste*); fashion and social life *(apparel, chair, checkers, chess, cloak, coat, conversation, dance, diamond, embroidery, falcon, flower, gown, jewel, kerchief, melody, mitten, ornament, sapphire, satin, taffeta, tournament,* and *veil);* court, government, and law *(acquit, assault, attorney, coroner, court, fraud, government, indict, jury, justice, libel, liberty, mayor, nobility, parliament, plaintiff, plead, reign, revenue, sentence, tax, traitor, treason, treasurer,* and *verdict);* religion *(cathedral, clergy, devotion, faith, mystery, prayer, preach,* and, by the way, *religion);* war *(battle, besiege, captain, combat, guard, lieutenant, sergeant, soldier,* and *vanquish);* and arts and learning *(beauty, ceiling, chimney, compile, copy, figure, malady, painting, palace, paper, pen, pillar, poet, porch, physician, preface, prologue, romance, sculpture, story, surgeon, tower, tragedy,* and *treatise).* The word *curfew* comes from *"couvre le feu"* (cover the fire), first introduced by William the Conqueror's attempt to control England by keeping Anglo-Saxons in their homes after dark. The expression *love* for a score of zero in tennis comes from the time when the game, popular with the French aristocracy, spread to England, and the French word *l'oeuf* (egg)—used to mean zero, just as we today use *goose egg*—was mispronounced "love." Living animals continued to be called by the Anglo-Saxon names used by the peasants who tended them and by the butchers who marketed them *(ox, sheep, and hog),* while French names were applied to their meat when set before the nobles (beef/*boeuf,* mutton/*mouton,* and pork/*porc*). The expression "just an average guy" comes from the days when the French name Guy (from the Latin Gaius for *male*) was in common usage.

It has been claimed that Mexican American Spanish (and indeed all American Spanish) is more closely related to Judeo-Spanish than to pure Spanish Castilian. While the Spanish language has taken most of its vocabulary from Latin, its grammatical structure has much in common with Semitic languages in general and Hebrew in particular. There are also phonemic similarities. The easy transition between the *b* (בּ or *beit*) and *v* (ב or *veit*) in Hebrew vocabulary (as in Arabic, where in medieval times there was a letter for *b* ب, but not for "v") is mirrored in the general lack of distinction between these letters in Spanish. Various words of old Ladino, the language of the fifteenth century Sephardic Jews still in use in Brownsville, include *belduque* (knife), *cuerta* (instead of *puerta* for *door*), *tristura* (instead of *tristeza* for *sadness*), *cochito* (instead of *cucharita* for *little spoon*), and *emboruje* (instead of *envolvió* for *get all wrapped up*).

The Impact of Early Linguistic Groups on Names

The most evident of the influences from all of these early ethnic groups is provided by the naming systems that stem from them. Names in the Borderlands reflect the succession of populations in premodern Spain and England. The derivations given are all from the sources cited.

Many Hispanic family names are Basque in origin, and the meanings of the names still suggest the concerns and lifestyles of the distant ancestors. Basque country is woody and mountainous, so it is not surprising to find many family names referring to heights and to woods: *García* and *Garza* (which coincidentally means *heron* in modern Spanish) come from the Basque word *gartza,* meaning *high crag; Mendiola,* Basque for *mountain spot; Mendoza* for *many mountains; Muñoz* from *munatz* (hill); and *Murillo* from *ribazo* (highland). The name *Zavaleta* by one derivation traces to *zabal* (widths) and *eta* (wide), meaning very wide passes or, in an alternate explanation to *abar* (oak thicket) plus *eta* (peak), meaning *oak peak. Medrano* comes from *edi* (fern grove), *Zavala* from *abar* (oak thicket), and *Zárate* from *zara* (wood) and *ate* or *athe* (door), for a pass through the woods. *Vidaurre* stems from *bidaurre* (on the road). The family name *Ibarra* derives from the Basque *ibai* (river), and *Peciña* from *eza* (bull rushes). *Tamayo* comes from *amai* (pasture), *Zúñiga* from a Basque word for *abundant pasture, Tapia* from *abi* (whortleberry), and *Orozco* from the Basque for holly grove. Salazar comes from *gorta* (a plot of ground). *Urbina* stems from Basque words meaning *two fountains,* and *Uribe* comes from *uri* (town) and *behe* or *bee* (lower), meaning *lower town.*

Family names known in the Mexican-American Borderlands and inherited from the Iberian period in Spain include *Carbajal,* from the pre-Roman Iberian word *carba* (oak thicket) and probably *Vega,* which is said to stem from the pre-Roman word *baika* (irrigated land). Thus, the shift from hunting to farming in the Iberian period is still commemorated in some Borderlands family names.

Celtic given and family names entered the Borderlands through both the Hispanic and British heritages. Their meanings still evoke the old Celtic emphasis on fighting and pride (as seen in the Spanish family names *Briones,* derived from *brigh* (force), and *Mata,* originating in *admata* (very good). These names also recall the (acquired) Celtic love of sailing, as seen in the "Anglo" names of Cordelia or Delia (Jewel of the Sea), Douglas (Dark Water), and Morgan (Sea Dweller).

A few Punic given names have been passed down, largely through the Bible to Christian Borderlanders. *Yishabel* (Woman of Bel), transliterated as *Jezebel* in English translations of the Bible story about the wife of King Ahab, has been transmitted in Spanish tradition as *Isabel.* Hiram (anointed) is a name that may originally have been a title applied to such Phoenician kings as Hiram of Gebel (or Biblos) and to Hiram of Tyre, the ally of King David and Solomon. Elisa (from *Elisha* [God is Savior]) was a name most famously born by the founding queen of Carthage, who was called Dido by the Romans. Like related Hebrew names, the Punic names thus evoke the religious involvement of the Phoenician people.

A Greek basis can also be detected for some Mexican American family names, including Sotero and possibly Sotelo from Σωτερ (savior). *Moreno,* once applied to the Moors, derives from the Greek word for black, μαυρος (*maurus,* a Greek transliteration of the Latin). First names with a Greek base generally have cognates with the Hispanic and Anglo forms. Border residents shift easily from one to the other form of their own names, as their mixed society puts them at ease with both cultural traditions. Examples of names include *Teresa* (reaper), *Andrés / Andrew* (manly), *Gregorio / Gregory* (vigilant, fast), *Nicolás* (victorious), *Felipe / Philip* (horse lover), and *Estéban / Stephen* (crowned). The Greek concern with ethics is seen in such given names as *Agata / Agatha* (good, kind), *Alicia / Alice* (truthful), *Catalina / Catherine* or *Kathleen* (pure), *Dorotea / Dorothy* (gift of God), *Helena / Helen* or *Ellen* (light), *Cristóbal / Christopher* (Christ-bearer), and *Timoteo / Timothy* (honoring God).

A Borderland reminder of the Roman presence in the Iberian Peninsula is the use of such family names as Balboa from the Latin *balbus* (stutterer), and as Macías, a reworking of the Roman family name Matia. *Saldaña* comes from the Latin *saldare* (to solder or fuse). Names in references to natural settings include Campos from the Latin *campus* or field, Perales from *pira* (pear orchard), Peña from *pinna* (peak), Soto and Sotomayor from *saltus* (forest). *Peralta* means a high lookout, and *Montalvo* comes from the Latin for a white mountain. The Latin *ramus* (branch) underlies *Ramos, Villa* refers to the Roman agricultural estates, and *Sepúlveda* comes

Some of the Names Mentioned in the Text

Basque names from woods and mountains	*Greek names from ethics*	*Germanic names from the military*	*Anglo-Saxon names from work and money*	*Hebrew names from religion*
García, Garza	Agatha, Inés	Alfonso	Beverly, Emma	Ann, Daniel, Eli
Medrano	Agnes, Alicia	Armando	Henry, Edmund	Elizabeth
Mendiola	Catherine	Bernard / Bernardo	Edward	Gabriel, Joel
Mendoza	Dorotea	Brunhilda	William, Baker	John, Judith
Muñoz, Murillo	Helen	Gary, Gertrude	Clark, Cooper	Miguel, Brito
Orozco, Zárate	Cristóbal	Harry, Herman	Méndez, Miller	Abadi, Curiel
Zavala, Zavaleta	Timothy	Herbert,	Potter, Smith	Ortiz
		Louise	Taylor, Tyler	
		Leonard	Corder	
		Leopold / Leopoldo		
		Matilda		
		Richard or Ricardo		
		Walter		
		Balderas		
		Gómez		
		Gutiérrez		
		Juárez, Suárez		

from the Latin word for a burial ground. Some Hispanic names come from the Latin terms for man-made objects associated with Roman times. *Paredes* comes from *parietis* (walls) and *Padilla* from *patella,* referring to a bread oven (the same source as for the name of the dish *paella*). *Quesada* comes from the Latin *caseus* (cheese). Many Latin-based first names, like the Greek, are found in Spanish-English counterparts. Examples of Latin-based given names include Alma (Soul), Bárbara (stranger), Emilia / Emily or Mimi (flattering), Laura (laurel leaf), Norma (model or pattern), Sylvia (of the forest), Victoria (victory), Virginia (maiden), Antonio (priceless), and Pedro / Peter (rock). Some of the names derived from Latin recall the Romans' military emphasis, including Marco / Mark (warlike), Martín (warlike), and Castro, which derives from the Latin *castrum* (fortified camp). Thus, while we sometimes refer to Mexican Americans as Latins, a good deal of Latin influence has come in via the Anglo heritage as well.

Many Anglo given and family names trace back to medieval English origins. Examples of Anglo-Saxon and other Germanic first names include those describing traits, such as Gail (gay or lively), Hugh (brilliant), Ethel (good or noble), Ethelbert or Bert (noble birth), Mildred (mild counselor), and Wanda (lithe). Traits of use in battle are especially prevalent as can be seen in Bernard (brave as a bear), Gary (spearman), Gertrude (spear-love), Herman (army man), Leonard (lion brave), Leopold (bold for the people), Louise (famous warrior-maid), Richard (powerful brave), and Walter (mighty man). Anglo-Saxon names often bespeak the pragmatic work and money-oriented mind-set still associated with Anglos, as can be seen in *Beverly* (beaver or worker), *Emma* (healer), *Edmund* (wealth protector), and *Edward* (wealth guardian). Anglo family names often designate the occupations of Anglo-Saxon ancestors, pointing back to a host of bakers, blacksmiths (Smith), clerks (Clark), coopers, millers, potters, tailors (Taylor), tilers (Tyler), and wood corders or pilers (Corder).

Many Mexican Americans still bear Germanic and especially Visigothic first names. This prevalence can be sampled by perusing any U.S. Borderlands telephone book. Among the commonest of names are *Alberto* (brilliant), *Alfonso* (eager for battle), *Armando* (Army Man), *Federico* (peaceful), *Fernando* (adventuring), *Francisco* (free man), *Gonzalo* (wolf), *Matilda* (mighty battle maiden), *Ricardo* (powerful brave), *Rodrigo* (rich in fame), *Bermudo, Brunhilda* (beautiful armor), *Dagobertos, Ramiros,* and *Rigobertos. Ruiz* means son of ruy, a shortened form of *Rodrigo. Carlos,* used as both a first and a last name, comes from the Germanic *Karl* (man). *Halderas* comes from the germanic *walde (power* or *rule). Gómez* traces from the Gothic *guma* (man), and *Gutiérrez* comes from the Old Germanic *walthari,* from *walt* or *wald (power* or *rule)* and *hari* (army), meaning command of the army. *Suárez* and *Juárez* trace back to *Sug-hari* (seemingly, *southern army*). *Guzmán* comes from the Germanic *gothsmanna,* from *goth* (apt) and *manna* (man), meaning a skilled man. *Méndez* traces back to the Gothic *Hermenegildo,* meaning he who is important for his herd (from *airmana* for *cattle* or *horses* and *gilds* for *worth*). *Salas* is traced back to the Germanic *Saal* (hall or dwelling). Thus, the Germanic heritage, while associated mainly with the "Anglosajones," has entered the Borderlands through Hispanics as well.

The family name Albornoz comes from the Arabic *al-Burnusi* for the wearer of a burnoose (an Arab hooded cloak). The family name Zamora derives from *zamr,* a musical instrument. Some Arabic first names have been perpetuated in both the Anglo and Hispanic Borderlands traditions. Examples include *Elmer* (in Anglo tradition) and *Almira* (always truthful), *Guadalupe* (from *wadi al-lub* meaning river of black pebbles), *Leila* (evening), *Saida,* and *Xavier* (bright).

Cases of Scandanavian-based given names in use in the Mexican-American Borderlands include military-based ones like *Erik* and *Erika* (ever-ruler or powerful), and *Harold* (army ruler), along with reminders of the Christian conversion of the Vikings around the year 1000, like *Oscar* (divine) and *Kirk* (church dweller).

Such originally French given names as *Luis* and *Rene* came via Castile to the Borderlands. The Gallicized Spanish names *Enrique* and *Felipe* early replaced the earlier Spanish forms *Enrico* and *Filipo*. The family name Cisneros derives from the Old French *cisne* (swan). English names were also affected by French influence. In the bilingual French-English society that followed the Norman occupation of England, an English man might carry a prestigious Norman name as well as a native Anglo-Saxon or Celtic-based nickname among his English friends. Thus William (an English reworking of the French Guillaume, which was itself a reworking of the Germanic Wilhelm) was paired with Bill, and Robert (popular with the French, though based in the German Rotbart) was matched with Bob. Other French-based first names that have come down through the Anglo tradition include evocations of chivalric love culture like Amy (beloved), Belle (beautiful), and Blanche (fair).

Hebrew-based names were a part of the Jewish heritage of the Mexican-American Borderlands. At his baptism, a medieval Spanish Jew was required to take a Christian family name, which was often a saint's name, a place name, or an occupationally related name. Some of the names favored by the Jews were passed on to Mexican-American descendents. Espinoza (or Espinosa) was one such name, made famous in the form *Spinoza* by the Sephardic Jewish philosopher of seventeenth-century Holland, Baruch Spinoza. The Gentile name Pérez, a patronymic meaning "son of Pedro," was attractive to Jews since it coincided with the Hebrew word *peretz* meaning *breaker*. *Gálvez* sounds like the Hebrew words for *found in a tree (nimtza ba etz)* or perhaps *saved by a tree (goel ba etz)*. The name Brito stems from the Hebrew *brit*, or covenant. *Abadi* is Hebrew for *my servant*. Borjas is a corruption of the Hebrew words *be'er has* (protected well). Jiménez (son of Jimeno) has been traced to the Hebrew name *Shimeon*. *Curiel* possibly derives from the Hebrew *zori-el* (my rock is God). *Ortiz* may come from *Or Eretz* (light of the earth). Sometimes Hebrew names were romanized, so that *Baruch* (blessed) became *Bendito*, and *Hayim* (life) became *Jaime* as a first name and *Vivens*, *Vivant*, *Vidal*, or *Vives* as a last name. Many other names have similar origins: *Enrique*, *Guzmán*, *Luna*, and *Mendoza* were all names borne by famous *converso* families in late medieval Castile.

Hebrew first names have remained popular in both Hispanic and Anglo traditions due to the influence of the Bible. Examples of first names popular with girls include Hanna/Anna/Ann (from *Hen* for grace or favor), Deborah (from *devorah* for *bee*), Elizabeth (from *Eli sheva* for *God is my Oath*), Judith (from *yehudit* for *thanked*), María/Mary (from *Miriam* for "Bitterness"), and Susan (from *Shoshana* for "Rose"). Hebrew names often given to boys include Aarón/Aaron (from *haron* for *mountain of strength* or *ark*), Abraham (father of a multitude), Adam (man, earth), Benjamin (son of the right hand), Daniel (god is my judge), David (beloved), Eli (my God), Gabriel (man of god), Jacobo/Jacob (from *ekev* for heel), Joel (the Lord is God), Juan/John (from *Yohanan* for God is gracious), Miguel/Michael (who is like God), and Moisés (from *Moshe* for drawn forth).

The Influence of Medieval Society in General on Borderlands Customs and Speech

A rich heritage of premodern customs and sayings, coming mainly from the High and Late Middle Ages and not linked to any particular linguistic group, has also been passed down. In their case, as well, Hispanic and Anglo Borderlanders share a common bond of heritage, with some significant variations. Here again, customs, folklore, and curious details suggest the survival of ancient influences from a common source. Even the most trivial surviving bits of folklore and custom harking back to medieval developments suggest more important influences that have helped to shape the peculiar culture of the Borderlands. While the impact of this general medieval background is detectable separately in both the Anglo and Hispanic worlds in general, those worlds meet and overlap in the Borderlands, producing this region's unique culture. First, the specifically Hispanic transmission of this heritage will be considered, then the Anglo, and finally the commonly shared influences.

General Medieval Influences via the Hispanic Route

Even though the rich native Mexican impact on Border Hispanic culture has redirected much of its focus away from medieval Castile, many medieval Spanish influences have survived. For example, Alfonso X's *Siete*

Partidas law code of the thirteenth century had a lasting effect on every aspect of Spanish culture, including language. The fact that the *Siete Partidas* was written in Castilian, since Jews and Moors were not trained in Latin, helped the Castilian language to reach its modern form earlier than English. Not until the sixteenth century did English governments grow sufficiently confident in and respectful of English to give up Latin as the official language of government record. Standard Spanish began to emerge from the court speech at Toledo, overriding the various regional dialects during Alfonso's reign. Border Spanish has preserved some medieval terms that have since passed out of favor in Castile, including *bravo* as well as *valiente* for brave, *prieto* as well as *moreno* for dark-complexioned, *caminos reales* instead of *carreteras* for highways (of the colonial period), *corral* instead of *cercado* for a fenced area, *chícharo* instead of *guisante* for pea, *chiflar* instead of *silbar* for whistle, *durazno* instead of *melocotón* for peach, *frijol* instead of *judía* for bean, *nieve* instead of *helado* for ice cream (a fifteenth-century invention using ice brought from nearby mountains), *palo* as well as *árbol* for tree, and *nomás* as well as *nada más* for nothing more. The lack of the Castilian lisp or *ceceo,* which was introduced in sixteenth-century Castile only after Mexican Spanish had already been launched, is another medieval trait. In contrast, *yeísmo* (pronunciation of Spanish *ll* as *y*) began in Andalusia early enough in the sixteenth century to be transferred to Mexico. The current Spanish of New Mexico, due to its relative isolation, has preserved some medieval words unknown in the rest of the Mexican-American Borderlands or elsewhere, including *agora, entención, pos, dende,* and *a ráiz.*

The *Lapidario,* which in the thirteenth century Alfonso X *el Sabio* ordered translated from Arabic into Castilian, shows an interest in the magical property of stones akin to that encouraged by Borderland *curanderos.* The *Lapidario* describes various stones according to the sign of the Zodiac ruling them, warning of Zodiacal periods when they should not be worked. The *chupacabras*—a mysterious unseen creature or force that, according to Borderland lore, sucks the blood from goats and other animals—is evoked by the *Lapidario's* blood-sucking stone, which draws blood toward it from either inside or outside of a body. Mention is also made of stones that turn water into blood, that flee from or attract wine, honey, or vinegar, and that appear in the sea when the moon, Venus, Mars, or Saturn rise or go down.

Another curious influence is seen in the American dollar sign. This symbol shows the two pillars of Hercules (standing for Castile's claim to the Straits of Gibralter, won by Alfonso XI), the *S* through them indicating the plural. It was originally used on Spanish currency to stand for Spain, accompanied by the motto *Plus Ultra* (farther on), in reference to Spain's mastery of the ocean west of the Pillars of Hercules. The way these symbols came to appear on the American dollar also testifies to the Anglo-Hispanic cultural interaction. The Anglo-American colonists became familiar with the symbol in the eighteenth century, when Spanish *pesos* or even just broken parts of them ("pieces of eight") were in high demand as currency. Benjamin Franklin's popularization of the Pennsylvania colonial money, the "dollar" (a name taken from the *Johannisthaler* or *Thaler* of Germany) brought Americans to speak of the peso as the "Spanish dollar." Due to the role of the Spanish peso in financing the American Revolution and guaranteeing the first U.S. paper money, the "Spanish dollar" became in 1775 the standard currency for the American rebels. On Thomas Jefferson's recommendation it was continued as the monetary unit of the United States in 1785. When an independent American silver dollar was minted, the symbol of the two pillars superimposed on an "S," along with the motto *Plus Ultra,* was retained, resulting in a combined homage to both the Hispanic and Anglo heritages.

General Medieval Influences via the Anglo Route

Anglo society, influenced far less than its Hispanic counterpart by the cultures of indigenous American peoples, offers a far greater array of lingering medieval European influences. The many connections between medieval English culture and modern Anglo American culture, while not unique to the Borderlands, have helped to shape its cultural blend as well. The examples cited in the next few pages should remind us of that vast heritage. The Anglo nostalgia for the medieval tradition is evident in the Borderlands, as can be seen in such annual events as the medieval festival at Edinburg, Texas, and the Scottish evening of the Rio Grande Valley Scottish Society. From English chivalry came the expression *by George,* still known if rarely used, from the custom of the English knights of swearing by St. George as the patron saint of their nation. The saying "to turn the tables" on somebody stems from these days of sparse furniture. Tables were usually mere boards set up on trestles. For meals, the smooth side was placed up, for writing on the rough side. If a guest was not wanted for dinner, the "tables would be turned" on him, so that the rough side was placed up by way of a broad hint. A related expression is *to give somebody the cold shoulder,* once meant to give an unheated shoulder of meat to an unwanted guest. Beds were so rare that when one royal family paid a state visit to another, the host queen was sometimes turned out of the royal bed, so that the two kings could sleep there, as befitted their dignity. Most people sat on benches or stools, and chairs were a status symbol. We still take note of a bishop's see (i.e., seat), since he and the king, if nobody else, were allowed to have a chair in church.

Many English-language sayings originated in (or are popularly believed to have originated in) late medieval England. In 1402 London's Hospital of St. Mary of Bethlehem began to specialize in cases of insanity. Locally, Bethlehem was commonly pronounced "Bedlam," the origins of that term's modern meaning for a chaotic and noisy uproar. Other lasting expressions resulted when Henry IV sent his son Thomas of Lancaster to govern Ireland. When Thomas found that he could not control most of the island, he fell back on a little strip of the coast around Dublin, and set up a system of watch towers along the border. This zone came to be called the Pale, from the pale or fence marking the first line of defense in front of the towers. The expression to go or to be "beyond the pale" for a person outside the control of the law was born at that time.

It is said that the vulgar custom of *giving someone the finger* originated at the battle of Agincourt in 1415. According to this explanation, the French had called for cutting off the middle finger of the bowstring hand of each captured English archer, rendering him useless as a bowman. After their victory, the English archers defiantly showed their fingers, still intact, to the defeated French. One of the French hostages from Agincourt was the poet Duke Charles of Orléans, cousin of the Dauphin. Sitting in his confinement in the Tower of London, on the feast day of the martyred St. Valentine, February 14, Orléans wrote a love poem to his wife back in France and doodled a design of hearts and flowers around it. Impressed, other lovers soon followed suit, in the first exchanges of Valentine Day cards. At any rate, an old custom had called for the choosing of sweethearts on that day because it was said that the birds did the same.

A royal postal service was introduced to England in 1482 by Edward IV. The term "postman" for a mailman is said to have come from the early days of mail carrying. To keep the noisy mail coach from waking people as it passed over the bumpy cobble-stone streets, the mail route was made to bypass the towns, and a post with a hook was set up on which the mailbag was hung. Each town appointed a postman to go out every day, get the incoming mail, and leave the outgoing mail on the post.

The stringent social-class distinctions of late medieval Castile and England have also left a mark. The elegant usages of the upper class gave us the bathrobe, a novelty first recorded as a possession in the wardrobe of King John of England, where it was described as a surcoat for use in getting up in the night. Upper-class luxury of the Late Middle Ages also gave us the fork; Edward II's favorite Piers Gaveston owned three silver forks kept for eating pears. Richard II introduced the handkerchief as a more refined replacement for the sleeve in wiping one's nose. The disparaging expression that somebody needs *to get down off his high horse* refers to the war horse of the medieval noble, which was significantly larger and heavier than the palfrey ridden by the commoner (or the noble himself when not outfitted for war or war games).

Whereas the secular life of the upper class was centered in the castle and its great hall, that of the average man focused around the tavern in the town. From the days of drinking in the inns come the expressions *to mind your p's and q's, to wipe the slate clean,* and *to start with a clean slate.* The innkeepers kept slates on which they wrote in chalk the draughts taken by a particular customer on credit. The "p" stood for a pint, and the "q" for a quart. To mind one's p's and q's was an admonition not to fall too far either into debt or inebriation. When an account was paid in full, a person would be able *to start with a clean slate,* with his subsequent drinking. While the tavern provided mainly wine in Castile and ale or beer in England, by the fifteenth century both wine and fermented grain malt were being used to make *whisky,* from *uisce* (water), the first of a two-word Gaelic phrase literally meaning water of life.

Some popular expressions have survived from medieval witchcraft. The term *hocus pocus* comes from a black mass performed using a cross turned upside down, the sacrifice and communal consumption of a pig, and the scrambling of Jesus' words *"Hoc est corpus meum"* (this is my body) into *"Hoc est porcus meus"* (this is my pig). The term *sinister,* literally meaning the left (side) in Latin and carrying the ancient connotation of something evil, is linked to the fact that in the Middle Ages witches used their left hands to cast spells, in contrast to Christian ritual blessings, which are signaled with the right hand. We still say "knock on wood" for good luck because people once knocked on trees to call on the fertility spirits to work their will. Another folk tradition inherited from the cult of the fertility goddess is that of throwing pennies into a well and making a wish. This practice originated as a propitiation to the fertility goddess in her water aspect.

One special category of cultural transmission is children's lore, through which as children we explore the childhood of our culture. Anglo society is unique in remembering early interests and events by incorporating them into nursery rhymes and fairy tales. There is no true Hispanic counterpart to the wealth of surviving early recollections passed down in this fashion in the Anglo tradition. This difference has been credited to the greater reluctance of the English to say good-bye to childhood. This Anglo trait underlies the practice of men calling attractive women "babes" and their girlfriends "baby" and has contributed to the whimsical twentieth-century concept of the teen-age years as a time of prolonged idleness and irresponsibility.

The earliest core of this English-language children's lore evokes the ancient and Dark Age inhabitants of Britain. Paleolithic society is recalled in English nursery rhymes regarding a cyclops. One English folk tale presents a man-eating giant who shouts,

> Fee-fie-fo-fum,
> I smell the blood of an Englishman.
> Be he alive or be he dead,
> I'll grind his bones to make my bread.[1]

Some rhymes hearken back to early religious beliefs. One details the gifts of various pagan deities, arranged according to birth days:

> Monday's child is fair of face,
> Tuesday's child is full of grace,
> Wednesday's child is full of woe,
> Thursday's child has far to go,
> Friday's child is loving and giving,
> Saturday's child works hard for a living,
> But the child that's born on the Sabbath day
> Is blithe and bonny, good and gay.

Anglo nursery rhymes have also passed down invocations originally intended to work spells. These chants include spells to guarantee good weather, like "Rain, rain, go away. / Come again another day. / Little Johnnie wants to play." Another surviving chant, "Wheat, peas, beans, and barley grow," was intended to influence a good crop yield. Still other chants were aimed at increasing the benefits of animal husbandry, including "Black sheep, black sheep, have ye any wool?" Another rhyme traces back to a chant sung in a cult of death and rebirth:

> Sing a song of sixpence, a pocket full of rye.
> Four and twenty blackbirds backed into a pie.
> When the pie was opened, the birds began to sing.
> Now, wasn't that a dainty dish to set before the king?

Similarly, an ancient belief held that correctly counting the destructive pigs of death, should they escape from the underworld, will send them back again. This idea is reflected in the popular rhyme used in counting a baby's toes:

> This little piggy goes to market;
> this little piggy stays home;
> this little piggy gets roast beef;
> this little piggy gets none;
> and this little piggy goes wee-wee-wee-wee all the way home.

Various fairy tales tell of conflict between the common folk and their leaders. The names Jack and Jill refer to the common folk of those times. The Celtic term *jars,* referring to a commoner, evolved into *Jack,* in contrast to *gan,* the Celtic word for a giant that gave rise to the name John for chiefs and kings, reinforced by its Biblical equation with the Hebrew name Jonathan. We still speak of a worker good at many jobs as being a "Jack of all trades" and revile an ignorant fellow as a "jack-ass." Popular Anglo culture today still repeats many reminders of this early class tension between the Jacks and the giants. "Jack and Jill went up the Hill to fetch a pail of water. / Jack fell down and broke his crown, and Jill came tumbling after" pictures what seems to be a human sacrifice by throwing people from a height. "Jack be Nimble, Jack be quick, / Jack jump over the candlestick" may refer to ritual leaps through bonfires.

Some hero tales popular with Anglo children trace back to the early Celtic period and tell about common Jacks who rebelled against the oppressive leadership of the giants, with their worship of the magical deities of death and human sacrifice. "Jack and the Beanstalk" narrates the exploits of a Jack who climbed a beanstalk (symbolizing the social distance between the commoners and the giants) to slay a giant who lived in a castle at the top. Jack then stole the giant's talking harp (the main instrument of the Celts) and his goose that laid the golden eggs (the *Gans* symbol of prosperity). "Jack the Giant-Killer" tells how a Jack killed a man-eating giant named Cormoran ("Sea Rock") at St. Michael's Mount, off the Cornish coast. This Jack dug a pit and covered it with sticks and straw. He then blew his trumpet, and Cormoran came running, only to fall to his death into the pit. St. Michael's Mount was then rededicated to the sun god Bel, under the name of Din-sul (Mountain of the Sun). Other tales poke fun at commoners. "The Little Tailor" tells how a tailor advertised that he had "killed seven," by which he meant seven fleas. However, it was assumed that he meant giants, and he thus found himself obliged to face a giant in combat. The name Tom, used for jokesters, gave rise to our terms of "tomfoolery" and "tommyrot." A comic tale about diminutive Tom Thumb relates how even he confronted a giant.

One nursery rhyme commemorates an ancient Roman victory. Constantius' defeat of the Saxon pirates, saving Colechester, prompted the mythical King Cole of Britain to a celebrate the victory remembered in the nursery rhyme:

> Old King Cole was a merry old soul,
> and a merry old soul was he.
> He called for his pipe,
> and he called for his bowl,
> and he called for his fiddlers three.
> Oh, there's none so rare as can compare
> to King Cole and his fiddlers three.

Children's lore incorporating political doggerel from the High and Late Middle Ages recalls the relatively free nature of English society, in which the common folk were able to repeat rhymes and tales of political significance. English-speaking children, including those in the Borderlands, may be commemorating an actual event when they play and chant "London bridge is falling down, / falling down, falling down. / London Bridge is falling down, / my fair lady." According to Snorri Sturluson's *Heimskringla,* in 1009 Norway's St. Olaf the Stout, ally of Ethelred the Redeless, sailed up the Thames against Danish-held London. Defenders fought back from London Bridge, shooting arrows and hurling rocks. Olaf had protective wicker-work roofs placed over his dragon ships and managed to get some of the ships under the bridge. There they hacked at and fastened cables around the supporting piers, then rowed hard downstream to pull the cables taut. The bridge collapsed with its load of fighters, and London surrendered.

Lady Godiva, the wife of Earl Leofric of Mercia, is still well remembered in English-language folklore as persuading her husband to lower the taxes of the Mercian capital of Coventry by carrying out her threat to ride through town naked. According to the story, Leofric forbade all men to look at her and was obeyed by everyone except "peeping Tom." It is claimed that the subsequent Lady Godiva procession was a transformation of an old pagan custom. Two figures, a black Hell and a white Holda (Love), were carried in an all-female procession, while men were forbidden to watch. One possibility is that Godiva defiantly took the role of the goddess Holda in this procession in order to express her sympathy with the townsmen who were protesting the tax. Popular memory records the event in the nursery rhyme:

> Ride a cock horse to Banbury [or Coventry] Cross,
> to see a fine lady upon a fine horse.
> Rings on her fingers and bells on her toes,
> she shall have music wherever she goes.

English resistance to King John's arbitrary taxation also left its mark on English vocabulary and folklore. According to a famous tale, when John placed a special tax on his towns, the residents of the Midlands town of Gotham, near Nottingham, pretended to have gone insane, since the mentally incompetent were exempted from taxation. As if to demonstrate their insanity, some of the citizens trapped cuckoos, a migratory bird, saying that by forcing the cuckoos to stay in town they hoped to win perpetual summer. This story gave rise to the term *to go cuckoo* for going insane. Three of the tricksters went out into the local Trent River in an unseaworthy boat or tub (the round-hulled northern boat, called a *Kogge* by the Germans, was a "tub" to the English). Two surviving nursery rhymes tell us the result of that experiment. One goes, "Three wise men of Gotham went to sea in a bowl. / If the bowl had been stronger, my song had been longer." A more widely-remembered rhyme goes:

Rub-a-dub-dub, three men in a tub,
and who do you think they be?
The butcher, the baker, the candle-stick maker.
Turn them out! Knaves, all three.

The trials and tribulations of the Late Middle Ages, with its epidemics and its class warfare, also left their marks on children's lore. A popular children's ditty still describes the response to and description of the Black Death in the fourteenth century—the quarantine of people exhibiting a rosy rash, the attempt to purify the air with flowers (posies), the sneezing and final collapse, with its "Ring-a-ring-a-roses, A pocket full of posies. A-tishatoo, a-tishatoo, we've all tumbled down." Henry V's English soldiers incorporated the fifteenth-century interest in witches into a marching song still included in some children books of English nursery rhymes:

There was an old woman tossed in a blanket,
  Seventeen times as high as the moon;
But where she was going no mortal could tell,
  For under her arm she carried a broom.
Old woman, old woman, old woman, said I!
  Whither, ah whither, ah whither so high?
To sweep the cobwebs from the sky,
  And I'll be with you by and by.

One Mother Goose Nursery Rhyme is a ditty people may have sung at the fall from power of the unpopular Richard III, referring to him as a hunchback (a "humpty dumpty"):

Humpty Dumpty sat on a wall.
Humpty Dumpty had a great fall.
  All the King's horses,
  And all the King's men,
Couldn't put Humpty together again.

This Anglo heritage of children's lore has acted as one of the bridges between the two Borderland traditions, as Borderland Hispanics have proven receptive to absorbing these tales and rhymes into their childhood experience. The fact that Spanish history shared some of the premodern experiences this lore recalls (such as cyclopes, pagan deities, witchcraft, Roman and Viking conquerors, and the Black Death) has acted as a catalyst to this acceptance. Children's literature reinforces both the cultural and linguistic tradition by familiarizing children with names and concerns that would otherwise have passed out of usage.

General Medieval Influences Coming by Both Hispanic and Anglo Routes

Many general medieval influences came to the Borderlands via both Hispanic and Anglo routes. Some of these influences have worked in Western society in general or become common to all of world culture. For example, knitting and buttons were developed in the colder climate of the fourteenth and fifteenth centuries for greater protection from the cold. The popular Borderlands custom of holding county fairs and church *kermesses* evince an influence from medieval town fairs. The term *kermesse* derives from the German *Kehr Messe* or Ash Wednesday mass at the start of Lent, when *Kehrauß* occurred (the sweeping out of the rubbish of the old year, also the name of the last dance of Carnival before the start of Lent). The adaptation of this German-based word into Spanish is explained by the prominence of German merchants in the Castilian economy and its fairs in the fifteenth century. England's Scarborough Fair was repopularized in the 1960s by the music of Simon and Garfunkel, which recalled the fair's fame for the sale of "parsley, sage, rosemary, and thyme," believed to be used for aphrodisiacs in the Middle Ages. The word *tawdry* (a contraction of St. Audrey) originated to describe the shoddy quality of the silk and lace necklaces sold at St. Audrey's Fair at Ely. The English word *cargo* was taken from pack-train references to *cargar* (to carry), tracing back to the medieval Andalusian donkey and mule pack-trains bringing goods to the fairs of Castile.

Various medieval sports, originally differentiated by what social class participated in them, have been passed down to the present. The aristocratic joust and duel are seen today in the Borderlands as occasional curiosities staged for medieval fairs. The custom of making men's shirts and coats button with the left side overlapping to the right side (while women's blouses and coats overlap to the left) is said to have originated with the joust. Had the heavy surcoats worn over the armor overlapped to the left, the lance held in the opponent's right hand might have caught inside the coat. The use of coats of arms stems from the symbols (called Charges) painted on a medieval shield for recognition in battles and jousts. Richard the Lionhearted, an impassioned jouster, elaborated many of the rules of heraldry and gave England its royal motto of *Mon Dieu et mon droit* (My God and my Right) and its emblem of three lions rampant. His brother-in-law Alfonso VIII of Castile added the castle symbol to the royal coat of arms for his kingdom. Such emblems are called arms because they were placed on shields, the shape of which they still retain. They were called coats (of arms) because when shields became too small or were abandoned, with the introduction of effective firepower in the fifteenth century, they came to be sewn on the surcoat worn over the armor. A *blot on the escutcheon* (or shield) indicates a negative reference like illegitimacy or treason. Commoners adopted emblems illustrating their line of work, and the practice of using insignia was soon adopted by medieval shops and other establishments, which placed their emblems on signs protruding into the street to guide the illiterate majority of their clientele. The continued use of a red-and-white-striped pole outside a barber shop evokes an arm running with blood (or the resulting blood-soaked rags hung out to dry), from the days when barbers also let blood as a medical practice.

Schools and colleges have elaborated these emblems, as can be seen, for instance, in the banners designed for the University of Texas at Brownsville. The banner of the College of Science, Mathematics, and Technology features a scallop, the symbol of the pilgrim to Santiago de Compostela, but here symbolizing travel to new worlds of learning. That of the School of Education has taken the fleur de lys symbol of Christ, adopted by the kings of France, in honor of teaching as the most royal of callings. The College of Liberal Arts features a gryphon, the guardian of treasure, which here denotes the treasure of knowledge. The School of Business shows the Phoenix, symbol of Christ's resurrection, to stand for the resurrection or birth of a new enterprise. The School of Health Sciences features the cross as the symbol of life and faith. Likewise, the mace, originally a weighted club used by knights to crush the armor of their foes and, by the fourteenth century, carried before a monarch is borne as a symbol of academic authority in commencement ceremonies. While the details of graduation regalia were not fixed until the seventeenth century at Oxford, compliments of William Laud, the gowns date from the need to keep scholars warm in the cold and drafty medieval university buildings.

Medieval coats of arms have also influenced the colors and symbols on flags. The red and gold of the state flags of New Mexico and Arizona indicate a Spanish heritage by using the colors of the flag of Spain. The red, white, and blue colors of the Texas flag are borrowed from the flag of the United States, itself an adaptation of the British Union Jack, which was an amalgamation of the medieval crosses of the patron saints of England (a vertical red on white for St. George), Scotland (a white X on blue for St. Andrew), and Ireland (a red X on white for St. Patrick).

The Borderlands derive some income from hunters visiting the area seeking white wing doves, deer, and javelinas. The hunt as sport is a typically medieval concept, as opposed to the Indian hunt for food. The English wrote various hunting guide books in the Late Middle Ages. Edward II's huntsman William Twiti wrote the *Craft of Venery* (versified by Julian Barnes as the *Boke of Huntyng*), and Henry V's cousin Edward, Duke of York, at the beginning of the fifteenth century, wrote *The Master of Game*. The boar and the deer were preferred game in medieval Castile and England, as in the Mexican-American Borderlands today, although the white-winged dove has taken the place of the pheasant. American hunting has been modified by native American influences. Anglo hunters on the early American frontier typically traveled together with Indian hunters, from whom they learned native hunting practices and where to hunt. Most English immigrants to America were commoners and thus untrained in hunting, which was mainly reserved for the upper class in England. The Indians taught them such information as calls, decoys, disguises, encirclement, fire hunting, and trail markings.

Wrestling, handball, football (i.e. soccer), and bowling, all popular with the common man in the Late Middle Ages, have remained in vogue in the Borderlands as elsewhere. Some English counties allowed wrestling matches with no holds barred, but others placed restrictions on the sport. The Lord Mayor of London sponsored wrestling matches every year on St. Bartholomew's Day, throwing bags of money to the winners. The expression *to get the upper hand over somebody* comes from arm wrestling. Football (meaning soccer) was particularly rowdy in the Middle Ages, a threat to property in the streets and churchyards where it was played. Archery was the sport most encouraged by the English government, in order to prepare good longbowmen for the military. Proclamations forbade men to play handball and football, the most popular alternatives, but some men stole away from the archery range to bowl or gamble.

Still other general medieval influences define only Hispanic and Anglo society. Legal expressions in both languages reflect the medieval heritage.

The feudal oath of a vassal to his lord lives on in *Lo juro* and *I swear to God,* as well as in oaths taken before legal testimony. The term *chiseler* for a crook comes from the practice of chiseling the edges off of the irregularly shaped coins of the day, in hopes that the next person to receive the coin would not notice. Various legal maxims in the Latin vocabulary of the medieval courtroom have survived even though not found in either statutes or court decisions. Examples include most famously *caveat emptor* (let the buyer beware), but also *audi alteram partem* (hear both sides), *ignorantia juris neminem excusat* (ignorance of the law excuses nobody), *qui facit per alium facit per se* (who acts through an agent acts through himself); and *salus populi suprema lex* (the welfare of the people is the supreme law). Surviving medieval English law practices include the robes of the judges (a typical medieval item of apparel), such legal phrases as *will and testament, law and order,* and *goods and chattels,* and Latin terms like *bona fide* and *vice versa.* The term *hoosegow,* comes from the Spanish *juzgado* for a tribunal but generally used to refer to a jail. However, most of the legal terms come from Anglo-Norman French, including *asset, embezzle, jury, larceny,* and *perjury.* The term *real estate* for landed property evokes the rural Middle Ages when the only real (i.e., significant) property was considered to be land holdings.

Some Borderlands family names record a commoner background by identifying the line of work of the paternal ancestors in the fourteenth century, when much of the family naming system was formalized. Hispanic examples include *Herrera* and *Herrero,* referring to iron workers, and *Madero* for a wood worker. *Hinojosa* implies a or livestock herder or worker in a field of hay *(heno),* and *Huerta* (garden) indicates a vegetable or fruit farmer. *Manzano* refers to an apple farmer, *Morales* to a black mulberry farmer, and *Olivares* and *Oliveira* to an olive farmer. Anglo examples, some of which we have already noted, include *Baker, Binder, Butler, Brewer, Carpenter, Carter, Clark, Cook, Cooper, Corder, Dyer, Farmer, Fisher, Fowler, Harper, Hatcher, Hunter, Mason, Miller, Parson, Potter, Shepherd, Shoemaker, Smith, Taylor,* and *Wheeler.*

On the folkloric side of cultural considerations, some Borderlands beliefs about the supernatural can be mentioned here, although religious traditions and doctrines will be considered in a later chapter. Hispanic and Anglo superstitions from early Europe still circulate in the Borderlands. Both language groups have continued the belief that the thirteenth of the month, especially on the night of a full moon, is unlucky. The number thirteen was a special holy number in the Celtic sidereal lunar calendar, which was based on thirteen moon cycles, counted as thirteen months of twenty-eight days each, in one solar cycle or solar year. As this calendar was replaced by the Roman system of twelve synodal lunar cycles, it was discouraged as unlucky. For Anglos, Friday the thirteenth is especially ominous. Besides Monday (moon day, *lunes*), Friday was a special day of the fertility goddess, as commemorated in the English word *Friday,* referring to the goddess Freya, and in Spanish *viernes,* referring to Venus. Throughout the Hispanic world, including among Borderland Hispanics, Tuesday the thirteenth (the day once holy to Mars, the god of war) is held to be the unlucky day. A saying warns: En martes no te cases ni te embarques (don't marry or start on a trip on a Tuesday).[2] The goddess's power was believed to be at its height during a full moon. It was believed that men could turn into werewolves under the influence of a full moon. The word *desastre* (disaster) literally meaning to remove a star, derives from the notion that a person's luck would sour when his lucky stars moved away from each other. The word *lunático* (lunatic) derives from the idea that the moon (*luna* in Latin) had the power to drive people crazy.

All of these general medieval influences over the Anglo and Hispanic worlds have a special significance for the Borderlands precisely because this is the unique region that blends and harmonizes these two traditions.

Concluding Remark

Linguistic, cultural, and folkloric considerations show that the Spanish and English societies were close cousins down to 1500, despite the greater Moorish influence in Spain and the more important Viking influence in England. Basque, Iberian, Celtic, Semitic, Greek, Roman, Germanic, and French threads were used to weave the two baby blankets of Hispanic and Anglo societies, wrapping them in similar garb in their infancy. Some of the linguistic and cultural similarities are so ingrained that it is difficult to know whether they are more Hispanic or more Anglo. The locally popular Spanish saying, "A los tres días el muerto y el arrimado apestan" (after three days, the dead and the imposer stink) parallels the English "Fish and guests stink after three days," which is found among Benjamin Franklin's "Sayings of Poor Richard" but may well go back to earlier times. Indeed, a book noting many such comparable English and Spanish proverbs has been compiled.[3] As Borderlanders blend into one bilingual identity, they are coming full circle back to an original Anglo-Hispanic linguistic-cultural relatedness from early times. Borderlanders of all backgrounds are becoming increasingly Spanish-English bilingual, and the Pocho mix of Spanish and Anglo influences (including children's lore), as well as the ongoing flip-flop tendency to move comfortably from one language to the other, is an unwitting acknowledgment of that early relationship. Despite the differences, the underlying resemblances between the two traditions form a bond that helps to explain the mutual affinity and rapid assimilation between Anglos and Hispanics in the Mexican-American Borderlands.

TWO

Political and Legal Influences

The political and legal foundations of the Spanish and English nations were established mainly during the High Middle Ages. Constitutionalism and representative institutions are among the most important heritages from that time, and Spain and England led the way in forming these basic elements of the state. A successful response to the challenge of almost total foreign occupation—by the Moors in Spain, by the French in England—helped to forge a basis for national identities in both cases. Each nation's reactions to foreign occupations will be considered in turn. During the High Middle Ages Castilian and English politics and law experienced a separate but parallel evolution, which we will review in order to reveal significant ties between Hispanic and Anglo communities that help to explain the relative congeniality of their blending in the Borderlands. Just as the political and legal institutions of Spain and England matured over a long period of time, their influences have also evolved in the Borderlands. Therefore, this chapter will first review these developments in Spain and England from the ninth through the thirteenth centuries, and follow with a consideration of Borderlands responses in these areas. Along the way we will note how some important Spanish and English differences created separate traditions that were eventually to meet in the border region. The chapter will conclude by considering the overall significance of both the shared and the contrasting political and legal heritages for the Borderlands.

Parallel Hispanic and Anglo Developments of the High Middle Ages

Close parallels in Hispanic and Anglo experiences run through the High Middle Ages, as can be seen in the similarities between the stages of their evolution in this period. In political and legal backgrounds Borderlands Hispanics and Anglos also share more of a common heritage than is sometimes remembered.

Start of National Unifications in the Ninth and Tenth Centuries

The development of institutional government in western Europe was a long and painful process covering the ninth, tenth, and eleventh centuries. The early Germanic tribal kingdoms had placed loyalty to individuals above adherence to abstract concepts or to institutions, which did not exist in any regularly functioning manner. From the ninth century, Spanish and English kings made use of a royal council (the *aula regia* or *palatium* in Spain and the *witan* or *curia regis* in England) composed of leading members of the king's court assembled to help with public affairs.

The concept of the modern state took shape in Spain and England as a result of military resistance to the invading Moors in Spain and to the Vikings in England. Castile's and England's reconquest efforts ran along parallel lines, even though starting earlier and lasting longer in Castile. The initiators, Pelayo in Spain (718–37) and Alfred the Great in England (871–99), were both leaders of the native peoples by right of birth, Pelayo as duke of Asturias, and Alfred as King of Wessex and *Bretwald* or High-King of England. Both leaders retreated to inaccessible terrain to form their resistance movements, Pelayo establishing his headquarters at Covadonga (*Cueva Dominica* or Cave of Our Lady) high in the Cantabrian Mountains, and Alfred hiding in the Isle (swamp) of Athelney. Both leaders endured contempt at the nadir of their careers. An envoy from the Moors, sent to argue Pelayo into surrender, contemptuously asked him how he could hope to hold out with such a small band, while Alfred was berated by a peasant woman for burning some pancakes she had asked him to watch. Nonetheless, Pelayo managed to defeat a Moorish army in 722 at the battle of Covadonga, assuring the continuation of a Christian Spanish kingdom in the north. Similarly, in May 878 Alfred defeated Guthrum at the battle of Edington and reestablished his rule of Wessex.

Alfonso III el Magno (the Great) (866–910) offers a contemporary comparison to Alfred. Alfonso launched the first vigorous southward push of the Spanish *Reconquista* by repopulating the north bank of the Duero Valley with Christian *Mozárabes* (Christians from Moorish al-Andalus). His success allowed his son Ordoño II (914–24) to shift the capital south to León. Alfred likewise encouraged his nobles to build *burgs* (wall-surrounded castles on high promontories) on the reconquered territory. Alfred's son Edward the Elder (899–924) reconquered Mercia, and his grandson Aethelstan (924–39) completed the reconquest of England by taking Northumbria. The national kingships thus established in England and Spain were still highly tenuous because they challenged traditional systems of local control and because enemy raids required every area to fight off sudden attacks unaided. Nonetheless, the structures of national bureaucracies began to take shape. Alfonso organized his royal council, using such palace officials as the *armiger* (royal standard bearer and troop commander), the *maiordomus,* the *notarius,* the *thesaurius,* and the *strator,* along with chamberlains and chaplains. Tenth-century England saw the introduction of stewards, butlers, marshalls, chamberlains, and sheriffs.

A Generation of Foreign-Imposed Royal Authority in the Early Eleventh Century

These experiments with more centralized governments were not sufficient to prevent brief but total takeovers of the two kingdoms by foreign rulers in the early eleventh century. Government still relied heavily on the personal leadership skills of the monarch, and when apt rulers were not produced, counts and earls went their own ways. In Spain, counts of Castile starting with Fernán González challenged the cohesion of the Kingdom of León, while in England various earls opposed weak kings. This defiance of the nobles encouraged a resurgence of raids from foreign invaders—Al-Mansur's Moors in Spain and Svein Forkbeard's Vikings in England—adding additional stress to the new nations.

Out of the resulting warfare, royal authority was reasserted by two conquering foreign kings: the Basque king Sancho el Mayor (the great or elder) in Spain and Knut, the Danish King, in England. Both of these monarchs were effective rulers who restored law and order and thereby won popularity with the peoples they conquered. Sancho el Mayor of Navarre (1004–35) occupied Castile in 1017 and León in 1033. Assuming the title of Emperor of Spain from the kings of León, Sancho minted the first Christian Spanish currency, and persuaded three of the Moorish *taifa* states to pay him tribute. Sancho's counterpart in England was Danish King Knut, son of Svein Forkbeard, who occupied and ruled England from 1016 to 1035. Honored as "Good King Knut," and by a carol entitled "God bless King Knut," he codified Anglo-Saxon law. The Basque hold on Castile was broken when Sancho el Mayor divided his realms in his will, leaving his son Fernando I with only the Castilian-speaking lands. After Knut's two sons died only seven years after him, English rule reverted to the native house of Wessex. Foreign rule and the strength of government it had brought disappeared from both kingdoms.

Return to Problems of Rule in the Mid-Eleventh Century

When the native element resumed control in the mid-eleventh century in the Kingdom of León under Alfonso VI and in England under Edward the Confessor, the problems of weak central government immediately resurfaced. Castile's Sancho II and El Cid made trouble for Alfonso, while this disruptive role was played in England by the Earls of Wessex and of Mercia. The resulting civil strife encouraged more foreign invasions, so that Castile was faced with a Moorish challenge from Yusuf ibn-Tashfin, and England was threatened first by the Vikings and then conquered by the Norman French.

When Alfonso VI (Fernando I's favorite son) ascended to the throne of León in 1065, Castilian opposition to León flared up again under Alfonso's elder brother, Sancho II the Strong. Sancho took Alfonso prisoner at the battle of Golpejera in 1072, exiling Alfonso to Toledo, but a Leonese noble subsequently infiltrated Sancho's entourage and pierced him through with a lance. This assassination allowed Alfonso to return to power, but Castile's defiance found a new leader in Rodrigo de Vivar, remembered as El Cid. When Alfonso banished Rodrigo in 1081, he found employment as a mercenary for the emir of Zaragoza. As El Cid won one battle after another for the emir, he gained the title of *el Cid* (from the Arabic *al-sayid* or *al sidi,* meaning Lord), and the Castilians began to sing a *cantar de gesta* about him.

England's central government suffered a similar pattern of stresses and threats at the hands of provincial loyalties and ambitious nobles. The accession of Edward the Confessor (1042–66) brought the throne back into the hands of the native house of Wessex. Edward was later honored as a saint, partly due to a meekness that made it difficult for him to impose royal authority. The king's position was especially undermined by a family feud between the houses of the Earls of Mercia and Wessex.

The Last Challenges to National Unification from Overseas

In a continuing community of experience endured by the Castilians and the English, their internal divisions encouraged renewed foreign invasions, of Spain by the Almoravids and of England by the Normans. In those distinct but oddly related military clashes, Alfonso VI (the defender in Spain) and William the Conqueror (the invader in England) both enjoyed an advantage gained from use of the saddle stirrup, which allowed heavily armored knights on horseback wielding heavy weapons to carry out shock cavalry charges. Alfonso VI alarmed the Moors by the incorporation of the central *meseta,* or plateau, into his realm. During a revolt against an unpopular Emir, al-Kadir, some of the Toledans asked Alfonso to take over direct rule of Toledo, which he did in 1085. Alfonso VI renamed the ex-emirate New Castile and changed his principal residence to Toledo, so that the name of the kingdom shifted from León to Castile. Al-Kadir was compensated by being declared Alfonso's vassal ruler for Valencia. In 1086 Alfonso began a campaign to conquer the emirate of Zaragoza, and it seemed that Muslim Spain might be reconquered by the Christians in short order. This hope was cut short when Sultan Yusuf ibn Tashfin arrived from Morocco with an Almoravid army and advanced on Toledo. At the battle of Sagrajas (or Zalaca), fought near Badajoz on October 23, 1086, Yusuf's forces won a sweeping victory. El Cid took charge of the Christian defense of Valencia and prevented the Moors from taking it. Only after the Cid's death did Ibn Tashfin finally capture the city, in 1101. However, Alfonso VI retained Toledo, foiling the last serious attempt of the Moors to reestablish hegemony in Spain.

At the same time, England was faced by a similar challenge from two groups of foreign invaders, first the Vikings and then the Norman French. After Edward the Confessor died in early 1066, Harold (II), Earl of Wessex, grabbed the throne with a questionable claim that encouraged foreign challengers. Norway's King Harold III Hardraada landed in Yorkshire in September, defeated one Anglo-Saxon army, and then met Harold of Wessex in the battle of Stamford Bridge. English victory was assured when Hardraada was hit by an arrow in his throat and fell dead. The English were given no opportunity to enjoy this victory, however, for an army of Norman-led French under Duke William of Normandy landed in southern England the next month, claiming that Edward had promised the throne to William. Harold rushed back south, not waiting to collect all of his troops, and took up a defensive position on Senlac Hill. At the battle of Hastings on October 14, 1066, Harold was killed by an arrow that pierced his eye, and his men were routed.

Political and Legal Developments of the Late Eleventh and Twelfth Centuries

A period of rapid modernization of government and law began in the late eleventh century in both Castile and England. The stability won with the waning of the Moorish and Viking attacks allowed for more attention to be given to internal improvements, while a population boom and increasing prosperity brought a new spirit of optimism. The growth of education allowed by the improved law and order brought a new professionalism to questions of government and justice, and the appeals made to Roman and canon law during the Investiture Controversy between Pope Gregory VII and Holy Roman Emperor Henry IV gave a boost to experimentation with the legal system. Also, the triumph of the papal Catholic Church in Christianizing European society lent force to its call for kings to provide justice and peace to their subjects.

Much of the development of the unified Hispanic and British kingdoms occurred in the High Middle Ages. The foundations of a stronger system of rule were laid down in Castile (León) under the long-lived Alfonso VI (ruled León 1065–, Castille 1072–1109), and in England under William I, the Conqueror (1066–87) and his son Henry I (1100–35). All three of these rulers made use of imported French feudalism, and all of them strengthened the crown's authority over the higher nobility. William I used a variety of local agents, from sheriffs (who replaced the earls as the main royal agent at the local level) and bailiffs to castle keepers and forest wardens, and in 1086 commissioned the so-called *Domesday Book* as a survey of the possessions of his subjects. Henry I centralized the English royal administration in London, with an exchequer office to which sheriffs brought collected tax revenues. Henry also introduced the office of chancellor, filling a secretarial role for matters of state and coordinating other departments, judges, the system of law and order, and the collection of revenue. Henry I sent out itinerant justices to relieve the sheriffs of most of their judicial responsibilities and to bring more objective legal decisions to the local areas.

In both Castile and England, a tug-of-war developed between those who wanted a tougher approach and those who preferred a more conciliatory policy regarding their subjects. Both royal families were divided in themselves on this issue. In Castile, Alfonso's wife, Constance, and his archbishop of Toledo, Bernard de Sédirac, opposed his conciliatory policy toward the Moors and Jews. In England, William I (like William II after him) bludgeoned his English subjects into obedience with curfews and a scorched-earth-policy in Northumbria, while Henry I took a more conciliatory approach. Indeed, Henry married Matilda ("Good Queen Maude"), a popular member of the old Anglo-Saxon royal house, and dressed in Saxon style, wearing his hair long in the Saxon manner.

In the late eleventh and early twelfth century, a town commune movement spread from France into both Castile and England, asserting town interests in defiance of the rural-based nobility. Alfonso VI and Henry I encouraged and benefited from this movement, making townspeople allies in their struggles to assert royal control over the nobility. Alfonso granted town charters *(fueros)*, bestowing the right to elect town councilors *(alcaldes)* to town councils *(consejos)* and to hold town meetings *(ayuntamientos)*. Large numbers of Frenchmen, spilling over the Pyrenees from a population explosion in France, settled in these towns, helping to repopulate and defend Castile and providing financial and military levies to the kings. In 1130 Henry I likewise granted the first English town charter, giving London a degree of local government. This concession set the model for town charters throughout the British Isles, allowing towns limited rights without challenging royal authority.

Setbacks in the Early Eleventh Century

The highly rural and local nature of both societies still made government centralization difficult to enforce. Disputed successions encouraged backlash as both Castile and England were shaken by civil wars under Urraca in Castile (1109–26) and Matilda in England (1135–53). The close parallels in the stories of these two queens are many. Both women inherited their thrones due to the premature deaths of their brothers, both opposed their second husbands, and both were faced by civil wars that undermined royal power, resulting in setbacks for their kingdoms. Urraca's second marriage, to King Alfonso el Batallador (the Battler) of Aragon and Navarre, was stormy. In 1112 Alfonso imprisoned her and for two years ruled Castile alone, until in 1116 he was driven back to his own realm. As a result, Aragon and Navarre again parted from Castile until the end of the Middle Ages. Portugal was also lost to Castile when Urraca's older illegitimate half-sister, Countess Teresa of Portugal, launched a revolt in 1117 that ended in her son Alonso Henriques declaring Portuguese independence in 1143. The splintering of the Castilian realm was continued by Urraca's son Alfonso VII, who at his death in 1157 left the kingdom divided between his two sons. Matilda's rule followed a similar course. Just as Urraca's second marriage proved disastrous, so Matilda's to Geoffrey Plantagenet, Count of Anjou, proved so incompatible that she refused for some time to live with him—for so long that it was only after six years of marriage that a child was born. Her succession to the throne in 1135 was challenged by her cousin Stephen of Blois, plunging England into a generation of civil war. Only after Stephen's son Eustache died did Stephen agree in 1153 to accept Matilda's son Henry as his heir.

The Recovery of the Later Twelfth Century

In the second half of the twelfth century, both Spain and England underwent a period of recovery, during the reigns of Alfonso VIII (1158–1214) in Castile and of his father-in-law Henry II (1154–89) in England. Between 1172 and 1200 Alfonso conquered the Basque provinces of Guipúzcoa and

Alava from Navarre, giving Castile control of the trade route that ran from the port of San Sebastián through Vitoria to Burgos. In 1198 with Aragonese help, he obliged his cousin Alfonso IX of León to ally with Castile, a pact sealed by the wedding of Alfonso IX to Alfonso VIII's daughter. The son born from that marriage, Fernando, inherited both Castile and León in 1217. Alfonso VIII also shattered the Moorish Almohad dynasty's hold on southern Spain with his victory of Navas de Tolosa in 1212. The resulting loss of prestige by the Almohads spurred revolts that broke al-Andalus from Morocco, leaving it more vulnerable to further attack from the Christian North. Alfonso VIII's father-in-law, Henry II of England, likewise expanded his kingdom's power. Henry managed to dominate King William the Lion of Scotland, to the point that William accepted Henry as his feudal overlord. Henry likewise imposed himself on the Irish as their king.

Royal power was enhanced by moves to encourage the cooperation of crown and people in the name of good government. In 1188 Alfonso VIII in Castile and Alfonso IX in León brought to their respective kingdoms the parliamentary system Portugal had introduced in 1143. While previous legislative assemblies, dating back to the Visigothic councils of Toledo in Spain, had included only the nobility and the clergy, representatives of the towns were now added to form a parliament, although it would be another two centuries before their votes were counted. The Castilian parliament concerned itself mainly with tax matters and rarely opposed the will of the monarch. While an English Parliament would not appear until the second half of the thirteenth century, Henry II stabilized his kingdom with the use of the jury system, used to handle the flood of disputes over lands and castles arising from the civil war between Stephen and Matilda. The jury increased the crown's popularity by restoring the Anglo-Saxon judgment by neighbors and equals. By 1189 it had become normal practice to hear and weigh evidence in cases where the evidence against the accused was not conclusive, and by the middle of the thirteenth century a grand-jury system had been established, wherein the grand jury established accusations in criminal cases and a petite or trial jury decided the verdict. The first guidebooks on government administration were also written under Henry II, including Glanville's treatise on English law, Richard Fitznigel's *Dialogue of the Exchequer,* and John of Salisbury's *Policraticus or the Statesman's Guide.*

The Rounding Out of National Definitions in the Thirteenth Century

The late thirteenth century brought consolidation and codification of the government changes in both Spain and England, under two cousins, Fernando III in Castile (1217–52) and Henry III in England (1216–72). Both Fernando and Henry were pious patrons of Gothic cathedral building. Fernando, now honored as a saint, prayed constantly, risked his life to help his friends in battle, and worked to bring proper justice to his subjects. He led the third main push of the *Reconquista,* recapturing most of southern Spain in the name of Christ. At his death he insisted on receiving mass while kneeling humbly with a rope around his neck. His tomb in Seville Cathedral was long opened twice a year to show that, like Jesus, his body remained uncorrupted in death. Henry III similarly aspired to become a saint, but his simplicity caused him to be taken less seriously. When an itinerant court entertainer commented that the king reminded him of Jesus Christ, Henry foolishly asked the jongleur to elaborate, only to be told that Jesus already at his conception was endowed with the mind of an adult in the body of a child, while Henry demonstrated the mind of a child in the body of an adult. Henry III's lack of discernment led to a baronial revolt that brought still more advancement in English popular rights and freedoms. His wife, Eleanor of Provence, wanted to make their younger son, Edmund Crouchback, King of the Two Sicilies, and she made every effort to bribe the popes into supporting him. Henry enacted special taxes for this purpose, in violation of the Magna Charta. This caused the barons to revolt under the leadership of Simon de Montfort. After de Montfort's forces defeated Henry's army at the town of Lewes on the coast of Kent in 1264, de Montfort convened England's first parliament. Members of the middle class were chosen by election of designated voters in their towns or regions.

Rounding Out of the National Monarchical Systems in the Late Thirteenth Century

In the late thirteenth century, capstones were placed on high-medieval national unification by two brothers-in-law with a reputation for wisdom:

Alfonso X el Sabio (the Wise) (1252–84) in Castile and Edward I, "the English Justinian," (1272–1307) in England. Alfonso added to his realm by taking Cádiz in 1260 and Huelva in 1262, and Edward conquered Wales in 1284 and (briefly) Scotland in 1296.

Both kings regularized their kingdoms' legal systems. Alfonso produced two works designed to create a more modern law code. Alfonso X's *Siete partidas,* or seven-part law code addressing in remarkable detail nearly every aspect of Spanish society, gave Castile a unified law code, his *Espéculo de las Leyes* (mirror of the laws) provided a guide for the royal court, and his five legal treatises rounded out the effort. These works emphasized the king's position as a sovereign over a united people rather than as a mere feudal suzerain over his barons. In this effort, he leaned on Roman law, which reinforced royal authority as well as the prestige of the nobility. Stress was placed on the king as God's vicar on earth in temporal affairs. Absolute royal power was encouraged, with judges acting as royal representatives. The state was viewed as an impersonal, abstract government standing above mere personal relations, a concept that would be brought to completion by the *reyes católicos* at the end of the Middle Ages.

In England, Edward I likewise worked to consolidate the power of the state. Parliament was used to win national assent for his tax and other government measures. Two supreme courts were set up at Westminster, the Court of King's Bench for criminal cases and the Court of Common Pleas for civil cases, while the Court of the Exchequer handled cases of royal financing and the Court of Chancery dealt with equity law. Statute law evolved, and two statutes concentrated authority more tightly in royal hands. The Statute of *Quo warranto* forbade the existence of all private courts not authorized by the crown, and the Statute of *Quia emptores* prohibited further subinfeudation. By the time Edward died, the English kings held sovereign power over a unified state, possessing the right to make laws and to tax lay subjects directly, including the clergy without papal consent. The principal English judicial institutions were now in place. Although both Castilian and Anglo societies would be thrown into economic and social disruptions during the next two centuries, the political and legal innovations made since the eleventh century would be consolidated. This is not to say that a modern state had been created in either Castile or England, even by the end of the Middle Ages, but that the foundations for two different models of the state had been laid.

Differences in the Hispanic and Anglo Developments of the High Middle Ages

Despite the many similarities outlined above, the Anglo and the Hispanic governmental traditions also experienced a certain parting of the ways in the High Middle Ages.

Spanish Christian society's mounting insecurity in the face of Islamic threats called for more solidarity behind the monarch, and a greater bond of trust developed between the monarchs and people of Castile, with its unbroken line of descent of native monarchs. In contrast, the English in this period were governed by foreign, French-speaking monarchs, who ruled by right of conquest. The unpopularity of their kings encouraged in English subjects the felt need to guarantee one hard-won right after the next, so that gradually their short-term misfortune was turned into long-term fortune. Less on guard against their own rulers, the Castilians would find that when their kings later turned oppressive, they lacked sufficient powers to protect themselves.

One important parting of the ways can be seen in their legal systems. Spain adopted the authoritarian tradition of Roman law in contrast to the more egalitarian common law followed in England. England had turned away from the Roman law tradition at the time of the Anglo-Saxon invasion, while Visigothic Spain had continued exposed to an influence from Roman law. Codifications of mainly customary law had been made in the seventh century in both Spain and England. The Visigoths had produced the *Liber judiciorum* (which survived as a source of written law in the kingdoms of Asturias and León, and in the thirteenth century was translated into Castilian as the *Fuero juzco* and used as town law by some cities). Some of the English customary laws or dooms had been codified between A.D. 601 and 604 by King Ethelbert of Kent as the *Dooms of Ethelbert*. In the late eleventh and twelfth centuries, Roman law gradually replaced common law in Castile, concentrating power in the hands of the rulers. At the same time in England, Henry I validated the laws and rights of the English people as they had stood in the freer days before the Norman Conquest. English common law (common to the whole realm) henceforth acted as a safeguard of the king's subjects, even allowing peasants the right to appeal to royal justice against a violent master. It fostered liberty from royal dictates, encouraged competition (from political debate to economic entrepreneurship), and may have fostered the particularly Anglo veneration of wealth and of the rich, who could best afford the high legal fees to win protection of their interests in the courts.

As a result of the favorable political climate in England, the church-led movement to free peasants from oppression by the nobles had notably more success in England than in Castile. As this movement, which had begun in the eleventh century, gathered momentum through the twelfth and thirteenth centuries, nobles increasingly agreed to lighten their demands. England's "best chattle" rule, whereby half of a peasant's property could be taken by his master at the time of the peasant's death, disappeared, and a class of relatively well-to-do land-holding English peasants arose.

Town freedoms fared better in England than in Castile, as well. Town governments in Castile for a time grew stronger than their English counterparts. The authority of Castilian town government extended over much of the territory around them (called their *alfoz*), although some sizable communities in the *alfoz* were allowed to have their own *alcaldes,* or town councilors. However, the Castilian middle class subsequently fared less well than their English counterparts. The inhabitants of the new Castilian towns began a series of revolts in the twelfth century, demanding the dissolution of restrictions imposed by seigneurial rights. The Spanish towns won so great an autonomy that the New Style monarchy of the Late Middle Ages began to subordinate the towns to royal control, nullifying the gains of the town movement. The nobles also tended to displace the middle class in power in the Castilian towns. In contrast, English town rights emerged from the Middle Ages intact by never having been much of a threat to royal power, and so continued to be a training ground for popular participation in government.

England's jury system instituted by Henry II guaranteed a fairer trial by bringing in the opinion of the defendant's peers, in contrast to Hispanic trials. Composed generally of twelve men by the middle of the thirteenth century, the English jury's duty was to render a final verdict on a preliminary judgment rendered by a grand jury. By 1220 all property disputes were being heard in royal courts. Participation on juries gave commoners such a boost in status that an English proverb sprang up, which Shakespeare (*Hamlet,* act 5), quotes: "The toe of the peasant comes so near the heel of the courtier, he galls his kibe [heel sore]."

Opposition to the tyranny of Henry I's son John (1199–1216) obliged King John on June 15, 1215, to sign the Magna Charta, enumerating the rights of barons, clergy, and townsmen. The concessions provided a useful precedent for later attempts to prevent arbitrary use of power. Especially noteworthy were the right to a speedy trial before punishment (one of the bases for the long-developing English legal principle of *habeas corpus ad subjiciendum*—literally, you should have the body for submitting—a check on judges' and royal authorities' use of unjust or unexplained incarceration or restraint) and the prohibition on any new tax without the consent of the royal council (the basis for the Colonial American axiom no taxation without representation). The charter stipulated that nobody (actually, no baron, clergy, or townsman) would suffer financial or physical loss until tried and judged by his peers. A council of twenty-five barons was instituted to keep a watch on the king and was empowered to take up arms against the monarch if necessary—the first written basis of an English institution designed as a check on royal authority.

Even though the English House of Commons was not yet treated as an essential part of Parliament, which began and ended without the Commons, and while it initially concerned itself mainly with interests of a local and restricted nature, a solid basis was laid for its later importance. More frequent in England than in Castile, departures from hereditary succession to the English throne (including the power grabs of Isabella and Roger Mortimer, of Henry IV, of Richard of York, of Edward IV, of Richard III, and of Henry VII) with their moves to win parliamentary approval, added to the importance of parliamentary approval of the succession.

As a result of all of these developments, by the end of the High Middle Ages crown authority and aristocratic prestige were more marked in Castile than in England. Educated English public opinion was being mobilized to preserve a standard of proper behavior and of respect for property rights. No longer as humble as his Castilian counterpart, the average Englishman was speaking his opinion in favor of a freer society. Castile and England thus shared many similar experiences through the prosperous High Middle Ages, reacted to them in somewhat distinct ways, and laid the basis for political and legal assumptions of the Mexican-American Borderlands.

Influences on the Borderlands

The forms of government and law assumed in England and Spain by the end of the thirteenth century shaped much of the medieval contributions in these areas. The following section focuses on this impact on the Borderlands, first in ways felt similarly by both Anglo and Hispanic communities and coming from both an English and Spanish heritage, and then in ways felt differently and from distinct origins.

Hispanic and Anglo Shared Influences from the High Middle Ages

The martial orientation of society during the High Middle Ages in both Castile and northernmost England, with their male-dominated, soldier, non-mercantile ethic, has left its stamp on Mexican-American border culture. In Castile, the many centuries of the *Reconquista* reinforced the Roman- and Moorish-based Hispanic machismo and patriarchalism, both characteristics connected with Mexican American society. The fighting ethic of the *Reconquista* is still evoked for Hispanic boys of the Borderlands, who are taught that a plate of beans and rice symbolizes battling Moors and Christians. As the boys eat, they decide whether the Moors (the dark beans) or the Christians (the white rice) are going to be left in possession of the battlefield (the plate) or whether they would make a truce (be mixed together).[1] The *Reconquista* is echoed in such Hispanic family names of Guerra and Guerrero (war / warrior), referring to battle sites and fighters. The name Guerra is documented as early as 1134. The great *Reconquista* fighting monarch San Fernando is himself commemorated by the San Fernando Valley in California. The castles built to guard the frontier with the Moors are mirrored in the presidios, or garrisons, left standing from the Colonial period throughout the Mexican-American Borderlands, from California's Santa Barbara to Texas' San Elezario on Rio Grande. A comparable Anglo tradition of feuds, violence, and male dominance has been brought to the Borderlands by the Scotch-Irish. Their route of migration traces back to the Anglo-Scottish border in the Middle Ages by way of Northern Ireland (in the seventeenth century) and the Appalachians (in the eighteenth century). The warfare begun by Edward I's conquest of Scotland and by Robert Bruce's successful independence movement continued to rage through the following two centuries, keeping the border between England and Scotland insecure and allowing local clans to carry out devastating raids.

One negative consequence of the introduction of written charters and land deeds in medieval Castile and England was widespread land-grabbing. Alfonso III (866–910) foreshadowed the great *empresarios* who settled Texas in the first half of the nineteenth century by making use of the old Roman and Visigothic principle of the *pressura* (land grants of vacant property belonging to the state) to claim territory deserted due to war with those who had cultivated and defended it, whether laymen or clergy, a process repeated on both the Hispano-American and Anglo-American frontiers in the eighteenth and nineteenth centuries. The use of land deeds became common in the late eleventh century in both Castile and England, due to the spread of literacy, to a more extensive government and legal administration, and to the appearance of many new landholders in the wake of the *Reconquista* in Castile and of the Norman Conquest in England. Castile's population and economy was built up by the granting of liberal land grants close to the dangerous frontier. Land speculators were quick to establish written deeds to land long held on a less formal basis by others.

Hispanic and Anglo land-grabbing traditions coincided in the Borderlands after the Mexican War, when the introduction of regularized surveying and land deeds was accompanied by widespread abuse. As the American frontier spread west, the first settlers (in the absence of properly trained surveyors and lawyers) established their land deeds with the help of poorly qualified agents. Many of the resulting deeds were vague, marking out so many paces from common objects like trees and rocks. With the development of the region, deceitful land grabbers employing professional surveyors and lawyers would write up more acceptable deeds for themselves and challenge the sloppily drafted frontier claims in court, often with success. Daniel Boone, who pioneered the Anglo settlement of Kentucky and staked out a claim to large tracts of land, lost all of it to this process, despite his great services and his international fame. Bitter, he moved on to Spanish-held Missouri, vowing never to cross back into the state which had treated him so badly.

The land grabbing in the Borderlands after the Mexican War often involved Anglo exploitation of Hispanics. Many Mexican Americans did not understand American requirements regarding land registration and, consequently, lost their titles. Some of the land grabbers, however, were apparently Mexican Americans who exploited their fellow Hispanics. Also, some Hispanics, a least for a while, continued to play a leading role under the new system. In California, Juan Bandini and José Antonio Estudillo of San Diego became the first county treasurer and the first county assessor, respectively. The Pachecos of San Jose provided a state senator and lieutenant governor, and the Sepulvedas of Los Angeles a judge, while Antonio del Valle's grandson Juan B. Castro was a prominent state politician, and Judge Covarrubias was married into the Carrillo clan. In New Mexico, the Oteros of Santa Fe provided a delegate to Congress, a vice president of the Atchison, Topeka, and Santa Fe Railroad, and a territorial governor from 1877 to 1906, and José Leandro Perea of Bernalillo left about 200,000 sheep when he died in the mid-twentieth century. In Texas, the Benavides clan dominated Laredo politics, while the Yturria and Fernandez families played a prominent role in Brownsville. Nevertheless, many Hispanics lost their lands and, thus, their prominence. Although the Treaty of Guadalupe-Hidalgo guaranteed existing land holdings in the newly conquered territories, the Land Law of 1851 still required proof of ownership. Inadequately prepared titles or problematic surveys and deeds were challenged in court, with widespread unfairness, intimidation, and even murder. The original land owners initially fared better in New Mexico, but they, too, eventually succumbed as Anglo farmers, ranchers, and sheepherders moved in.

Contrasting Hispanic and Anglo Influences from the High Middle Ages

Medieval Hispanic and Anglo political and legal traditions have differed in several important respects in the Borderlands. In this section we will consider differing views concerning group orientation as opposed to individualism, personal as opposed to institutional approaches, and respect for authority as opposed to an emphasis on popular rights and liberties.

The *Reconquista* left Hispanic society more group oriented than its Anglo counterpart, incorporating more concern for the feelings of others, reflected in greater formality and polite respect. Group cohesion in the face of an external threat is a well-known sociological principle, bringing a reaffirmation of a society's values, norms, and beliefs. The Spanish language tends to place less emphasis on the individual than does English, achieving this through the use of reflexive verbs, which tend to defer attention away from the speaker. For example, whereas in Spanish one would say *"Se me cayó el vaso"* (the glass fell itself from me), in English a person would say, "I dropped the glass." This distinction is likewise seen in the proverbs favored by the two peoples. Popular Hispanic *dichos* like "por la boca muere el pez" and "en boca cerrada no entran moscas" (the fish dies because of its mouth, and flies don't get into a closed mouth) urge people not to be too outspoken, while Anglos often remind each other that "the squeaky wheel gets the grease."

The *Reconquista's* prolonged need for strong local military leadership made Castilian society more aristocratic and more based on personal relationships. The Castilian brand of feudalism was looser than the English and never subordinated the noble as much as was the case in England. In the Castilian *behetría,* a *rico hombre* (higher noble) granted his protection to an *hidalgo* (lower noble) in exchange for certain services or payments, an agreement sealed by a mutual oath of fidelity but without the *rico hombre* having the right to withdraw ownership of the land from the *hidalgo.* A Castilian vassal *(vasallus* or *criado)* might be either a freeman with a fief (*préstamo* or loan) or a tenant farmer *(solariego).* While Castile did not make feudalism central to its society, never standardizing or codifying its feudal laws, feudalism was elaborated into a comprehensive and tightly regulated system in William I's England. Most of the Anglo-Saxon nobility was displaced, and the new French barons were given scattered holdings, with the requirement that all vassals and subvassals swear an overriding "liege homage" directly to the king. Border Hispanics still share a penchant for looking to personal relationships in business and government dealings rather than to impersonal principles. The elaborate stylization of social relations and greater care with courtesy accompanying the feudal system were transmitted to border Hispanics, along with, it has been claimed, a less idealized view of work as ethic or principle.

It has been observed that Hispanic practice emphasizes respect for authority, while the Anglo approach values constitutional pluralism. The weakness of Castile's Third Estate (the political status of common people), heavy reliance on Roman law, lack of a jury, and need for a powerful king and nobility due to the prolonged military demands of the *Reconquista* laid the groundwork for the more authoritarian Hispanic tradition. The Castilian ethic thus moved away from the emphasis on representative government, a free press, and distinctions between branches of government, which were developed in Anglo tradition. The very *Reconquista* that had stimulated the rise of town communes and of parliaments in Castile gave the monarchy such prestige and power that it eventually crushed their power. This fact, plus the emphasis placed by Roman law on executive authority over the nation and on the father and husband's authority in the family, have been passed down to Borderlands Hispanic society, along with a greater concern with law and order. Thus we find that Borderlands Hispanics have often given more support for the military and police than for democratic rights. This influence is manifested in the Borderland's local boss-dominated politics, low voter turnout, and emphasis on personal ties rather than on professional expertise in hiring.

In contrast, English society placed a premium on popular rights. England's smaller size allowed the English kings to travel regularly throughout the entire realm, providing the stability in which the middle class could thrive and assert itself. England's stronger House of Commons, common law, and jury system all pointed the way to the Anglo world's democratic orientation, a social view that has worked at odds with the border Hispanic's heritage of respect for authority. While town government and the parliamentary system built upon it both started earlier in Castile than in England, it was in the latter society that both systems put down deeper roots. The powerful and unpopular kings of high medieval England spurred their subjects to struggle against royal power. The United States Constitution with its guarantees of the right to a speedy trial, to no taxation without representation, to due process of law, and with its concept of checks and balances traces back through many intermediary stages to the influence of Magna Charta.

The different approaches to law developed in medieval Castile and England have created a unique blend of laws in the Borderlands. The impact of Alfonso X's *Siete partidas* can be seen in legal concepts inherited via the sixteenth century Laws of the Indies. The Texas legal code of 1841 accepted various aspects of Spanish law. The *sistema de bienes gananciales,* a system of communal or shared property rights between a man and his wife, was adopted in Texas, New Mexico, Arizona, and California. Its provisions once allowed Texans to pay lower taxes than citizens of other states, until the tax burden was equalized by the United States Congress. The "ganancial" system's concept of a community of property interest between spouses protects the wife's equal say in the disposition of the couple's holdings. This provision contrasts with the concentration of property rights in the hands of the husband in English law. Joint filing of income tax is, likewise, an extension of the ganancial principle. Children of recognized legal unions do not lose their legitimacy if the marriage is subsequently declared invalid. Adoption as a legal procedure, unknown in English law, was accepted in Texas law in 1850. As in Spanish law, adopted children were given full rights of inheritance, while still being able to claim inheritance from their biological parents. However, Arizona law follows the Spanish precedent of opposing common-law marriages, in contrast to the provisions of English common law. From thirteenth-century Castilian law the principle of debtor protection eventually found its way into Texas' homestead law of 1839, which protected from seizure the debtor's principal residence with its basic furnishings, personal clothing, and items needed for work. In 1840 the Republic of Texas decided to continue the Castilian unitary system of civil courts rather than the dual Anglo system distinguishing between courts of law and courts of equity, although retaining law and equity decisions. Texas also followed the Castilian legal principle that trials must be held in the locale of greatest convenience for the defendant. Another Castilian legal custom followed in Texas and Arizona, as well as in several non-border states, is a provision allowing for the appointment of an independent estate executor, with powers normally allowed only with a court order.

The medieval Castilian system of land deeds has influenced the Mexican American Borderlands. Many of the region's farms and ranches are divisions of grants still known by their Spanish names. Two land grant practices from the Spanish *Reconquista* influenced New Mexico. First, the state's private land grants trace back to attempts to raise one's social status, a heritage from the days when Castilian monarchs lacked other resources to reward their soldiers. Second, the New Mexican community land grant whereby pueblos administer surrounding lands *(ejidos* or *montes)* in accordance with local custom traces back to the defensive and colonizing role of new towns established on conquered lands during the *Reconquista.* As Spanish law was elaborated in other specializations during the *Reconquista,* further precedents were established for legal principles found in the Borderlands, regarding mines, water rights, women's property rights, and many other concerns. The Kearny Law Code, continuing those Spanish and Mexican laws not incompatible with the laws and principles of the United States, was adopted for New Mexico in 1846 by Governor General Stephen Kearny and published in both English and Spanish. It is still the basis for New Mexican state law, including Spanish mining and water law provisions also found in Texas, Arizona, and Colorado law.

Texas at first had taken a similar approach. Spanish civil law not incompatible with the new Constitution was continued by the Texas Republic in 1836 but was replaced in general by English common law (as in other states) in 1840. Even then, Spanish laws survived where English law was lacking in whole or in part. Spanish law is considered valid in legal cases referring to the Hispanic period. Some of Texas' and Arizona's water laws are drawn from the Hispanic heritage. The community sharing of water rights for power generation or irrigation, regardless of the ownership of the surrounding lands, is a survival of the early Castilian system. Community *acequia* and water-rights organizations have copied the rules and regulations of *Tribunales de las aguas* of the Spanish Levant. Those seaside land grants that date from before 1840 reserve a wider stretch of beach for the state. Likewise, pre-1840 riverside land grants stopped at the water and restricted water use beyond domestic and livestock consumption, and usually irrigation rights as well. Another surviving Spanish legal principle is government grants of rights to mine or otherwise use land, rather than selling or giving it to private owners. When Texas adopted the Anglo-Saxon common law in 1840, it retained the reservation of subsoil mineral rights to the government, a provision dating back to medieval Castile. The Texas government used its 5 percent portion of the gross receipts from mineral concessions to endow its public system of education. California recognized Spanish land grants and kept other elements of Spanish law, including those concerning water rights and trespassing. Texas was influenced by the Spanish land grants to perpetuate large ranching estates. Because Texas validated grants made by the Spanish and Mexican governments, around one-seventh of Texas' private lands have titles originally granted by Spain or Mexico.

The use of statutory law (statutes issued by a representative body), most notably in regulations issued by state governments, traces back its development to England under Edward I. The English common-law doctrine most commonly expressed in the phrase "a man's home is his castle" led to the safeguard of the search warrant, requiring probable cause before law officials can invade a person's house. The warrant stems from the medieval principle, never accorded true legal validity (even though enunciated by William Pitt the Elder in the eighteenth century), that a lord could not be touched by the royal bailiffs so long as he remained inside his own castle. The English jury system, renowned as a safeguard of individual liberties from government oppression, has been a mixed blessing due to differences between medieval and modern societies. Law has grown so much more complex that today we joke that a jury is a panel chosen to decide which side has the better lawyer. In commercial law various devices have had to be introduced to restrict issues before they come before a jury.

Borderland local governments stem from the medieval English system. The administrative division of the shire (often called a county after the Norman Conquest), with its sheriffs (shire reeves), is one Anglo-Saxon contribution to the Mexican-American Borderlands and to the United States as a whole. Surviving elements include the terms *alderman* (older man) and *mayor,* derived from the Latin *major* meaning greater and first used in twelfth-century London when its port-reeve became the town mayor. Many town councils in the Borderlands are designated Boards of Aldermen. The term *by-law* for a town ordinance came from *bȳr,* an Old Norse name for a town, an operating procedure meaning literally a "town law," and not, as is sometimes assumed, a marginal or minor law. Finally, the English system of circuit judges is one of the many lasting English heritages in the Borderlands.

Concluding Remark

High medieval Castile and England left a distinct mark on the political and legal aspects of Mexican-American Border culture. Both traditions, the English and Spanish, developed from a common starting point, a need for law and order after brutal invasions of their countries' vulnerable regions. The two traditions took alternate paths, the Hispanic toward placing a priority on law and order, the Anglo on popular participation. Both traditions contained the possibility of excess. In one direction lay a future of corrupt Spanish and Latin American dictators, in the other the social rot attendant on a self-indulgent American society. But both contained the seeds of future success: the stability inherent in respect for authority and the strength of unity that develops from participatory democracy. Combining both traditions, the Mexican-American Borderlands might be said to have achieved something of a balance between the two, combining a degree of respect for authority with a feeling of freedom to speak out. Border residents can aim for the best of both worlds.

The separate political and legal developments in medieval Castile and England influenced a parting of the ways between Spanish and English economies and the class structures built upon them. The next chapter considers the economic and social class heritage.

Three

Economic and Social Class Influences

Mention of the Mexican-American Borderlands often calls to mind ranches and ranch bosses, irrigation agriculture and farm workers, factory developers and barrios. These images stem from traditions launched in medieval Castile and England, now blended in the U.S. Southwest. In the Late Middle Ages, a subtle shift occurred in the focus of political power that brought two centuries of social class conflict. Instead of concentrating on the development of national systems of law and government, emphasis was now placed on rivalry (most significantly between the middle and upper class) for control of the central governments. The middle class had prospered during the economic upswing of the High Middle Ages, putting it in a position to challenge the military aristocracy for power in the fourteenth and fifteenth centuries. This chapter begins with a brief summary of those economic developments, as they affected both Castile and England. We will then note the differences between the Castilian and English experiences of the Late Middle Ages. Then the parallel developments in the late medieval social class history of Castile and England will be treated reign by reign, followed by a survey of differing developments in this area. Finally, we will consider the influence of these various developments in Spain and England, similar and contrasting, in the Mexican-American Borderlands.

Parallels in Hispanic and Anglo Economic Developments in the Middle Ages

Just as in the cases of linguistic, political, and legal heritage, so also have economic developments in Hispanic and Anglo societies been molded by many similar influences from the Middle Ages. Castile and England shared a similar economic background from the Dark Ages. After an initial vigorous development as parts of the Roman Empire, both areas had been devastated by the Germanic invasions at the start of the Dark Ages. Many towns from Mérida to York had been left in ruins, and forests had spread back over extensive areas. A slow effort to reestablish farmlands had been begun by monks and had been followed by mixed groups of settlers seeking a fresh start. Alfred the Great in England and Alfonso III in Castile encouraged the movement, as did later kings of Castile and England in the eleventh, twelfth, and thirteenth centuries. In the unsettled conditions during the centuries of warfare against Moors in Castile and Vikings in England, the tribal system of property ownership on which ancient land holdings had been based was ignored. The final beneficiaries of the movement were the kings and the military aristocracy, who took control of most of the land and of its agricultural economy, the nobles realizing benefits either by grants from kings or by the use of force against commoners. This concentration of control in royal and noble hands occurred step by step in Castile, as new lands gained in the *Reconquista* were placed largely in the hands of *ricos hombres* and *hidalgos,* and it was sealed in England with the imposition of the Norman feudal system, beginning in 1066. England was especially affected, changing from having been one of the most wooded countries of Europe to becoming the most deforested, with a total extermination of its wolves.

Pilgrimages fostered business in both countries, most notably those to Santiago de Compostela and to Canterbury. So numerous were pilgrims on the roads in both countries that merchants often masqueraded as pilgrims to avoid paying road tolls from which pilgrims were exempt. In the eleventh century, French businessmen serving the pilgrims on their way along the Cantabrian coast to Santiago de Compostela helped to establish and develop towns along the route, including Pamplona, Burgos, León, Lugo, and Santiago itself. The population was not only growing but shifting. Improvements in the agricultural economy freed new sources of human labor. The introduction of the three-field system, the horse collar, horseshoe, tandem harness, moldboard plow, and water-powered mill played a major role in England, while in Spain the water mill and a widespread move from use of the hoe to the plow were especially significant. In contrast, the population of Islamic Spain was static. The agriculture of both kingdoms prospered, allowing them to export wheat, ham, bacon, lard, and tallow, as well as olive oil and wine from Castile. The English developed deep-sea fishing. Mining activities increased in both countries, with the mining of tin in Cornwall, lead in Derbyshire, copper in various parts of England, iron in Sussex and Vizcaya, and mercury in Almadén. Toledo made use of iron to produce armor and weaponry, and both England and Castile exported salted meat. The currencies of both England and Castile would be strengthened in the thirteenth century by the striking of gold and silver coins. The growth of towns in the High Middle Ages encouraged fairs as a major new economic development. Stourbridge Fair in the West Midlands, St. Ives Fair in East Anglia, and Scarborough Fair on the northeast coast became especially famous in England in the eleventh through thirteenth centuries, while Castile's newly important fairs included those of Valladolid, Medina del Campo, Belorado (near Burgos), Sahagún, Moyá, and Seville.

In the twelfth and thirteenth centuries, first the English and then the Castilian economy came to focus (eventually competitively) on wool exports to the Flemish cloth industry. Wool provided a fifth of England's public revenues (from the customs duty on sheep fleece). English merchants operating in Bruges established the Hanse of London, which regulated the English trade in wool and other items. In 1267 England's Company of the Merchants of the Staple was founded by traders exporting English wool, metals, salted meat, butter, and cheese to the "staples" (i.e., markets granted a monopoly of handling this trade) of Bruges, Calais, Antwerp, and Dordrecht. In 1326 it was arranged that the English staple would be shared among nine English, two Welsh, and three Irish towns. Castilian wool was purchased in Medina del Campo's two annual fairs in May and October, as well as at lesser fairs. Santanderino and Basque merchants transported the wool (along with iron, wine, and honey) from Burgos by mule trains to Santander and Bilbao, where it was shipped to Flanders. Genoese merchants in Cádiz, Sevilla, and Córdoba also purchased large amounts of Castilian wool. As early as 1280 Castilian merchants in Bruges were important enough to be representing German trading interests as well as their own.

A national economic policy gradually emerged under the guiding hands of the Castilian and English monarchs in the fourteenth and fifteenth centuries. Royal support now favored expansion of farming communities, construction of drainage ditches and embankments, emancipation of serfs, protection of waterways and woodlands, and introduction of new industrial skills from abroad. While Castilian expeditions probed the coast of northern Africa and claimed the Canary Islands in the fourteenth century, the English pushed ahead with a merchant marine whose trade was based in such ports as London, Bristol, Hull, and Newcastle. In the mid-fourteenth century, Edward III's Queen Philippa of Hainault settled Flemish wool weavers in Norwich where they established a thriving textile business, turning English wool into cloth for export. In 1486 the crown officially recognized the Merchant Adventurers, organized to carry English cloth abroad.

Differences in the Hispanic and Anglo Economic Developments in the Middle Ages

Despite the similar developments noted above, important distinctions also arose between the Castilian and English economic and social class situations. Generations before the Norman Conquest, the economic stimulus brought by the Vikings, especially under England's King Knut with his capital at London, established England's reputation for being wealthier than its neighbors. In the High Middle Ages the contrasting political developments of Castile and England set their economies even more clearly on different paths. The hostilities of the *Reconquista* prevented Castilian merchants from participating in the business strength of Islamic Spain, while diverting support and wealth to the military aristocracy. As the Christians conquered to the south, Muslim businessmen tended to emigrate without being adequately replaced by non-Muslims, to the detriment of manufacturing and commerce. The formation of big ranches made it difficult to develop a well-to-do peasantry. Castile did not import food stuffs, being independent in that regard, and so did not manufacture items to trade for imported food. As a result, merchants were not numerous outside of Burgos, Medina del Campo, and Seville, and even in Seville they were mostly Genoese. Despite a theoretical government commitment to foster manufacturing, there was little protection or stimulus for industry in Castile. In contrast England's combination of strong central rule with prolonged peace fostered the emergence of an increasingly mercantile society. As a result, despite parallel economic experiments through the Middle Ages, the English economy gradually grew stronger than that of Castile, a distinction clearly marked by the start of the fifteenth century.

Edward III's Queen Philippa reopened coal mines on her English estates, so that a start was made on exploiting both coal as well as wool, England's two main industrial assets. The English business world labored under fewer restrictions than the Castilian; in 1394 Richard II intervened to allow artisans to operate in defiance of gild monopolies. By the end of the fourteenth century, the English had ousted the Castilians as the leaders in lucrative wool exports. The average Englishman greatly benefited from an improved standard of living. Day laborers in England saw their wages treble, and they pushed for pay in money rather than kind and for a five-day work week. England's population rebounded to replace the two-and-a-half million people lost to the Black Death. English peasants were among the most prosperous in Europe, and the observation was made at this time that more English folk were dying of overeating and overdrinking than from hunger. By the Late Middle Ages, the economic disparities between Castilian and English societies were sufficiently great to mold different social class structures in the two lands.

Similarities between Hispanic and Anglo Social Class Developments in the Late Middle Ages

The social class history of late medieval Castile and England discloses still more parallels between the Hispanic and Anglo heritages. Both Castile and England were thrown into a social crisis at the turn of the thirteenth to the fourteenth century. As the climate cooled, the customs of the upper class diverged from those of the commoners. Whereas previously everyone in a castle had lived together in the great hall, now the upper class spent more time in smaller rooms heated by fireplaces. Europe's prosperity declined in the period when Mongols under Hülegü, a grandson of

Genghis Kahn, devastated the Persian Gulf region and Chinese fleets dominated the Indian Ocean trade. European trade with China under Kublai Khan, Hülegü's brother, was directed mainly across Central Asia—an arduous route, involving expensive land travel over vast distances. At the same time, the immense Mongol polity, which dismantled long-established travel barriers across Central Asia, facilitated the spread of the Black Death. Vast numbers of Europeans died. After its first appearance in Castile and England in the middle of the fourteenth century, the plague recurred four times in Spain between 1381 and 1444 and five times in England between 1361 and 1391. It took the lives of between a third and two-thirds of the inhabitants of the two kingdoms. Caught in the economic turmoil, nobles divided into factions and closed ranks against the emerging middle class.

Moreover, many of the functions once making the nobility important were fading. The three original bases for upper class status had been military service, land holding, and government office. The military importance of the upper class had rested on its ability to maintain expensive armor and horses and on its expertise in heavy cavalry charges. However, the growth of a money economy allowed kings to hire mercenaries. With the new use of pikesmen in close-order formation, of longbowmen, and eventually of firearms through the Late Middle Ages, the importance of the mounted knight in heavy armor diminished, and they were eventually displaced by commoner infantrymen. Pikesmen in a close hedgehog formation proved able to turn away cavalry attacks, while arrows shot in rapid succession from masses of longbows, and then balls shot from muskets and cannons, made nonsense out of armor. Experimentation with guns that could be shot from horseback began in the early fifteenth century. The nobility's control of the land, which had been an integral part of the feudal system, was losing importance with the emergence of fluid capital wealth. The upper class, reticent to engage in trade, found that bourgeois families were surpassing them in wealth. The nobility's role in government was also eroded as increasing complexity and professionalism in government required trained personnel, usually commoners.

The Onset of Social Instability

Close parallels can be noted again in the Late Middle Ages, as in the High Middle Ages, between contemporary reigns of several English and Castilian sovereigns, but with different outcomes that would determine views on social class in Hispanic and Anglo societies for centuries to come. The first signs of the new troubles occurred at a time of weak leadership in both Castile and England. Sancho IV (1284–95) and Fernando IV (1295–1312) both died young of tuberculosis, leaving the Castilian government in the care of María de Padilla (1295–1321), who struggled to enforce her will first as queen mother and then as queen grandmother. In England, Sancho's and Fernando's cousin Edward II (1307–1327) relied on insolent and grasping advisors, who made him unpopular with his nobles.

In 1275 a Castilian civil war erupted over the succession to the throne between Alfonso the Wise's grandson Alfonso de la Cerda and Alfonso's second son Sancho. When Alfonso died in 1284, Sancho became king as Sancho IV. He felt obliged to allow the formation of a brotherhood *(hermandad)* of town governments, as an aid to law enforcement, even though this undermined royal power in favor of the towns. Then, just as he seemed on the verge of stabilizing his rule, he died at age thirty-five. In England, Edward II antagonized the nobles by the favor he showered on the sarcastic Piers Gaveston. In 1310 a group of nobles forced Edward to authorize a committee of twenty-one lord ordainers to oversee (through Parliament) royal appointments, declarations of war, and royal trips abroad, and Gaveston was put to death. In 1322 Edward resumed control, repealed the reform measures, and promoted another unpopular favorite, Hugh le Despenser.

In each kingdom, strong queens stepped into the turmoil. Since Sancho IV's son Fernando IV was only nine years old when he became king of Castile in 1295, his mother Maria de Molina assumed the regency. Through years of civil war, she gradually got the kingdom in hand, passing on a calmer realm when her son attained his majority in 1301. But when he also died, in 1312, followed by his wife shortly after, Maria de Molina (now as regent for the infant King Alfonso XI) was thrown back into a long fight with the unruly nobles, a struggle that continued until her death in 1321. In England, a focal point for baronial opposition emerged in the person of Edward II's Queen Isabel. Disenchanted with her husband, Isabel and her paramour Roger Mortimer raised an army, rallying many of the barons. Edward II was obliged to abdicate in 1327, was imprisoned, and was soon announced to have died.

Start of a Pro-Noble Policy

A period of appeasement of the nobility followed under two flamboyant warrior kings and second cousins: Alfonso XI in Castile (ruled León 1312–, Castile 1325–1350) and Edward III in England (1327–77). In both cases, a regency government at the beginning of each reign helped to incline the young monarchs to a pro-noble policy. In Castile, Juan Manuel, regent from 1321 to 1325, predisposed Alfonso XI toward a policy of appeasing the nobles. In England, Roger Mortimer and Queen Mother Isabel likewise influenced Edward to appease his barons. These two kings established glittering courts to amuse the high nobility, who vied for membership in new social orders of knighthood. At his new Mudéjar-style convent-palace of Tordesillas, Alfonso founded the *Caballeros de la banda,* distinguished by the award of a decorative band. Edward III filled his court at Windsor Castle with festivities, pageants, and dances and introduced the Order of the Garter. These two monarchs also kept their nobility placated by sharing booty gained in military campaigns. Alfonso led wars against Granada (no longer submissive) and in 1340 won a victory at the Rio Salado. Then, in 1341, with the help of the Genoese, Aragonese, and Portuguese fleets, he sank a Moorish fleet at the naval battle of the Straits of Gibraltar, which he claimed for Castile. Like Alfonso, Edward III was relieved of some of the pressures from his restless nobles by their preoccupation with war booty from successful engagements during the turmoil of the French-English Hundred Years War: in 1340 an English fleet defeated a French fleet off the Flemish town of Sluys; in 1346 Edward defeated a French army at the battle of Crécy, and conquered Calais.

The reverse side of Alfonso XI's placation of the nobles was the increased tax burden he placed on the middle class, introducing the *alcabala* (a sales tax) and an export tax (mainly on wool), in addition to the *quinta* (a fifth of all gains from border raids). By the end of the fourteenth century, all of the nobility, both the higher *ricos hombres* and the lower *hidalgos,* had won exemption from most taxes, thus unifying the solidarity of both levels of the nobility against the middle class. Alfonso also curbed the growing independence of the town governments, making lifetime appointments of royal *corregidores* to oversee town councils and breaking up the Castilian *hermandad,* the town-based law enforcement organization. In contrast, the importance of the English middle class was advanced with the strengthening of Parliament. In exchange for financial grants, in 1340 Edward conceded that henceforth only Parliament could enact a non-feudal tax. In 1341 it was further granted that tax money might henceforth be spent only as directed by Parliament. With this step, Parliament could and did prevent the hiring of a standing army in peace time, thereby depriving the kings of an instrument for crushing the will of the people. The House of Commons also got a boost in social prestige and in its social base in 1339 when the Knights of the Shires were excluded from the House of Lords by the higher nobility and were obliged to sit with the town representatives in the House of Commons. Middle class figures began to play a role in national government, William de la Pole, a wool merchant of Hull, selected as Edward III's principal financier and his son Michael created duke of Suffolk. Edward III sometimes socialized with the London merchants, drinking with them and staying overnight in their homes.

Two Sets of Warring Brothers

The Castilian and English social class tensions of the Late Middle Ages grew more strident in the 1360s and 1370s, when two sets of brothers exerted power in the two kingdoms. Castile in the 1350s through the 1370s was dominated by the half-brothers Pedro el Cruel and Enrique de Trastamara, who hated each other and vied for power, while in England Edward, the Black Prince, and his admiring younger brother, John of Gaunt, took leading roles in government. In each case, the younger brother, in alliance with the nobles, moved to reverse the more liberal policy of his elder brother after his death.

Alfonso XI, disliking his Queen María, had virtually abandoned her and their son Pedro to live with his mistress Leonor de Guzman and his ten illegitimate children by her. The subsequent clash between the legitimate heir and his illegitimate half-brothers offered a new outlet for class confrontation. After Pedro became king (1350–69), his mother had Leonor put to death. Pedro tried to soothe the feelings of Leonor's son Fadrique, Master of Santiago, in 1353, by giving him the honor of escorting to Spain his new bride, Blanche, a niece of King Jean the Good of France, only to have Fadrique impregnate his bride en route. Pedro ordered Fadrique's murder and commanded that Blanche be transferred to the Alcázar of Toledo, where her death was soon announced. When Pedro attacked Aragon in a war that lasted from 1356 to 1366, the higher nobles *(ricos hombres)*, feeling neglected by Pedro's pro–middle-class (and pro-Jewish) policies, failed to support him. Pedro, consequently, had to rely on the less effective *hidalgos*. In reaction to Pedro's attack, the king of Aragon sent a rebel army into Castile under Fadrique's twin brother Enrique de Trastamara. Enrique proclaimed his championship of the nobility. While Pedro fled to Portugal and ultimately to Aquitaine, triumphant Enrique showed his contempt of the townsmen by raising taxes without bothering to get the approval of the *Cortes*, or parliament.

In 1367 Pedro managed to regain his throne for a time, thanks to the brief military intervention of English troops led by Edward, the Black Prince, Edward III's son. Pedro rewarded his middle-class supporters by granting the towns the right to appoint twelve *procuradores* to sit henceforth on the royal council (an innovation Enrique de Trastamara would later feel obliged to accept in letter, though not in spirit). Yet, since Enrique had already done so, Pedro also dared to raise taxes without the approval of the *Cortes*. Pedro's triumph was short-lived. Besieged in Montiel Castle near Ciudad Real in March 1369, Pedro was lured to a midnight parlay and stabbed to death by Enrique. The new king, Enrique II (1369–79), rewarded his noble followers with titles and lands and grants of entails *(mayorazgos)*, whereby estates were passed on intact to one male heir. Unprecedentedly powerful noble families emerged. At the same time, a blow was struck at the middle class's Jewish component. The Jews of Burgos and Toledo were fined, and Jews were obliged to wear Magen David badges and to live separately from gentiles in Jewish *alhamas*.

Civil discord also divided English society in this period. In 1376 the "Good" Parliament removed two royal officials from power in England's first impeachment. The next year, the "Bad" Parliament, under the control of the reactionary faction of John of Gaunt, imposed an unpopular poll tax on the country. The result was the Peasant's Revolt, to be considered in the following section.

The Town Revolts of the 1380s and 1390s

The rebelliousness of the commoners came to a head in the 1380s and 1390s under two kings both entranced by the panoply of chivalry, and both of whom died tragically with hints of suicide: Juan I (1379–90) in Castile and

Richard II (1377–99) in England. After demonstrating suicidal tendencies, Juan died spurring his horse into a freshly-plowed field, where the animal toppled, killing the monarch. Having been overthrown, Richard died of starvation, officially announced as self-determined. Commoners in both kingdoms moved to increase their powers. For the first time the Castilian *Cortes* or parliament became a set institution, meeting regularly. In 1385 it was decided that, henceforth, four of the twelve people in the royal council were to be from the Third Estate, the common people. In 1386 the *Cortes* established a national police force, the *Hermandad* (not to be confused with the town league *hermandades* founded in 1282 in Sancho IV's revolt, crushed by Alfonso XI). The Third Estate also won the right to review the crown budget and war plans. In 1387 the *Cortes* ruled that the king had to present his financial accounts to every *Cortes* for inspection. However, even then, laws were still issued by the king, and the Castilian parliament had no right to legislate, control taxation, or even to deliberate on royal policy.

Similarly, English commoners assailed Richard II with demands for more power. Son of the Black Princc, Richard was ten years old when he came to the throne in 1377. Four years later, England was shaken by the so-called Peasant's Revolt of 1381, which was actually as much an uprising of the middle class as of the peasants. The rebel demands included the abolition of the poll tax, an end to class distinctions, and the dissolution of church wealth. Manors were occupied and members of the upper class were murdered. When a mob grabbed control of the city of London, the royal advisors fled with the boy king into the Tower of London. Young Richard met with Wat Tyler, the main rebel leader, at Smithfield, to the east of town. An argument arose, and Tyler was struck down. Seeing their leader fall, the rebels drew their longbows, but Richard rode up to them and assured them that he himself would protect their interests. Taken off guard by such courage and seeming sincerity on the part of their fourteen-year-old monarch, the rebels disbanded and order was restored. Richard's Council, however, failed to honor this promise, and he subsequently grew tyrannical, imposing arbitrary fines and new controls over speech and correspondence. However, in 1391 he twice demonstrated sympathy for the commoners, first by vetoing a bill that would have forbidden the schooling of villeins, or village peasants, and next by requiring that when a church was appropriated to a monastery, a portion of the realized profits had to be set aside for the parish poor.

Resurgence of Noble Power

The nobility in both countries reasserted itself at the turn of the fourteenth to the fifteenth century under two ailing kings: Enrique III (1390–1406) in Castile and Henry IV (1399–1413) in England. The two men were brothers-in-law, Enrique being married to Henry IV's half-sister Catalina. Enrique III el Doliente (the sickly) was physically weak from childhood and died at twenty-seven. Henry IV suffered from some disfiguring illness, possibly leprosy or a venereal disease, which ended his life at forty-six.

The Castilian nobles took advantage of the minority of Enrique III to attack and divide the middle class. The Spanish noble class was greatly strengthened in 1390 when the Christian segment of the middle class was turned against its Jewish counterpart, a development impossible in England, where the Jews had been expelled in 1290. Based on ignorance and suspicion of Jewish cabalism and its esoteric religious teachings, Castilians charged local Jews with performing sacrificial rites and summoning demons. The Jews were presented with a choice of conversion or death, and so many Jews were killed or forcibly baptized that very few unconverted Jews were left in Andalucía. In 1412 the remaining nonconverted Jews were excluded from government service, obliged to live in separate ghettos, wear a Magen David badge on their clothes, and forbidden from serving Christian clients. The Castilian middle class, divided along religious lines, was thus beaten back at the very moment it needed unity to consolidate parliamentary gains. As a result, the middle class component in the Castilian Parliament lost most of its power and importance. In 1391 the Madrid *Cortes* created a regency council of eight nobles, including the Chancellor Pedro López de Ayala. At the *Cortes* of Burgos in 1391–92, nobles intimidated the city representatives into retracting their demands. Recent middle class gains were lost. In 1395 the government expanded the practice of appointing royal *corregidores* to sit on town councils. The towns came to be dominated more and more by nobles, as *hidalgos* and even *ricoshombres* came to live in the towns, bringing with them their disdain for work.

In England Henry IV (1400–13), after overthrowing his cousin Richard II, justified his assumption of the throne by claiming the act was the will of the people as expressed in Parliament, further strengthening parliamentary power in England while it was waning in importance in Spain. This resulted from the efforts of barons working with townsmen to bolster the English Parliament as a way to keep the king in line, since it was as yet unclear which group would dominate that institution. In 1407 the House of Commons killed an attempt by the House of Lords to legislate on its own. So many of the nobles rebelled against Henry's rule that the principal focus of his reign was kept on keeping them in line.

Heroic Warfare in the Early Fifteenth Century

In the 1410s, the nobles of both countries indulged in a frenzy of warfare under two short-lived military heroes, Fernando de Antequera (1406–16) in Castile and Henry V (1413–22) in England. Fernando de Antequera directed the Castilian government during the infancy of Juan II, who was only one year old when he inherited the throne of Castile in 1406. Fernando became a military hero by repulsing an attack from Granada at the battle of Antequera in 1410. In 1412 he was "elected" King Fernando I of Aragon but continued to exert influence in Castile. After a debilitating illness, however, Fernando died relatively young, in his mid-thirties. Henry V, who took the English throne in 1413, reopened the Hundred Years War. In 1415 he won a victory over the French at Agincourt. He followed up on his victory by conquering Normandy between 1415 and 1419. In the latter year, Northern France went into revolt against the Dauphin Charles and invited Henry V to marry Catherine, daughter of the aged Charles VI the Crazy and sister of the Dauphin, and be their next king. However, Henry fell ill and died in 1422, about the same time as his father-in-law.

Height of the Chaos of Feudal Warfare

Fighting between feuding noble factions peaked during the reigns of Juan II (1406–54) in Castile and Henry VI (1422–61) in England. The two governments were further weakened by insanity in the royal families as a result of porphyria ("the purple disease"). In this genetic blood disorder, red blood corpuscles escape from the cardio-vascular system into the general body fluids. The urine turns bluish or purple, and thought processes are confused by the effect of chemical reactions in the brain. Juan II's second wife, Isabel of Portugal, and Henry VI were both victims of the disorder. In Castile, noble clans fought each other for land and power, while the *Cortes* continued to decline in importance. Many towns lost representation altogether, while the crown took over the selection of the *procuradores* of those towns that still participated. After 1432 only nobles could be town representatives. The nobles led by the sons of Fernando de Antequera repeatedly kidnapped the king, who was repeatedly saved by Álvaro de Luna, a nephew of Archbishop Pedro of Toledo. The dissatisfied nobles in 1453 found an ally against de Luna in Isabel of Portugal, half-insane, possessive, and resentful over de Luna's influence over her husband. Isabel persuaded Juan II to arrest de Luna, who was beheaded in 1453. Juan II died the next year, while Isabel went completely mad.

Factional hatreds also shook English society. Frustration rose as England was gradually pushed out of France at the end of the Hundred Years War. Henry VI invited defiance of the crown first by being too mild and eventually by the force of his encroaching insanity. Henry's childhood years, like those of Juan II, were spent at a Court torn by rivalry between two factions, one headed by Henry's paternal uncle Humphrey, Duke of Gloucester, and the other by Henry's great-uncle Cardinal Beaufort. Beaufort's peace policy with France was adopted in 1445 and sealed by the marriage of Henry VI to Margaret of Anjou, niece of Queen Marie of France. Acting in support of the Beauforts, Margaret rapidly won influence with Henry VI. Just as Isabel of Portugal six years later would use her influence with Juan II to destroy Álvaro de Luna, so Margaret of Anjou brought Henry VI to arrest Humphrey of Gloucester in 1447 on a charge of treason. The shock caused him to die from a stroke. Cardinal Beaufort followed his enemy Gloucester to the grave half a year later.

Richard, Duke of York, a distant cousin of the king, soon began to foment opposition to the crown. He had been displaced as the king's heir in 1453 when Margaret of Anjou gave birth to Prince Edward. However, when Henry VI fell ill with porphyria in 1454, Parliament appointed Richard Lord Protector. Porphyria usually manifests itself initially in only a brief spell of insanity. The brief onset is followed by a long period of sanity, with later fits being more prolonged and the intervals of lucidity less extended, until permanent insanity sets in. When after a short time Henry VI recovered his senses and control of his own government, Richard determined to grab back power by force. In 1455 he opened the War of the Roses, spreading the rumor that Prince Edward of Wales was illegitimate, but he met defeat and death at Wakefield in 1460. His son Edward, the new duke of York, was declared king as Edward IV by a council of nobles and managed to defeat Margaret of Anjou in March 1461 at the battle of Towton. Margaret and Prince Edward fled to France, and Henry VI was imprisoned in the Tower of London.

The Resurgence of Middle Class Power

In the third quarter of the fifteenth century, both Enrique IV of Castile (1454–74) and Edward IV of England (1461–83) looked to the middle class for support. In both kingdoms the hostile reaction of the nobles led to the overthrow of these kings' heirs, who were violently replaced by figures linked to the nobility. Enrique lived a simple, unpretentious life, not letting anybody kiss his hand, addressing everyone with *vos,* that is, without regard for social station, and preferring the company of common folk. Distrusting the high nobility *(ricos hombres),* he surrounded himself with lesser nobles *(hidalgos)* and bourgeois, using Jewish and *converso* administrators and Moorish guards. He built up a rich treasury and stimulated Segovia's textile production. The Castilian economy briefly blossomed for the last time for centuries, as foreign merchants turned Segovia, Burgos, Valladolid, and Toledo into major European trade centers. In England Edward IV also introduced a program favorable to the middle class, working to end the feudal chaos and to improve the economy. He, too, encouraged cloth manufacturing. The thick English wool, which had previously been exported by the Merchants of the Staple for sale to the cloth-weaving industry of Flanders, was increasingly turned into cloth in England and then sold abroad by the Merchant Adventurers. Law and order was enforced, making the roads safe again for commerce. More middle-class bureaucrats were hired to government administrative positions, and the crown itself invested in business ventures. Nobles who continued to disturb the peace found themselves brought before the new Court of Star Chamber (held in a room of Westminster Palace with stars painted on its ceiling), where they were subject to torture, conviction without witnesses or defense, and summary death sentences.

Enrique IV and Edward IV and their wives were both involved in sexual scandals that undermined acceptance of their children as their heirs. Enrique, remembered as *el Impotente* (the impotent), blamed his dysfunction on his first wife, whom he divorced, remarrying Juana of Portugal.

When Juana gave birth to a daughter, the suspicion was voiced that the real father was the dashing young courtier Beltrán de la Cueva, and skeptics called the girl Juana la Beltraneja. In contrast, Edward IV was a womanizer who seems to have cajoled Eleanor Talbot, daughter of the first earl of Shrewsbury, into his bed by arranging a secret wedding ceremony with her. This charge threw into question the legitimacy of Edward's subsequent marriage to Elizabeth Woodville, a widow with three children. The pro-bourgeois policies of these two kings stirred opposition from the nobility. In 1465 a group of rebel Castilian nobles launched a revolt, crowned Enrique's eleven-year-old half-brother Alfonso as king, and suppressed municipal liberties. In 1467, after the rebels took Segovia, Enrique surrendered. In England, Edward IV's policies antagonized some of the very nobles who had put him in power. The earl of Warwick made contact with Margaret of Anjou in France. In 1470 Edward IV's forces were defeated, and Edward fled to Flanders. However, in March 1471 Edward IV reinvaded England and won back the English throne at the battles of Barnet and Tewkesbury. Edward, Prince of Wales, was killed, Henry VI was murdered in the Tower of London, and a broken Margaret was eventually sent back home to France.

New Style Monarchy

The Middle Ages ended with the reigns of two red-headed, strong-armed "Machiavellian" monarchs. In Castile, now loosely joined with Aragon in the first step toward the unification of Spain, Isabel la Católica (1474–1504), wife of Fernando of Aragon, filled this role, while in England it was Henry VII (1485–1509). The monarchs in both kingdoms were iron-fisted disciplinarians who held a tight reign over themselves and their subjects. Isabel seldom or never drank wine and spent very modestly on food and other daily needs for herself and her family. Card games, cosmetics, and other frivolities were banned from her court over her husband's futile objections. In England, Henry VII was tight-lipped and coolly calculating, a penny-pincher who personally audited all royal accounts and built up a strong treasury.

Each of these monarchs had come to the throne through rebellion after a suspicious death of a royal prince had cleared their path to the throne. Isabel had received the support of the rebel nobles in 1468, after her younger brother Alfonso had died of some kind of poisoning (which the historian Palencia suspects was intentional). Henry VII had likewise come to the throne by the elimination of a young king (and his brother). When Edward IV died in 1483, his sons Edward V and Richard were twelve and ten years old respectively. Edward IV's brother Richard, Duke of York, in his capacity as regent, had housed both boys in the Bloody Tower of the Tower of London, from where they soon disappeared forever. After declaring them illegitimate, Richard had assumed the throne in 1483. The French government had accused Richard of murdering his nephews, and suspicion of Richard's guilt had weakened his position, but he had made no move to produce them or to explain their disappearance. Instead, Richard III had allied himself with reactionary barons, winning support from members of the old nobility. It is true that the Parliament of 1484 had passed legislation against unfair taxation, unwarranted arrest, and jury intimidation, as well as granting the right of bail, as an attempt to increase the usurper's popularity. However, Richard increasingly trampled traditional rights and customs, calling up an old-fashioned Great Council (in 1485) consisting only of nobles, in place of a parliament, and ruthlessly executing those who opposed him, violating sanctuary, and imprisoning bishops. In 1485 Henry Tudor, Earl of Richmond (of a Welsh family but with some royal English blood from his mother), challenged Richard for the throne. Although Henry had brought only a small force with him when he landed in England, many Englishmen rallied to his cause. Even the traditional Yorkist towns of London, Gloucester, and Worcester refused to aid Richard, and the troops sent by York arrived too late to participate. At Bosworth Field in August 1485 Richard fought bravely, but by the time the battle commenced, Henry's army had grown to ten thousand men, against only eight thousand for Richard. The battle ended when Richard was pulled off his horse and killed.

Isabel and Henry VII both drew strength from their marriage partners. Isabel married the heir to the throne of Aragon, Fernando, in 1471, and induced Enrique IV to accept her as his heir. After Enrique died in 1474, Alfonso V of Portugal, who in old age had married his niece Juana la Beltraneja, invaded Castile claiming the throne. The Catholic monarchs, as Isabel and Fernando (Ferdinand) are remembered, repulsed his army at the battle of Toro on the Duero. Henry VII's marriage to Elizabeth of York, daughter of Edward IV, ended the Wars of the Roses by uniting the

York and Lancaster factions, thereby adding legitimacy to Henry's claim to the throne.

In this age of the so-called New Style monarchs, rulers enhanced the power of their central governments (in contrast to the decentralized type of rule that had marked the Middle Ages). Isabel managed to consolidate the New Style monarchy in Castile by an alliance with her nobles, while Henry based his version on cooperation with the middle class. In both cases, the monarch was allying with the strongest class in the land, which happened to be the nobility in Castile and the middle class in England. Isabel took her route because of the ongoing vulnerability of the Spanish middle class. Some of the towns resisted the *corregidores* which Isabel appointed as royal-appointed watchdogs on the town councils. In 1484 a *corregidor* was denied admission into the Burgos town-council meeting, which then voted in 1485 to refuse to pay a new tax that violated their town charter rights. A fight resulted between the town fathers and Isabel's *Hermandad* police, which was imposing royal authority with a policy of amputations and executions by arrows. As towns all over Spain prepared to follow the Burgos example, a new institution helped to break their opposition—the Spanish Inquisition. Even though the attacks on the Jews at the end of the fourteenth century had temporarily weakened the Castilian middle class, the effect of the forced conversions brought the bourgeoisie new vitality by the mid-fifteenth century; By becoming at least nominal Christians, Jews had removed the principal impediment to their marrying Gentiles. Given the wealth of these Spanish *conversos,* the Gentile Christian middle-class families were eager for such marriage ties. The intermarriages proceeded so fast, that the saying arose, "Scratch a Spaniard and a Jew will bleed." The middle class had thereby gained a solidarity it had hitherto lacked. Enrique IV had seemed to be guiding Castile toward a more mercantile future. But this program was now abandoned as the enemies of the middle class accused its Jewish-blooded members of being insincere Christians ("crypto-Jews"). Since many of the *conversos* did hold secretly to Judaism, the charge was all the easier to make against anybody with a *converso* heritage.

The Spanish Inquisition was established on paper in 1482 and was in place by 1485. (The Papal Inquisition had never been introduced to Castile, although it had operated in Aragon.) This institution was run by Dominican friars under the control of the Spanish crown. It drew up lists of "purity" of bloodline, placing many middle class families under suspicion and social ostracism. Some of the arrested *conversos* were subjected to burning or garroting in autos da fe (actos de fe), although others bought release from prison by quickly handing over their fortunes to the crown. The Inquisition brought the queen great sums of money, with which she consolidated the power of her central government. Additional sums were brought into the royal treasury by Isabel's expulsion of the Jews from Spain in 1492. That same year, Isabel and Fernando completed the Spanish *Reconquista* by conquering the last Moorish state of Granada.

Following the old theory of divine right of kings, which claimed that the monarch's responsibility was directly to God, Isabel legislated without parliamentary cooperation. The last time that laws were issued based on the petitions of town representatives was at the 1480 Parliament of Toledo. At the same time, Castile was given a general law code called the Ordinances of Montalvo, further centralizing the legal system. The royal council's role was enhanced and divided into five departments: justice, external policy, internal policy, the Santa Hermandad, and matters of Aragon, Valencia, Cataluña, and Sicily. Isabel stabilized the currency with a new gold coin, the *excelente*. Nobles were granted an important place in her system of government, provided they accepted stronger crown controls. They were allowed continued possession of their vast estates, an elevated social status, and an outlet for gaining wealth through booty in war. In a more positive vein, Isabel ended serfdom, razed to the ground some castles of recalcitrant nobles, attacked robber-baronage, gave preference to trained *letrado* commoners in the civil service, held crown control over the three military monastic orders, and continued a strong crown-controlled *Santa Hermandad* police force. The *Mesta,* an association organized to promote the production of sheep and wool, was incorporated into the government.

In contrast, Henry VII consolidated the bourgeois-oriented rule pioneered by Edward IV. He promoted English trading companies, especially the Merchant Adventurers, who sold finished cloth in Flanders. He subjugated the guilds to royal control in 1504, since their regulations had been stifling competition and business growth. He continued to place trained commoners in high government offices, and improved the equality of the laws. He forbade nobles to keep private armies, accelerated the use of the Court of Star Chamber to crush his opponents, and executed some of the leading nobles. As a result, disaffected nobles mounted two major revolts aimed at toppling the new Tudor dynasty, one in 1487 and the other in 1496, but both failed to unseat the increasingly powerful Henry.

Differences between Hispanic and Anglo Social Class Developments in the Late Middle Ages

Despite the many close parallels in their histories, an important difference between Castile's and England's approach to social class status emerged by the end of the Middle Ages. The economic pinch of the Late Middle Ages was greater in Castile than in England, yet a Castilian knight would be stripped of his spurs and sword, losing his knighthood, if he ventured into trade. While Castilian nobles could be seen begging, many English knights turned from a military career to merge with the small freeholders, forming a viable gentry living from estate administration. By the start of the fourteenth century, English society had abandoned the rigid class divisions that still marked Castile for centuries to come, with blurred divisions between the high nobility and the gentry, and again between the gentry and the yeomanry. The fact that the social class hostility of the fourteenth and fifteenth centuries was more pronounced in Castile than in England resulted in a more drastic attack on the middle class in Castile, reaching its height under Isabel la Católica.

As a result of Isabel's negative impact on the middle class, Spain ended the Middle Ages without a strong middle class. Only the gold and silver of the New World would allow Spain to maintain a facade of greatness for the next three centuries. Whereas in Castile, the nobility maintained a good deal of power (even in the towns), many English commoners (including mercers, dyers, cooks, and blacksmiths) became landowners, prospered, and occasionally managed to send their sons to college. In the mid-fourteenth century English alliterative poem *Wynnere and Wastoure,* the king promises to knight Winner, head of an army of commoners hostile to the military class. Richard II did knight some London aldermen for helping to crush the Peasant's Revolt, and Edward IV started a tradition of royal knightings of the mayor of London. A middle-class, mercantile orientation was thus stamped on Anglo society, while a strong class ethos took root in Spain by the end of the Middle Ages.

Results of Economic and Social Class Concepts for Mexican-American Society

Various influences have come to the Borderlands from medieval economic and social class developments. Some are shared from a common heritage, while others have come in two forms, one Hispanic and one Anglo, which have blended into unique patterns in the border region.

Hispanic and Anglo Shared Influences from the Late Middle Ages

Medieval knighthood bequeathed a sense of obligation to serve and a code of honor still felt today by political office holders. The office of justice of the peace developed out of the 1351 Statute of Laborers, which established justices as keepers of the peace to enforce the statute. Although Edward III's Statute of Laborers proved unenforceable in the face of economic change, the office of justice of the peace was passed down, in altered form, to Anglo-America.

One of the more important influences on the Borderlands from late medieval economic developments has been in the field of ranching practices. Many medieval nobles found a new source of wealth and power as ranching barons with extensive estates in the south of Castile and the north of England—a development unique to these two kingdoms. The Castilian *Reconquista* and William the Conqueror's devastation of northern England made vast lands available for grazing. In Spain Muslim farms were abandoned by flight or expulsion, and since the Castilians lacked sufficient Christian farmers and the knowledge of irrigation techniques to maintain them, the lands were converted to huge ranches or *latifundios*. Huge flocks of merino sheep originally imported from the Maghreb were established, although the wool produced was not as high in quality as that from the English sheep. In the thirteenth century, extensive grazing of sheep and cattle was introduced to newly reconquered Andalucía and Extremadura, large herds grazing especially in the Guadiana Valley. In 1273 wealthy Castilian sheep-breeders, including nobles, the church, and military orders, formed the *Mesta*. Sheep were driven in October and April along set routes between summer pastures in the north and winter pastures in the south. Under the supervision of *Mesta* officials, four principal *cañadas* or sheep walks of over 240 feet in width were laid out and kept open. The most westerly ran from the vicinity of León through Zamora, Salamanca, and Badajoz to the area of Huelva. The next sheep walk to the east began in the region of Burgos and Palencia and wound south through Segovia and Ávila to the vicinity of Mérida. The third trail linked Longroño (near the Navarrese border) with Sevilla, via Soria, Madrid, Toledo, and Córdoba. The most easterly *cañada* began around Cuenca and ran across La Mancha to the upper Guadalquivir Valley and the region of Murcia. Herds of a thousand sheep were moved each year over hundreds of miles between summer pastures in and near Galicia, Cantabria, and the Pyrenees and winter pastures in Extremadura and Andalucía. The herds were moved south in September and October, returning north in April and May, when they were sheared on the way. Mule trains carried provisions, sheepdogs helped to keep the sheep in line, and other animals were at times herded along, including horses, donkeys, cattle, goats, and pigs. The *Mesta* set up markets and fairs, supply points, rest areas, and toll centers for fees owed to the crown. It maintained law and order and established its own court to resolve problems. The *Mesta* received royal support to the detriment of the of other farming interests.

Cattle ranching also increased in the lands taken by the Castilians from the Moors. The small Spanish cattle herds consisted of Moorish semi-feral longhorn breeds adapted to life on the arid *meseta*. The cattlemen, coming mainly from the lower nobility and lacking social standing, set up no comparable organization to the *Mesta,* although some royal charters of permission to hold cattle drives were obtained. The main cattle trail route ran from León and Salamanca through Extremadura to the Guadalquivir Valley. While many of the ranchers castrated their calves, producing steers more docile than bulls that could be herded by men on foot, other ranchers let their cattle run wild until a roundup in which the herds had to be managed with considerable skill from horseback.

England saw a parallel development of sheep- and cattle-ranching. William the Conqueror's scorched-earth policy in Northumbria left the northern lords deprived of adequate laborers for agricultural work so that in the twelfth century they also turned extensively to sheep-raising. Sheep herding came to represent half of England's landed wealth. Cattle herding was also developed, mainly in the agriculturally marginal hill country of the northern border region with Scotland. The English herders also made seasonal migrations of their various breeds, which were created by interbreeding of beef and milk cows. In the fifteenth century, most of the prisoners brought before any royal commission of assize and gaol delivery in England's northernmost counties were cattle-thieves. With the conversion of Castilian and English land to ranching purposes, Prussia, Poland, and Hungary replaced Castile and England as leading grain producers.

These medieval developments laid the basis for ranching in the Borderlands. The New Mexican sheep-raising industry was started from herds brought by Juan de Oñate's expedition in 1598, while Nuevo Santander's sheep-raising practices after the mid-eighteenth century influenced Texas. The mountainous and arid regions from California through Arizona and New Mexico to West Texas proved to be especially suitable for sheep ranching, due to the sheep's ability to graze on slopes and to make better use of marginally productive lands. The two main types of sheep introduced from Castile—the *churro* or scrub, a small and lean animal with coarse, lightweight wool, and the thicker-wooled *merino*—were both well adapted to the semi-arid conditions prevailing from Texas (now the leading American sheep breeding state) to California (the second most important). Castilian sheep-raising customs, practices, institutions, and organization developed in the Late Middle Ages were also passed down to the Borderlands, where many remain in place to this day, in spite of the fact that Anglo-American shepherds took over much of the sheep raising industry in the nineteenth century. The chain of command from the ranch owner or *patrón* through a *mayordomo* to a range boss, to a mounted rider, to two or three shepherds was Spanish in origin, as was the assigning of fixed grazing rights to individual owners. As in Castile, sheep walks (herding paths) were fixed by law. The California gold rush brought an increase of the sheep population in that state, as herders joined the miners. A surge of commercial ranching followed in Texas during the Civil War.

Francisco Vásquez de Coronado first introduced cattle to the Borderlands during his expedition into New Mexico in 1540. Cattle ranching became especially important for the Hispanic colony in Texas, starting with the missions of Nacogdoches in 1690. In 1721 the Marquez de San Miguel de Aguayo, a wealthy Coahuila nobleman, came to San Antonio to replace Martín de Alarcón, the first Spanish governor of Coahuila in Texas. His expedition of 500 hundred men with approximately 3,000 horses, 6,500 sheep, and 4,800 cattle has been called the first big cattle drive in Texas history. Cattle were more emphasized than sheep in the eastern half of Texas from the earliest Hispanic settlement, due to their better adjustment to hot and humid conditions and to their immunity to malaria. The longhorns herded in medieval Castile were mixed with cattle types introduced by the French into Louisiana and by the Anglos into a broad region extending from South Carolina to Texas. Cattle ranching was spread to California by Junípero Serra's expedition in 1769 and to southern Arizona by 1790. The herds increased so rapidly that by the end of the eighteenth century there were approximately a million head in California. Beef became a food staple there, and hides and tallow were marketed to South America and to the United States in the early 1800s. Although cattlemen had been assigned a lesser social status in Castile, where the word *charro* referred to a bumpkin, in the Borderlands they became cattle barons, and *charro* took on the meaning of *elegant.* The cattle industry, however, did not really develop until the 1800s. From about 100,000 in 1830 the number of cattle increased to over 380,000 in 1846, and at least 80 percent of these were the *cimarrones* (wild descendants) of Spanish cattle. Their offspring would become the so-called Texas cattle herded on vast cattle drives to the railheads in Kansas and shipped to the stockyards in Kansas City and Chicago. From this same stock came the cattle that were later used to stock the ranges of Wyoming, Montana, and Colorado. The California cattle industry began its decline at about the same time that the Texas industry began its rise during the American Civil War.

The Castilian cattle ranch likewise laid the basis for the Borderlands cattle culture, with its cowboy outfit, methods, and lingo. The early Californio organization of roundup judges to settle ranching disputes was modeled on the Castilian *Alcaldes de la Mesta.* Branding is known from tenth-century Spain, and the branding laws and registration, fence and range laws, and toll systems developed from practices brought over from Spain. Other elements transmitted from medieval Castile ranching practice include the corral, branding in the spring (practiced from the tenth century on), registration of brands in official books (from the thirteenth century), selection of cattle for sale in the fall, the Texas longhorn (first bred on the Spanish *meseta*), the cattle drive (as livestock were to market or from one pasture to another with the changing seasons), and herding from horseback (unique to the Castilians in the Middle Ages). The virtuosity of the medieval Adalusian cattlemen in the late fifteenth century inspired the first rodeos, with their displays of roping cattle and of grabbing cattle by the tail, seizing the horns, twisting the head, and throwing them to the ground. Gear has also been inherited from medieval Castile, including the harness, bridles *(brida),* bit *(embocadura),* starred spurs *(espuelas),* chaps *(chaparrajos),* horse feedbags *(morrales),* halter, prod, ropes *(mecates),* and lasso or lariat. The cowboy saddle is based on the horned saddle copied by the Spaniards from the Moors. Spanish words for these and other practices, gear, and associated references are still clearly heard in the English words for beef jerky *(charquí),* buckaroo *(vaquero),* burro, calaboose *(calabozo),* chaps *(chaperreras),* cinch *(cincha),* desperado, the double-loop knot called the dolly welter *(de la vuelta),* hacienda, lariat *(la reata),* lasso *(lazo),* mustang or bronco *(mesteño),* palomino, pinto, ranch *(rancho* or *ranchería),* stampede *(estampada),* and vamoose *(vamos).* While a *mesteño* (of the *mesta*) was an unbranded cow belonging to the *Mesta* organization of Castilian herders, its Anglicized equivalent of "mustang" referred to a wild horse. The everyday cowboy dress traces back especially to Andalucía. The colorful *charro* or dressy cowboy costume (like the *china poblana* for women) stems from the Spanish province of Salamanca, where the term *charro* was applied to the residents of a group of towns including Alba, Vitigudino, and Ledesma. This was the area where Spanish livestock breeding had first been developed in the twelfth century. The broad-brimmed hat (but now turned up slightly at the brim), short, open jacket, wide sash over tight-fitting trousers, and spurred boots had spread from this region to southern Spain with the *Reconquista* of the thirteenth century. The name for the ten-gallon hat is a distortion of *sombrero galoneado,* a fancily decorated hat.

The medieval English cattle industry contributed the whip and bulldogs, the provision of cattle salt licks, and burning of the range lands. The early tension between English sheep herders and cowboys was also perpetuated in New Mexico, where Hispanic shepherds faced off in range wars and conflicting land-grant claims against Anglo cowboys coming in from Texas. The Anglo settlers of Texas added their own contributions to Borderlands cattle ranching. Castration of bull calves left the male animals tame enough to be herded on foot, even by women, older folk, and boys (the origin of the term *cowboys*). Whips were employed, and bulldogs and other breeds were trained and bred to help control the cattle. Overgrazed fields overrun with bushes were burned to renew them. When such methods proved inadequate in England, overgrazing caused many of the English cattle herders to migrate in the second half of the seventeenth century first to Jamaica and then on to South Carolina. They then followed the westward move of Anglo settlement across the Deep South into Texas. In the Mexican-American Borderlands, as in medieval Castile, many ranches owed their vast acreage to land grabbing as the border shifted. In Castile ranches had been formed out of lands taken after the victories of the *Reconquista* (as mentioned earlier), and, similarly, in the Borderlands the Mexican War allowed resulted in seizure of lands vacated by former owners loyal to Mexico. As one of the main features of the Borderlands, ranching was introduced, developed, and strongly influenced by both the Castilian and English ranching practices.

Various medieval technological developments have become hallmarks of the Mexican-American Borderlands. The production of wire, which would be applied to the barbed-wire fences of the cattle ranches, developed in the early eleventh century by use an invention called a drawplate and by use of a wire mill (using waterpower for the wire drawing) by the late fifteenth century. The horizontal-axle windmill dates from late twelfth-century Europe, while the suction pump that made it effective in the Borderlands was added in the fifteenth century. The Conestoga wagon, which brought many of the Anglo immigrants to the area in the nineteenth century, was based on the *longa caretta* of the early twelfth century. Both types of wagons were made possible by the tandem harness, itself made feasible by the medieval inventions of the horse collar with lateral shafts (of the ninth century), the nailed horseshoe (also of the ninth century), and the whipple-tree rod to equalize the pull (from the eleventh century). The stage coach's basic principle of a compartment suspended on springs can be traced back to the first half of the eleventh century in England. The Andalucian system of donkey or mule pack trains was also adopted to the Borderlands, where they played a central role in transportation down to the arrival of the railroad.

Contrasting Hispanic and Anglo Influences from the Late Middle Ages

Late medieval developments also molded the dichotomized Hispano and Anglo class-linked attitudes of the Borderlands. The defeat of the middle class in late medieval Spain consolidated the aristocratic ideals already fostered by the *Reconquista.* In *El Libro de los ejemplos de conde Lucanor,* merchants are dismissed as crassly concerned with profit. One of them at the time of death tries to bribe his soul not to leave him; the heart of another merchant is found not in his body but in his treasure chest; and a third is drowned rather than letting go of heavy jewels. The complaint that materialism has triumphed over idealism, leaving the old aristocracy poor and despised, is found in many of the six hundred songs by fifty authors between the 1370s and 1440s, collected at the Castilian court into the *Cancionero de baena.* The aristocratic pride and disdain of materialism often expressed in medieval Castile was less commonly encountered in England. The English, with their more assertive commoners, tended rather to show contempt for pride, which was viewed in a more positive light by the aristocratic Castilians. In Chaucer's uncompleted *House of Fame,* an eagle carries the poet to view the House of Fame, which is built on a mass of melting ice. He sees the names of the famous, futilely chiseled as a memorial into the ice, which is disappearing before his eyes. The goddess of fame is shown to be arbitrarily assigning and denying her gift with little reference to merit. In "The Former Age," Chaucer asserted that pride played its part in wrecking the happy equality of the original Golden Age. In the cycle known as the *York Plays* of late medieval England, the great lords are mocked as braggarts and are repeatedly dragged out of bed for some trivial reason or for comedy at their expense. Pride is also excoriated in the figure of Lucifer in the "Pageant of the Creation." While other angels sing God's praises, Lucifer grouches that he, despite being superior, is nothing more than a mere angel.

An Anglo-Castilian dichotomy of social values was thus already delineated by the close of the Middle Ages. Hispanics were conditioned to be disinclined toward materialism or a strict work ethic, while fostering a hierarchical and paternal social structure and a respect for tradition. The class tensions and group confrontations of the fourteenth and fifteenth centuries in Spain reinforced the family and group orientation still central to Mexican American society. The border custom of embracing is part of this package of group-oriented customs. It has been noted that Hispanic students differ from their Anglo counterparts in their preference for a structured approach to learning, an authority figure in charge of a class, collaborative work with their peers, and attending class in the evening.[1]

In addition to these Hispanic forces working in Mexican American border culture, there are values coming in from the Anglo heritage, tracing back to the Late Middle Ages in England. A more self-assertive attitude vis-à-vis the government and important individuals was carried by Anglo farmers and handworkers across the Atlantic, in contrast to the deference shown to the privileged hierarchy of secular and ecclesiastical nobles that accompanied the Hispanic migration to America. The relative success of middle class goals by the end of the fifteenth century in English society helped to develop such values as individualism, thrift, industry, and a fascination with progress. This complex was especially represented by the second wave of Anglos into the Borderlands, coming from the upper Midwest in the twentieth century.

The Horatio Alger–style Anglo-American rags-to-riches dream of rising to success by business ingenuity is still nourished by the children's tale of fifteenth-century English hero Dick Whittington. This story encourages entrepreneurial poor boys to stick to their dreams by telling how young Dick Whittington comes into London penniless and becomes a scullion boy for Sir Hugh Fitzwarren. He invests his only possession, a cat, in a trading voyage of his merchant master. Discouraged, he decides to leave London, but as he walks down Fleet Street, the bells of St. Mary Bow seem to say, "Turn back, Dick Whittington, Lord Mayor of London." He returns to his job, and when his master's ship returns, he learns that his cat has been sold for a high price to a Moorish king plagued by rats. Launched into wealth, he goes on to become London's mayor. The real Dick Whittington did become a patron of London, providing church buildings and a public library. The closest medieval hero emphasized in Spanish-language children's literature current in the Borderlands is Cristóbal Colón (Christopher Columbus). While Columbus certainly has his entrepreneurial side, this is balanced by his role as an explorer and conquistador, which evokes such values of the feudal nobility as courage, fighting skill, and adventure. The imaginative dreamer Columbus has little in common with the pragmatic, stay-at-home bourgeois Whittington, whose great achievement is to win wealth in business and political office. Furthermore, Columbus is often presented in a negative light in local Hispanic literature as the cruel exploiter of native Americans.

The chivalric romantic view has shaped different views of love and manners. Although now in rapid flux, Hispanic society has traditionally given women less encouragement toward independent behavior than Anglo society. A local Hispanic stereotype of the Anglo-American woman disparages her as shamelessly aggressive. Peter Ramirez's comic strip "Raising Hector" recently featured a Mexican American family struggling with feelings of remorse over the mother's employment. The roots for this attitude go back to the days when Spanish society was more resistant than the English to female self-assertiveness. Castile's more aristocratic warrior society tended to subordinate the woman to the man more than was the case in England's more peaceful mercantile setting. It is true that in Christian Castile men and women were equal in the eyes of the law: both the father and mother gave away the bride at her wedding, a wife's property, although administered by the husband, remained her own, and widows held tutelage of the children and could make legal contracts. Nonetheless, women were expected to follow the biblical injunction to be obedient to their husbands. In Castilian literature, praise often focused on the model of the Virgin Mary, caring and pure. Gonzalo de Berceo, a mid-thirteenth century cleric, in his verse *Milagros de Nuestra Señora* (miracles of Our Lady) presented the Virgin as a firm but loving mother figure. In his *Cantigas de Santa María* (as in his *Siete partidas* law code), Alfonso X encouraged women to occupy themselves with pious and modest activities, to be virtuous, and to avoid displays of temper. A model of romantic married love is presented by the Cid and his obedient wife Jimena in the *Poema del Cid,* presumably written in the mid-twelfth century; the pair part so reluctantly from each other that it is like pulling a fingernail from a finger. The *Poema de Fernán González,* written in the mid-thirteenth century, presents the resourceful princess Sancha, who, while fully capable of fending for herself, acts to help her future husband.

In contrast, the literature of more middle-class medieval England frequently described women who dared to challenge both their husbands and conventional behavior. Marie de France, an author writing for the court of Henry II around the year 1170 in Anglo-Norman French, who may or may not have been writing in England, wrote *Lays* or verse tales, some of which arouse sympathy for women. In the "Lay of the Werewolf," a woman discovers that her husband is a criminal werewolf. She hides his clothing one night so that when he returns from a murderous night in town he is obliged to remain in his animal shape. Eventually, the king discovers what she has done, restores the man to clothes and human form, and banishes the woman for her marital betrayal. Marie's "Lay of the Two Lovers" presents a man too stubborn to take good advice from a woman. While proving his love for a princess by carrying her to the top of a mountain, he grows exhausted, but spurns her urgings to take a drink of her magic liquid to restore his energy. Impelled by a "macho" impulse to do the feat on his own strength, he makes it to the summit, only to drop dead. In the 1190s, in Nicholas of Guildford's Middle English poem *The Owl and the Nightingale,* an owl, representing learning, accepts that adultery is justified for a woman with a worthless husband. Geoffrey Chaucer's Wife of Bath in *The Canterbury Tales* represents the point of view that women should hold a more dominant place in society, expressing the wish that husbands be meek.

Many ideas of courtesy and romance, which have largely passed out of fashion since the mid-twentieth century in the Borderlands as elsewhere, were also shaped by the courtly love movement originating in Medieval France, England, Spain, and Italy. Customs such as holding doors and adjusting chairs for ladies to help them push up to a table, and helping ladies in and out of vehicles, increasingly antiquated today, trace back to the civilizing of the English and Spanish nobles as a result of the chivalric love movement. These courtesies, now of dubious practical worth, were originally anchored in common civility, given the awkwardness of a lady having to hold up her long, heavy skirts in such maneuvers. The tradition that men should walk on the outside of a sidewalk, still repeated today, came from the need to protect women in a narrow medieval street from slop thrown out of overhanging, second-floor windows to collect in the gutters. The custom of a man tipping his hat to a lady, which lasted into the mid-twentieth century, originated with the courtesy of a knight removing his helmet or raising his visor to identify himself to a lady, thereby putting her at ease. The children's game of blindman's buff was once popular with court ladies. Certain concepts about romantic love, including the notion of love as a sickness, as inspired by the meeting of eyes and on first sight, of the woman as beyond the reach and station of the longing suitor, first appeared in the romantic verse that blossomed in Spain and England in the High Middle Ages, lives on especially in Hispanic songs.

Town layouts in the Borderlands also very much reflect medieval heritage: Hispanic-founded town plans rooted in the military emphasis of the Castilians, Anglo-founded towns either in the mercantile or legal concern of the English. As the medieval Castilians founded new towns in the southern move of the *Reconquista,* they employed the pattern the ancient Romans had used for their establishments in Spain, creating garrison towns to concentrate population into more-easily protected units. A gridiron of streets intersect at right angles to facilitate rapid troop movement. Easy to survey, these towns center in a plaza at the crossing of the two main streets, where the town hall and church (if not on a square nearby) and other public buildings are located. Whereas in most towns of medieval northern Castile the streets followed a rabbit warren of directions and there was no plaza, new or refounded and planned Castilian towns created during the southward push of the *Reconquista* tended to be laid out on this grid pattern. Briviesca, relocated in 1208, is one example of a planned plaza and gridiron town. This pattern looked back to early Greek towns, the Roman military camp, and Spanish Roman towns like Italica and Mérida. It was reinforced in early modern times by the prestige of *De architectura* by Emperor Augustus's architect Vitruvius. The Spanish crown through the Laws of the Indies called for the new colonial cities in America to conform to this type, so that the pattern is found in the original sections of Mexican-American Borderlands towns founded under Hispanic rule, including San Diego, Los Angeles, Santa Fe, Albuquerque, and San Antonio. Leading Borderlands towns from San Antonio and Laredo through El Paso, Albuquerque, and Santa Fe, to Los Angeles and San Diego were founded in the Spanish colonial period and show this pattern.

Anglo settlements looked back instead to one of two different models of town planning, both of which were applied on the East Coast and were subsequently spread westward with the expanding Anglo-American frontier. The first type traces directly to medieval England, where towns grew up as markets stretching out along one major street, with stores and inns to attract the attention of potential customers passing by. Such towns grew up where there was a castle on the road to offer them protection and ideally a church to provide moral support. When this system was first transplanted to New England, the early meeting house provided military and religious support in one combined structure. New York City was founded on this same concept by the Dutch, around Broadway as the central commercial street. Brownsville, founded by Yankee Charles Stillman, was laid out along Elizabeth Street as its "Broadway." The second type of Anglo town plan brought to the Borderlands (influenced by medieval England's emphasis on popular participation in the legal system) was first developed in the town plans of the Colonial South. Too rural to support true market towns, the southern settlements centered on the courthouse. This pattern spread westward to the Borderlands with southerners. It can be seen in Edinburg, Texas, with its central courthouse square, among other examples. Thus the echoes of medieval town plans still resonate on the Mexican-American border.

Concluding Remark

Thus many features of Borderlands life were given their distinctive form in the Late Middle Ages. Ranching, farming, mining, business, trade, coinage, technology, and class interrelationships were all affected. Despite parallel developments in the social histories of the two societies due to similar geography, climate, proximity, and trade, differences emerged in class relations and value systems. Social class distinctions also added fuel to the religious distinctions between the two societies, as will be explored in the next chapter.

FOUR

Religious Influences

The Borderlands have inherited a marked religious piety from both medieval Castile and England. Indeed, it might be argued that the religious flavor of Borderlands society is its strongest tie to the Middle Ages. This chapter will first consider historical influences on border Hispanic and Anglo spirituality such as European pre-Christian cults, early Christian zeal, and witchcraft. Then the different religious developments of the medieval Hispanic and Anglo worlds will be discussed, in order to understand the blend of thought that produced differing effects in religious traditions of the Borderlands.

Hispanic and Anglo Shared Religious Developments in the Middle Ages

Early Spain and England exhibited a strong commitment to Christianity, with several shared characteristics that arguably set them apart from even their neighbors within the body of Latin Christendom. Similarities include their indigenous pre-Christian emphasis on deities of life fighting the forces of death, the early date of their Christianization, their role in the

Christianization of societies, and their prolonged defense of Christianity in the face of conquering infidels. We will first consider the pagan cults of pre-Christian times, because their influence continued to live on as part of medieval society and, hence, has passed on certain traits to Borderlands culture. Here, again, a common heritage can be noted for both Hispanic and Anglo cultures.

Early Commitment to Benevolent Pagan Deities of Life

Pagan cults emphasizing the sun's life-preserving qualities of warmth and light in early Spain and Britain (both Celtic and Anglo-Saxon) prepared the way for an enthusiastic acceptance of Christianity. The sun god was called Abellion by the Celtiberians in Spain and Lug or Bel by the British Celts. Both Spanish and British societies gave him a primary emphasis. In Spain a sun temple was erected on the site of Seville, and sun boats for transporting the dead to the next world were depicted at passage graves near Antequera, north of Málaga, about 2,345 B.C. The Spaniards honored the sun god on the spring equinox by burning giant wickerwork animal figures, a custom preserved along with firecracker fights by the *nit del foc* during Valencia's Las Fallas festivals. Britain was once called *Logres*, meaning Lug's Land, while the name of London derives from *Lug Dun* (Lug's City). He was honored with bonfires at his festival of Beltaine on the first of May, symbolically marking the start of the light half of the year. On the mid-winter solstice (once celebrated on December 25), he was worshipped with the burning of a Yule log, representing the sun's fire, and by a boar feast in which the boar's head was placed on a platter with a baked apple representing the sun in its mouth. British priests went from house to house in a tradition to be continued later under the Germanic name of wassailing, scaring away evil spirits by throwing objects at trees and then drinking a toast. An ancient pilgrimage route through Gaul connected the sun shrine at Compostela in northwestern Spain to the ring of standing stones at Stonehenge in Britain, where, it was believed, the sun god would arrive on earth. The tomb of Saint James at Santiago de Compostela was constructed over the ancient shrine to the sun, while the tomb of Thomas Becket in Canterbury Cathedral lay approximately on the ancient pagan pilgrimage route to Stonehenge.

Lug/Bel anticipated Jesus in various ways. He was depicted in victory over a boar, a symbol of the forces of death. The Welsh *Mabinogion* (writings of the poets) narrates the victory of the forces of light over those of darkness. Llew (Lug) dies on a tree. As Llew's flesh decays, it falls to the ground, where it is eaten by a sow, symbol of death. However, Llew is then brought back to life by his father and flies as an eagle, symbol of the spirit, into the sky. Some of the early Christian missionaries equated pagan gods of light and life to the God of the Bible. Lug (Llew) was equated with the God of the Bible, as well as with Jesus. The tree on which Lug died, before his resurrection and ascent into heaven, seemed to prefigure the cross of Jesus, which was rapidly identified by early Christians as the World Tree. The story of Lug suffering a triple death (attacked by a trinity of deities, according to Irish tradition), paralleled Jesus' three-fold wounding from flogging, crucifixion, and a posthumous spear wound.

Like the Celts before them, the Anglo-Saxons converted to Christianity smoothly because of similarities between their pagan beliefs and the new faith. The Anglo-Saxon counterpart of Lug was Woden, whom they invoked for healing, while the Anglo-Saxon god of death and war was Donner. In the *Edda,* Odin (Woden) opposes Thor (Donner). The Anglo-Saxon god Woden, like Jesus, suffered death (or was prophesied to do so) through self-sacrifice, hanging on the World Tree that connected Heaven, Earth, and Hell and being stabbed in the side. He, too, suffered from thirst as he died, called out at the moment of death, descended to the world of the dead, rose triumphant to new life, and promised salvation to his followers. Pope Gregory the Great, whose missionaries began the conversion of Latin Europeans to papal leadership in Spain and England, urged conversion of the pagan Anglo-Saxons by degrees, by rededicating pagan temples as churches, and adapting pagan practices into Christian worship.

Impact of the Early Pagan Cults on the Borderlands

The above-mentioned pagan cults, by leaving their mark on the medieval period, have left a trace on Anglo religious customs in the Borderlands as elsewhere. Thus evergreens, once symbols of eternal life, are still used to decorate interiors. Sprigs of mistletoe, once believed to have been used by the ancient priests to ward off evil, are still hung over doors at Christmas (and as an old English excuse for kissing, as holy to the goddess of love). Branches of holly, also still displayed at Christmas, were brought into houses in early England. Tradition held that if the holly had spiny leaves the man would dominate the family for the coming year, if smooth the woman would hold the upper hand. The tradition of Santa Claus, as popularized by Clement Moore's poem "'Twas the Night Before Christmas" in early nineteenth-century New York, grew partly out of the pagan Anglo-Saxon concept of Wodin riding on an eight-footed horse at Yuletide to reward true believers and punish offenders. In Christian England, Wodin was reworked into the transitional figure of Father Christmas, included as a character in mumming plays and greeted in a fifteenth-century carol with a "Hail, Father Christmas, hail to thee!"

Spring fertility customs have also exerted a lasting impact. The depiction of a goose-footed early Celtic mother goddess, whose cult paralleled the devotion later shown to the Virgin Mary, may have influenced the concept of the modern Mother Goose. Early British sayings and tales came to be lumped together in the form of teachings for children under the rubric of Mother Goose nursery rhymes. Borderlands and broader American Easter customs stem from a blend of influences found in both early Spain and England. Although the Anglo-Saxon historian Bede argued that the Anglo-Saxon goddess of spring and dawn, Eostre, lies behind our word *Easter,* another derivation traces the word back to the Phoenician goddess Astarte, a form of the Babylonian deity Ishtar. Eostre's and Astarte/Ishtar's sacred hare, the bearer of eggs as a symbol of new life, has become our Easter Bunny. The universal American custom of giving gifts of eggs as a symbol of new life at Easter originated with the Spring festival of these goddesses throughout wide areas of the ancient world. The presentation of eggs as dues to the lord of a manor on Easter in the feudal period reinforced the continuation of this practice in the early Christian period.

Both decorating (using greenery in fourteenth-century England) and dancing around the maypole, originally a phallic symbol decorated with flowers, accompanied pre-Christian fertility festivals on the first of May. Known in both Hispanic and Anglo traditions, this custom is perpetuated by children in some Borderlands schools. Mayday festivities also once included playing the (originally rough) war game of the hobby horse, where men rode on stick figures of horses. This activity has given us both the children's hobby horse and the term "horse-play." Carnival, with its Borderlands variations such as Brownsville's Charro Days and El Paso's Sun Bowl Carnival, likewise came via medieval Castile from pre-Christian spring fertility rites. The custom of eating pancakes on Shrove Tuesday (before Ash Wednesday) dates back to the time when stored foodstuffs still on hand as winter ended were consumed in a celebration ritual. The Borderlands custom of burning firecracker-filled piñatas to fill the night sky with their flaming missiles harkens back to the pagan sun cult practice of burning huge wickerwork statues of animals. The most spectacular event of this sort is the burning of the fifty-foot-high *Viejo Zozobra* or "Old Man Gloom" on the main plaza in Santa Fe every fall, as part of the celebration of the Hispanic reconquest of New Mexico in 1692, after Pope's Indian Revolt.

The most widely spread heritage of the pagan death cult is Halloween. Tracing back to the Celtic festival of Samain on the night of October 31, this ritual originally marked, not a harvest festival, but the start of the barren second half of the year (lasting until Mayday six months later). Beginning a time of food shortage, and associated with the slaughter of those animals that could not be maintained through the winter, it was a gloomy commemoration of the forces of death. Hailing the period when the nights grew longer than the days, it included the lighting of night fires to ward off the unleashed spirits of darkness. Ghosts of the dead were believed to haunt the living. About 998, Abbot Odilo of Cluny tried to Christianize the popular festival by instituting the feast of All Souls on October 31 to commemorate the dead souls of the faithful. The date for All Souls was later moved to November 2, and to it was joined All Saints or All Hallows Day on November 1. From this festival came the name of All Hallow's Eve or *Halloween* for the night before. Mexican American culture has continued this medieval homage to death, reinforced by Aztec motifs on this theme. Awareness of the fleeting nature of life led to an emphasis on death in the Spanish tradition and to a stress on morality in the British outlook. Fourteenth-century Castile shared with much of Europe the motif of the *danza macabra,* showing death leading off his victims in a grisly dance. This tradition fed into the tradition, shared by the Borderlands with Mexico, of the production of candy and models of skulls and visits to family graves on the *día de los muertos* on the second of November. This emphasis has also been passed down to the Mexican-American Borderlands in part from early Spanish and British worship of gods of war and death.

Christian Zeal in Medieval Spain and Britain

The fact that the Christianity was established early in Spain and Britain contributed to their special commitment to the new religion. Both lands claimed to have been evangelized by the first generation of apostles. Paul in Romans 15:24 and 28 wrote of his intention to visit Spain and is believed to have done so. British tradition also asserts that the apostle founded St. Paul's Cathedral as London's first church on the site of a shrine to Lug. British tradition also states that Joseph of Arimathea came to Britain, settling at Glastonbury. Roman soldiers may have practiced Christianity in Britain in the first century; Aulus Plautius, the general who commanded the Roman invasion of Britain in A.D. 43, was married to a Christian.

The Christian ardor of the early inhabitants of Spain and Britain was heightened by their success in holding to their faith despite persecution. Spaniards were prominent among those who defied Diocletian's attempt to root out Christianity. Santa Eulalia of Mérida spit in the face of the torturer who was slicing off her breasts. Prior to conversion, the British martyr St. Alban hid a Christian who had run for shelter into his house and was converted by his guest.

Christian zeal was further increased by the shared role of Spaniards and British in Christianizing other peoples. Spanish and British troops in the army of General Constantine fought the battle of the Mulvian Bridge at Rome in 312. Constantine's soldiers were said (at his bidding) to have borne crosses as their insignia, along with the letters IHS for *In hoc signo vinces* (in this sign you will conquer). Their victory allowed Constantine to end the persecution of Christianity by the Edict of Milan in 313. In 394, Emperor Theodosius, a Spaniard from Segovia, declared Christianity the official religion of the Roman Empire. The British missionary St. Patrick began the conversion of Ireland in the fifth century. Britain's own Christianity was briefly threatened when the island was conquered by the pagan Anglo-Saxons in the fifth and sixth centuries. However, the Anglo-Saxons were rapidly converted and showed such zeal for their faith that they in turn sent out such missionaries as St. Boniface, who won converts in Germany, and laid down his life evangelizing among the Frisians.

The commitment to Christ was further strengthened by the vigorous Christian resistance to conquests by foreign unbelievers: of Spain by Muslim Moors and of England by pagan Vikings. In 718, Pelayo established his center of resistance to Islam at the one-time cave home, Cova Donga (Cueva Dominica or the Cave of our Lady), of the Christian hermit San Millán. Alfonso II, el Casto (the Chaste) (791–842), after absorbing Galicia into his realm, emphasized the veneration and tomb of St. James. Sancho el Mayor and Alfonso VI encouraged French Cluniac monks to establish monasteries in Spain. Alfonso sent to Abbot Hugues le Grand part of the booty from his capture of Toledo, with which wealth Hugues built a new church at Cluny, with a chapel dedicated to prayers for Alfonso's soul. Santiago and other saints were believed to be fighting on the side of the Christian armies in the *Reconquista*. Patron saints arose for particular communities, people, or problems. For example, San Isidro of Madrid, a farmer born about 1080, became the patron saint of farmers and of Madrid. A cult of devotion to particular statues proliferated, and some of the statues were believed to be endowed with miraculous powers. One legend tells how the Cid's horse stumbled while passing a mosque that had once been a Visigothic church. When the mosque was converted back into a church, according to the legend, an ancient statue of Christ that had been plastered over in a niche at the start of Islamic rule was found with a candle still miraculously burning after all of the intervening centuries. When a woman tried to kiss the foot of the statue, the statue pulled its foot back, and an investigation disclosed that the statue's foot had been smeared with poison.

Christian enthusiasm for the *Reconquista* spilled over beyond the mere goal of reconquering Spain. Alfonso X, the Wise, planned a joint Castilian-Aragonese crusade to the Maghreb, and the Trinitarian and Mercedarian orders were dedicated to ransoming Christian captives from the Moors. Castilians launched a major effort to convert the Moors in the fourteenth century by founding of a trilingual college in Arabic, Hebrew, and Chaldean at the University of Valladolid for the preparation of Christian missionaries to the Muslims. A drive to convert the natives helped to spur on the Castilian conquest of the Canary Islands in the fifteenth century and motivated Columbus's crossing of the Atlantic at the end of that same century. Indeed, Columbus was convinced that he was destined to bring the message of Christ to the pagans across the Atlantic Ocean.

A similar religious spirit met the Vikings in England. When Danes conquered Northumbria in 865, English monks fled with the relics of St. Cuthbert to keep them out of pagan hands, while King Edmund of East Anglia was elected to sainthood after he was killed in 869 trying to stop the Vikings. It was said that his detached head called to his friends after the battle, from the paws of a wolf. At the end of the ninth century, Alfred the Great of Wessex took a vow to give half of his mind and body every day and every night to God. As he pushed the pagans back to the north, he required that the Vikings he defeated convert to Christianity, a demand continued by his son Edward the Elder and his grandson Aethelstan, as they completed the reconquest of England from the Vikings.

Pilgrimages to Spanish and English shrines also heightened devotion. In the eleventh and twelfth centuries, Spain and England developed the two most important Christian pilgrimage shrines after Jerusalem and Rome. After Beato de Libana's *Comentario sobre el Apocalypsis* claimed that St. James or Santiago, brother of John the beloved disciple, had evangelized in Spain, Floro de Lyon's *Martirologia* went on to claim that in the seventh century James's body had been brought on God's orders in a miraculous boat with neither sails nor oars and reburied in Spain. A body unearthed in Compostela was claimed to be that of the supernaturally transported saint, and a church was built over his tomb. In the second half of the eleventh century Alfonso VI's encouragement increased the number of pilgrims considerably, and Santo Domingo de la Calzada improved the roadway to Compostela. In 1170 the murder of Thomas Becket in Canterbury Cathedral reestablished England as an important pilgrimage destination. Contemporary Spanish art recorded Becket's martyrdom. The Castilian and English pilgrimage routes were significantly interlinked. The pilgrimage to Santiago de Compostela was popular with the English (including Chaucer's fictitious Wife of Bath and Henry II's son Henry the Young King), most of whom took the sea route, less safe and less comfortable but cheaper, on ships that sailed regularly from the south-coast ports of England. The most precious relic at Reading Abbey was one of St. James's hands, and King John donated money to build a shrine in its honor.

Christian values and themes were spread through both Castilian and English literature. In the thirteenth-century *Gesta de Fernán González,* San Pelayo, San Millán, and Santiago ride with the Christians to fight the Moors. *Pastorela* shepherd plays enacted the Christmas story to musical accompaniment. Castilian Chancellor Pedro López de Ayala in the *Rimado del palacio* (poem of the palace) in the late fourteenth century confesses his faults and condemns all types of sin). Moral lessons are presented in Juan Manuel's 1335 *El conde Lucanor o el libro de petronio.* One tale tells about a man who makes a pact with the Devil, who treacherously facilitates his hanging, and another about a person who confesses Christ superficially on his death bed but goes to hell anyway. In England in the fourteenth and fifteenth centuries, gilds enacted mystery plays; the cycles of Chester, York, and Coventry have been preserved. Parades of large carts moved through the streets on holy days, each with its own stage, scenery, and props for enacting of one scene, presented by a particular gild. The wagons followed each other in order of scenes, which were performed in succession at designated points of the route. Performed at various festivals through the year, the plays enacted the mysteries of the church, each town's yearly cycle treating all of Bible history from Creation to the Last Judgment. In addition, English songs called for adherence to truth. One fourteenth-century song admonishes, "Always try to say the best," while another announces that "truth is best."

Impact of Medieval Castilian and English Piety on the Borderlands

The intense religious involvement of both medieval Castilians and Englishmen created a basis for the ongoing piety of Mexican American Borderlanders. Christianity was first brought to the region in 1598 by Franciscan missionaries entering New Mexico. Missions were also founded in Arizona in 1700, in Texas in 1718, and in California in 1769. Parishes under secular priests were established by the end of the eighteenth century, one in New Mexico and two (San Antonio and La Bahia) in Texas. California and Arizona joined the list by the middle of the nineteenth century. In California the first diocese was established in 1840, in Texas in 1847, in New Mexico in 1853, and in Arizona in 1897. The English also brought this spirit to America, beginning with John Eliot and the Algonquian Bible, the first printed in North America, in early seventeenth-century Massachusetts. The medieval monastic approach of equating native sky and creator gods with God of the Bible, as well as pagan gods of death with Satan, was perpetuated by some of the Catholic leaders in Colonial Mexico, including Sor Juana Inés de la Cruz with her equation of Quetzalcoatl and Christ and Juan Diego with his vision in Mexico City of the Virgin of Guadalupe at the shrine of the Aztec mother goddess Tonantzinon on Tepeyac Hill. In Protestant America, John Winthrop's *Good Newes from New England* likewise saw the Christian God in the Algonquian deity Kiehtan, and Satan in

Hobbamock. John Winthrop's grand-nephew Jonathan Edwards, minister in Northampton, Massachusetts, in 1730 wrote *Surprising Conversions* as a handbook of his First Great Awakening, a major missionary movement that stirred a massive new enthusiasm for Christianity. In the early nineteenth century, Jonathan Edwards's grandson Timothy Dwight, then president of Yale University, stirred still another wave of missionary spirit that broadened into the Second Great Awakening. This movement swept over the Trans-Appalachian area, spreading Christian fervor all the way to the American Southwest. Missionary work is still active among Borderlands Catholics and Protestants alike, both Spanish- and English-speaking. Busloads of Christian youths from various parts of both countries head for the Borderlands each summer for work building churches and holding vacation Bible schools.

Baptism, in its two ongoing forms of immersion and sprinkling, is part of the medieval heritage. The original form of baptism by the Christian missionaries in Spain and Britain was by total immersion, at first in natural bodies of water and later in baptismal basins. Sprinkling first originated as a reminder of baptism performed before Sunday mass. Immersion in Europe's cold winters threatened to cause pneumonia, especially in the baptism of infants, demonstrated in the death of the first-born son of Clovis, king of the Salian Franks (481–511), and baptisteries required extra space and expense for congregations. As a result, baptismal fonts, which were small enough to require no special baptisteries to house them, appeared for pouring water over the heads of those being baptized as an alternative to immersion.

The common custom of crossing one's fingers for good luck (effective in the minds of some practitioners as a charm asking for forgiveness even when telling a lie) comes to us from the days when this was seen as one way to make the sign of the Cross, along with the more noticeable gesture of crossing oneself from head to chest to shoulders. The southern European tradition of placing a large rosary or decorative chain over the shoulders of the bride and groom at a wedding, representing their linked Christian commitment, is perpetuated in the Borderlands. Medieval Spanish saints are still honored by Borderlands Catholics; San Isidro, the Madrid farmer, is especially venerated by rural New Mexicans. Votive offering has roots in an ancient practice. It was practiced in ancient Spain and in the temples of Asclepius in the Greek settlements. Ex-voto or votive requests in the Borderlands are presented to miracle-working community saints who are honored with pilgrimages and festivals. In many Borderlands Catholic churches, statues of saints are hung with ex-voto figures made of wax, silver, or tin, representing an ailing person or a member of his or her body (like an arm or leg) or a sick animal. The supplicant lights a candle in front of the image and prays. If the prayer is heard, a painting on wooden or tin sheets illustrating the illness or accident is subsequently left beside the statue, witnessing that a miracle has occurred. Votive offering traces back almost to the beginning of civilization in Spain, as is evidenced by the clay feet found in the ruins of Numancia.

Some Borderlands customs connected with religious festivities derive from medieval Castile and England. The *pastorela,* or shepherd play, was introduced by the Franciscan friars into the Borderlands for the purpose of evangelizing and instructing, along with *Las posadas* (a reenactment of Joseph and Mary's search for lodging in Bethlehem celebrated on the eight nights before Christmas). While the *posadas* derive from sixteenth-century Mexico, the *muñeiras,* sung as part of the *posada* request for sweets or toys by the children, are Galician in origin. San José Mission in San Antonio and San Juan Bautista and the Presidio of Santa Barbara in Southern California are three locations that have regularly staged *pastorelas* at Christmas time. Luis Valdez, playwright and founder of El Teatro Campesino, incorporated into his film version of *La pastorela* the questions about the meaning of the star and the angelic voices posed by the shepherds in the medieval prototype. On the *día de los reyes* (Epiphany) on the sixth of January, the custom of placing a tiny doll representing the baby Jesus in a *rosca* (a wreath-shaped cake) so that the person who gets the piece is expected to host the next year's celebration stems from a similar medieval Spanish tradition. In the fourteenth century at the court of Navarre, a bean was placed in a cake eaten on January 6, the recipient of the piece with the bean winning a year of presents and deference as King Bean. Candlemas, the Feast of Lights held on February 2 (with antecedents in pre-Christian Europe), has been maintained by both Catholic and Episcopal traditions in the Borderlands.

Such Borderlands celebrations as Brownsville's Charro Days and Los Angeles's Rose Bowl Parade are influenced by medieval festivals, of which Carnival was the most outstanding. The Spanish word *carnaval* is traced by one etymology via the Romance term *car navale* to the Latin *carrus navalis* (naval car). A ship on wheels containing an image of Dionysius was once pulled through the streets amidst singing and revelry in a tradition that spread from Greece to Spain. The celebration of *carnaval* in medieval Spain extended from *jueves gordo* (Fat Thursday) to Shrove Tuesday and Ash Wednesday marking the start of Lent. Some of the border activities descend from practices that accompanied the Carnival festivities. Borderlanders still break *cascarones,* or confetti-filled eggs, over one another's heads.

The breaking of the piñata, both as part of the *posadas* and on birthdays, also traces back to medieval Spain, even though the custom has died out in Spain since then. The first Sunday of Lent was then called *domingo de piñata,* from the Italian word *pignatta,* a suspended candy-filled, pine-cone-shaped clay or framework container decorated with colored paper. The piñata was suspended in the center of a room during a masked ball and jerked up and down by a cord while blindfolded participants tried to hit it with a stick. Once it was hit, its candies spilled on the floor, to be gathered by the guests.

The earliest mention of the weaving of the palm leaves carried by worshippers on Palm Sunday, in emulation of Jesus' royal reception into Jerusalem, comes from the area of Alicante in southern Spain. The *penitente* brotherhoods of New Mexico have perpetuated the medieval Easter-time passion plays. Playing the parts themselves, the Brothers reenact Jesus' final hours, complete with the man playing the role of Jesus being whipped, crowned with a wreath of thorns, dragging a cross, and being tied to and raised on that cross. Passion plays are still presented annually at Tomé and Talpa, New Mexico (as in other parts of the Borderlands and the world).

The Corpus Christi festival, authorized by Pope Urban IV in 1264 and implemented by Pope Clement V in 1311, became a virtual national Spanish feast day in the late fourteenth century. Held at first on the Thursday after Trinity Sunday, it was transferred in 1969 to the Sunday after Trinity Sunday (the eighth Sunday after Easter). The Spaniards gave it special emphasis because a miracle that had occurred in Spain had persuaded the Papacy to institute this youngest of the major church festivals. At the battle for Chío Castle outside Valencia in 1238, the Moors had attacked while Berenguer de Entenza's Aragonese were attending mass. After the Moors had been defeated, the Aragonese had pulled the communion wafers out of cracks in rocks where the priest had hastily hidden them in the emergency. The wafers, which had just been consecrated when the attack began, were supposedly found to be exuding Christ's blood. The medieval importance of this feast in Spain is evoked by the name of Corpus Christi,

Texas. This settlement began as a trading post established in 1839 by Col. Henry Kinney of the newly independent Republic of Texas, and it was incorporated as a city in 1852, in the wake of the U.S.-Mexican War.

The medieval practice of making a *promesa* or promise to go on a pilgrimage in thanks for answered prayer is still common among Borderlands Catholics. Pilgrimages are made to such Borderlands shrines as that of Our Lady of San Juan, Texas. The medieval pilgrimage also left a mark on family names. In each group of pilgrims to Santiago de Compostela, there was a contest to see who would be the first to make it to the top of the hill on the road from where Santiago's church could first be spied. The winner would be awarded the title of the "king" of the pilgrimage tour group and would sometimes advertise the honor back home by assuming this title as a last name, in the days when family names were coming into fashion. From this custom such family names as Reyes and King (as in the King Ranch) have come to the Borderlands. The practice is also reflected in the children's game of "King of the Hill (or mountain)," in which boys push each other off a small hillock and then shout, "I'm the king of the hill."

The Episcopal Churches of the Borderlands have maintained various English medieval touches in their holidays. Parishioners were once shriven (absolved of sins after confession) for the start of Lent on Shrove Tuesday, and a pancake dinner is still held on this occasion. They may wash feet on Maundy (*mandatum* or command) Thursday, the anniversary of the Last Supper, when Christ commanded his disciples to love one another and washed their feet. Edward III and other English kings were known to wash the feet of poor men on this day, and noble and wealthy householders traditionally washed the feet of their servants. Ashen crosses are still marked on parishioners' foreheads on Ash Wednesday, just as in the Catholic churches. God's blessings on the crops were until recently invoked on Rogation (request) Sunday, the fifth after Easter.

Witchcraft

A widespread belief in magic and witchcraft is the reverse side of the religious intensity described above. Various influences were absorbed into medieval witchcraft from the ancient death cults of the druid priests. The Spanish Celts had immolated male goats, stallions, and men in honor of Bran (Crow), the god of death and war. The British, who had dangled the heads of vanquished enemies from their chariots, had worshipped Bran at Avebury Ring (thirty miles north of Stonehenge) and at the adjacent Silbury Hill (the largest artificial tumulus in Europe). The Romans had massacred the druids, while permitting temple building to the non-druidic Celtic gods. The original meaning of a druid was later confused by the fact that at the end of the Roman imperial period the term *druid* came to be applied to the priest of any Celtic god. With the coming of Christianity, the pagan magic cults that worshipped Bran, the god of war and death, were absorbed into Satan-worship cults.

Christian opposition to witchcraft, rooted in biblical warnings, first aimed at Satan and symbols of Satan more often than at his witch devotees. In the Anglo-Saxon poem *Beowulf,* the hero as a champion of God fights three Satanic dragons. The thirteenth-century Castilian *Poema de Fernán González* tells how Fernán survives the attack of a fire-breathing dragon sent against him by the Moors. A late example is provided by the fifteenth-century Castilian chivalric romance *Amadís de Gaula,* which was known in a fourteenth-century version as well, in which Amadís comes to the island of the Devil and slays a fire-breathing, winged dragon, the Devil escaping from its mouth and flying away with a great roar.

In the Late Middle Ages, witch trials and burnings proliferated. England's Avebury Ring was partially destroyed in the fourteenth century on orders of the local bishop in hopes of discouraging witchcraft ceremonies being held there. A twelfth-century font in a church built just outside the ring of stones displays a dragon (symbolizing Satan) biting the bishop's foot while the churchman strikes it with his crozier. The fad for black magic affected Jewish circles as well, even though Rabbis Rashi and Rashbam of France had rejected mystical interpretations in the eleventh century, and Maimonides (Rambam) had issued strong warnings to the Spanish Jews against the growth of black magic among them in the twelfth century. The Cabala (received [lore]) is a collection of books of Jewish mystical teachings influenced by Gnosticism and opposed to both the spirit and the letter of the Bible. Of the four methods for interpreting the Torah, it favors *sod* (secret) and *derash* (symbolic) over *peshat* (literal) or *remez* (contextual). Emphasis was placed on *gematria* (playing with words' number values) and *notarikon* (constructing sentences from words by considering them as acronyms). The *Sefer yezira* (book of creation), the oldest book, apparently written in Alexandria during the Roman Empire period, taught how to use the holy consonants JHWH for magical creation of life (the *golem*). The Tetragrammaton (four letters) or four consonants of God's personal name (JHVH or YHWH) was used as a powerful symbol. At the start of the fourteenth century, Moses of León wrote another of the books of cabalistic lore, the *Sefer ha-zohar* (book of splendor), emphasizing magic, reincarnation, and formulas for controlling demons. These Jewish teachings mingled with other sources of Christian witchcraft, especially after Alfonso the Wise commissioned a group of Jews to translate cabalistic writings. Tarot cards, which had appeared by the fifteenth century, were influenced by the Cabala.

Accusations of witchcraft peaked during the late fourteenth and through much of the fifteenth century. Alice Perrers, mistress of Edward III in the 1370s, was believed by many Englishmen to be using wax images, potions, and incantations to undermine the king's health. Dowager Queen Joanna of Navarre, the widow of Henry IV, was imprisoned for four years in Pevensy Castle in Sussex on the charge of using witchcraft in an attempt to cause the death of her stepson Henry V. In 1447 Eleanor Cobham, wife of Henry VI's uncle Duke Humphrey of Gloucester, was accused of trying to cause the death of the king by witchcraft and was banished to the Isle of Man. In Castile, Juan II indulged a secret interest in magic, and a witch was consulted by some of his courtiers about the fate of his minister Álvaro de Luna, who was soon executed on the charge of having practiced black magic. Juan's daughter, Isabel la Católica, was a collector of the witchcraft-influenced paintings of the Dutch artist Hieronymus Bosch. One witch coven was exposed in Vizcaya in 1500.

Witchcraft Influences on the Borderlands

The Borderlands' medieval heritage is a spotted one, as much a patchwork of positive and negative traits as the human psyche itself. Various folkloric influences from European medieval witchcraft can be noted. Fascination with the occult in medieval Castile helped create a Hispanic interest in magic, reinforced by Anglo witchcraft tradition, which still plays a major and controversial role in Borderlands society. Hispanic tradition blends the medieval heritage with Mexican Indian folk beliefs. *Brujas* (witches) use black or malevolent magic, while *curanderas* (folk healers) restrict themselves to white or benevolent magic. Spells are cast to influence a lover or to eliminate a rival, and cards are read to tell the future. *Hierberías* sell herbs in fresh, dried, or prepared form, as well as amulets, talismans, and books on the occult. The common border preoccupation with the *mal de ojo* or evil eye traces back to a treatise on the subject written by the Castilian Enrique de Villena, who died in 1434. Franciscan Alphonso de Espina's *Fortalitium fidei,* written between 1459 and 1461 and once considered authoritative, explained the nature of *duendes* (poltergeists), still an important element of Borderlands culture.

Border incidents apparently involving demons in the form of poltergeists, like the attack of brick-throwing ghosts on the house of Brownsville resident Adolph Glaevecke in 1879, have medieval antecedents. Stories of witches able to work powerful magic in matters of love, sometimes with fatal consequences, trace back to Fernando de Rojas's 1499 *La Celestina,* and beyond this play to medieval folktales on the subject. Medieval accounts of witches both alive and dead who assume the shape of black cats have found a place in Borderlands folktales. Stories about supernatural animals guarding buried treasure have precursors in medieval stories about buried hoards watched over by dragons, as found most famously in the epic of *Beowulf.* Legends of ghosts haunting buildings connected with their previous existence are as rife as their medieval antecedents, which in England were often told in connection with castles. Ghosts come riding back from the grave on horseback to protect people just as Santiago and other saints once rode along with the Christian warriors in the campaigns of the *Reconquista.* Sightings of ghost ships hark back to such medieval tales as that of the wandering Jew. Accounts of dead souls appearing from graves to bewilder the living descend from the medieval stories of the will-o'-the-wisp. Claimed appearances of headless ghosts as transmitted by Washington Irving's "Legend of Sleepy Hollow" are reminiscent of medieval ghosts at the Tower of London. Around 1310 the introduction from Spain to England of the Middle Eastern formula for staining glass a golden color (in a chemical reaction using silver salts) may underlie stories of base metals being magically converted to gold; it is said that Spain's Ramon Llull "the alchemist" worked such a conversion for King Edward of England at about that time. Some modern musical rock groups have further encouraged interest in witchcraft.

Witchcraft continues to exert a tragic grip on the Borderlands today, as the world was reminded by the group responsible for the Santa Elena Ranch massacre in 1989, which included some students at Texas Southmost College in Brownsville. Unfortunately, even concepts of witchcraft conform to the general pattern of how medieval traits have followed their separate Hispanic and Anglo paths to rejoin in the Borderlands, but the fact that this is so reinforces the importance of that phenomenon.

Contrasting Hispanic and Anglo Religious Developments in the Middle Ages

Since both Borderlands societies were influenced by medieval Castilian and English traditions, many religious customs are shared as well. For example, both Catholic and Protestant churches may celebrate the Christmas season with elaborate manger scenes. The popularity in medieval Castile of miniature manger scenes or *nacimientos* (an innovation brought by Franciscans from Italy and dating back to the eighth century) is manifest in the especially elaborate *nacimientos* in the Borderlands tradition, which show the Christ child in the stable surrounded by visitors, and often depict the entire town of Bethlehem. The Spanish tradition of going forward in church to kiss the figure of the infant Jesus in his manger has become part of the uniquely Catholic tradition in the Borderlands. Also, the common Hispanic Catholic emphasis on the dead and dying Christ, shaped by the violence of the *Reconquista* and the Inquisition, perpetuates another medieval Castilian tradition. More than is acceptable in Protestant churches, the pain Christ suffered for the sake of mankind is conveyed, as seen already in Gregorio Fernández's fifteenth-century statue of the dead Christ. The contrasting doctrines and views of papal authority and church leadership can also be traced to pre-Reformation developments in Spain and Britain. A brief explanation of these aspects of Borderlands religious life may give a clearer understanding of our multicultural society.

Differing Hispanic and Anglo Views of Church Leadership

Already in the Middle Ages, Hispanic society showed a greater degree of respect for episcopal and papal leadership than did the English. The English also did not exhibit the same enthusiasm for the monastic tradition as did their Castilian counterparts, and by the late Middle Ages, the number of monks, friars, and nuns in Castile was far greater, both relative to population and in absolute terms, than in England. Castile's aristocratic bent naturally placed more emphasis on the regular clergy as a special holy group set apart from the masses. Castile's creation of the Dominican Order of friars entrusted with the work of the Inquisition, and of the fighting monastic orders of Santiago, Calatrava, and Alcántara have no counterparts in any such orders born in England. England's more egalitarian contribution lay more in the realm of the secular clergy and their congregations of laymen, most notably with the creation of the proto-Protestant Lollard movement.

The two regions also had differing relationships with the papacy through the Middle Ages. The foundations of episcopal power in Castile were laid down in the Visigothic period. In 612 Bishop Isidro of Seville put his former student Sisebuto on the throne in the place of Recaredo's son Suintila. When Suintila sat on the throne from 621 to 631, he tried to counter Isidro's power by making the monarchy officially hereditary, but Isidro finally overthrew him and replaced him with another student, Sisenando. It was at Sisenando's coronation that Isidro first introduced the anointing of Christian kings with holy oil as the sign of God's choice as expressed through the religious leaders. Isidro then guarded against another attempt to make the monarchy hereditary by calling the Fourth Council of Toledo in 633, which made a clerically guided elective kingship official. A formula was adopted for saluting the new kings henceforth with the words "Rex eris si recte facias; si non facias, non eris" (you will be king if you do what you should; if you do not do so, you will not be). Even after Isidro died in 636, the priest-dominated system he had established continued on, as we can see in the votive crown offered to the church of Garrazar near Toledo by Recesvinto in 653, as a symbol of the submission of the Visigothic monarchs to the Spanish church. The bishops gained such power that the Visigothic nobles competed to have their sons made bishops. Ecclesiastical authority remained strong in the Christian North despite the Moorish conquest. Even in the Anglo-Saxon period in England, church leaders were subordinate to the secular rulers in politics. Dunstan, archbishop of Canterbury, played a central part in shaping English government policies in the tenth century, but his efforts mainly worked to strengthen the position of the kings, rather than to empower the ecclesiastical hierarchy.

The importance of the pope's support for the ongoing *Reconquista* further explains why papal opinion was more important in medieval Castile than in England. Castile strove to maintain friendly relations with the popes, at the cost of accepting papal claims that were rebuffed in England. In return, the church lent support for the campaigns against the Moors and provided other favors. With the help of Archbishop Bernard of Toledo, Alfonso VI persuaded the pope to elevate five new churches to episcopal sees. For his part Alfonso VI adopted the Roman Church ritual at Gregory VII's urging. Since many Castilians were opposed to abandoning their native rite, Alfonso submitted the question to a trial by battle, but the man championing the Mozarabic rite (the liturgy used by Christian Moors) defeated the champion of the Roman ritual. On the reasoning that the fight had not been fought fairly, Alfonso submitted the question again, this time to judgment by fire. While the Roman ritual book burned rapidly, the Mozarabic Ritual book remained mainly intact. At that point, Alfonso shoved the Mozarabic ritual book deep into the flames, commenting that what the king wills is law. Only in Toledo were the *Mozárabes* allowed to continue their own ritual. The Leonese-Castilian bishops freely traveled to the papal court and sent legal appeals to Rome. Later medieval kings of Castile maintained the close cooperation with the papal church established by Alfonso VI. In 1212 Pope Innocenzo III called a Crusade to push back the Almohad offensive against Castile and pressured Castile's rivals, Navarre and León, to join in the cause. In 1236 Fernando III acquired the right of *patronato real* (presentation to church office) for the kings of Castile.

Greater controls were imposed over religious life in Spain than in England. The Castilian church permeated all aspects of life, teaching intolerance for differing religious opinions. In the thirteenth century, San Fernando III was zealous in branding, hanging, burning, and boiling the unorthodox. Alfonso el Sabio's legal codes, the *Espéculo de las leyes* and the *Siete partidas,* accepted papal supremacy in spiritual affairs, reserving for the king a comparable position in temporal matters. Pope Nicholas III felt free to chide him, and the Castilian bishops sometimes bucked him. The tradition of loyalty to the papacy was reinforced in the mid-fourteenth century by Gil de Albornoz, the fighting archbishop of Toledo, whose army resubjected rebellious Rome and its hinterland to the authority of the popes.

England, usually free from threat of conquest in the High and Late Middle Ages, had no such pressing need for papal cooperation. On the contrary, tensions developed between the English kings and the archbishops and popes. William the Conqueror took steps to insure that the church would not undermine royal authority. He decreed that no churchman could sit in his royal council, the *curia regi,* as representatives of the church. Those churchmen who were members of the council were there strictly as functionaries of the monarch. William's archbishop of Canterbury, Lanfranc, held loyal to William, insulating the English crown from papal pressures. However, his son William II (William Rufus) clashed with his archbishop of Canterbury, Anselm, who took refuge across the English Channel and urged the pope to take strong action against the English king. This rift was healed only in 1107, when William Rufus's brother and successor Henry I agreed that the king of England would no longer be dispenser of the bishops' ring and staff, but that the bishops would continue to honor the king for endowing them with their lands. Nevertheless, the crown still controlled appointments. Long before the Reformation the common English resentment of the papal church was expressed under Henry II by the courtier Walter Map in his use of the word ROMA as an acronym for "radix omnium malorum avaritia" (the root of all evil is the love of money). One of Map's poems, referring to the four beasts of the Apocalypse and identifying the lion as the pope, accuses the papacy of honoring silver mark coins more than St. Mark.

Henry II, however, made a dramatic miscalculation when he appointed Thomas Becket, his royal chancellor, as archbishop of Canterbury. As chancellor, Becket had been a loyal servant of crown interests and a congenial personal friend to the king. Yet once he was archbishop, Becket became a fervent champion of church rights. In a dispute over the respective judicial prerogatives of church and crown, the church made three claims: that the court of last appeals for England was that of the pope; that "criminous clerks" or clergymen found guilty of a crime, even if defrocked, could still not be called before a secular court for that crime; and that the church had jurisdiction in all cases where a question of morality was involved. Becket imitated Anselm by fleeing to France until 1170. When he finally returned, he excommunicated the bishops who in his absence had crowned Henry II's eldest son, the short-lived Henry, as co-ruler, throwing doubt on the legitimacy of the coronation. Henry flew into a royal rage (a term he might well have inspired) and cried out asking who would rid him of Becket. Four of Henry's knights who were present made their way to Canterbury and there murdered Becket inside the cathedral. The shock spread as far as Spain, where a medieval wall painting depicting the murder of Becket is still to be seen in Cataluña. Henry was publicly whipped by the clergy, received a vial of Becket's blood to wear around his neck as a momento of his sin, and he had to abandon his legal claims.

Relations between king and archbishop deteriorated still more under Henry II's youngest son, John. In 1205, after the cathedral clergy of Canterbury dared to elect their own candidate as archbishop, John obliged the cathedral chapter to switch their vote to his own choice instead. Faced with two appointees, Pope Innocenzo III made his own selection, an English cleric named Stephen Langton. When John refused to accept Langton, Innocenzo placed England under an interdict, whereby all the churches of England were closed. Nobody could be properly married, or buried on holy ground, and baptism and extreme unction were the only sacraments allowed. John retaliated by seizing all church property. Innocence then excommunicated John, obliging the faithful to shun contact with the king. In 1213 with the king of France preparing to invade England as a champion of the pope, John saved his throne by capitulating, making England a papal fief. For the next century the pope was the theoretical overlord of England, sending legates to guide the kings. The pope's right to appoint all English ecclesiastical leaders in disputed elections was acknowledged, and John agreed to pay a large, new rent to the pope.

In Edward I's vigorous reign (1272–1307), Edward began to reassume the powers lost to the papacy by his predecessors. Edward's skill in rallying popular support by recourse to Parliament and by running an efficient administrative and legal machine undermined support for the popes in England. When Pope Boniface VIII refused to allow the English clergy to pay royal taxes without papal permission, Edward responded in 1296 by outlawing the clergy. This drastic move brought Boniface to concede that the clergy could pay royal taxes in an emergency. English society grew even more hostile to the papacy during the Hundred Years War between England and France, due to the relocation of the papacy at Avignon, located in the French sphere of influence, and to papal support to the French side. An English poem claimed that while the Pope had become French, Jesus himself had become and Englishman. Edward III's Parliaments struck down the prerogatives gained by the papacy from Henry II. The Statute of Provisors in 1351 stipulated that the pope could henceforth appoint foreign clergymen to English church posts only with the approval of the English king. Two years later, the Statute of Praemunire stated that

English churchmen were not permitted to appeal legal cases to the pope. While both pieces of legislation remained theoretical for the time being, a strong opposition to the papal church emerged among the English. In contrast, Castile, as an ally of France, continued to support the Avignon popes, paying large amounts into the papal treasury. The Avignon popes worked to counteract English influence in Castile. Pope Urban V did not hide his partisanship, financing Enrique de Trastamara's attack on King Pedro in 1366, for which he received strong support from Enrique when he grabbed the throne. The extent of deterioration of respect for episcopal authority in England by the end of the Middle Ages can be seen in the fact that two bishops were murdered by the mobs stirred up by Jack Cade's Rebellion in 1450.

Differing Hispanic and Anglo Doctrinal Leanings

Protestantism represents the culmination of certain (partly English) medieval religious currents. The distinct doctrinal leanings of medieval Spanish and English societies can be detected in the heresies to which each was prone. Spain's heretical inclination ran to Arianism and Gnosticism, both rooted in a disinclination to accept Jesus as both man and God. The teaching that God stooped to become man seemed to clash with Spanish pride and respect for authority. In contrast, the favorite British doctrines of Pelagianism and Lollardism proclaimed great independence for individuals, the former denying original sin and both emphasizing a person's ability to choose the correct religious path. This tendency may have had its roots in a tribal spirit venerated in Britain from ancient times and in the prospering medieval English commoners' disinclination to accept dictation from above.

The first heresy manifested in Spain in early Christian times was Arianism, which held that Christ was a mere man, being God's son only in the same sense applying to Adam, that is, being made and not begotten. Bishop Hosius of Córdoba became a key figure in condemning this view at Constantine's Council of Nicaea in A.D. 325. The resulting Nicene Creed declared that Jesus was begotten, not made. Despite his role at Nicaea, Hosius subsequently became an Arian himself and suffered from the persecution he himself had initiated. Spain's Arian leanings were reinforced when the Arian Visigoths conquered Spain in the fifth and sixth century.

In 576 King Leovigildo's heir Hermenegildo converted to Catholicism and started a revolt. In a brief campaign Leovigildo defeated Hermenegildo, who was put to death. These events drove the Spanish Catholics to such a fever pitch of agitation that in 586 Leovigildo on his death bed convinced his surviving son and heir, Recaredo, to make peace with the Catholics. As a result, Recaredo in 589 converted with all of his Visigoths to Catholicism.

The Gnostics claimed that Jesus was a spirit but not God and not man, and that he had taught a secret magic knowledge to allow people to escape the evil material world created by the petty God of the Bible. The *Gospel of Thomas,* one of the Gnostic Gospels, declares that Jesus did not really die on the Cross. In the second half of the fourth century, a Galician named Priscillian led a Gnostic movement that spread rapidly through Spain and Southern Gaul. Priscillian's supporters were sufficiently strong to elect him Christian Bishop of Ávila. In 383 Maximus, another Galician, who had been sent as a Roman general to Britain, seized control of Gaul, brought Priscillian to trial in Trier, had him decapitated, and drove the sect underground. However, the First Council of Braga in 561 still viewed Priscillianism as a serious threat to the church.

Both Arianism and Gnosticism reasserted themselves in Spain later in the Middle Ages. Arian influence continued to be reflected in the adoptionist views expressed in Spain's Mozarabic or Visigothic ritual, claiming that Jesus was only God's adopted son. In late medieval Castile, the belief that Jesus was less than God arose among some *conversos* (Christians of Jewish descent). This question, involving the doctrines of the Trinity and of Jesus' divinity, were naturally brought from their Jewish background along with problems with salvation and predestination. Isabel la Católica's Spanish Inquisition, designed in part for political and economic reasons, attacked this heresy with the use of torture of the auto de fé. The Gnostic challenge reemerged in the early thirteenth century in the form of the Albigensian heresy spilling over into Spain from Southern France. The Albigensians rejected the authority of both Bible and papal church and condemned the physical world as evil. Santo Domingo de Guzmán (St. Dominic) of Palencia became the most effective of the preachers inveighing against the Albigensian heresy. He inspired a band of followers, whom he organized as the Dominican Friars, for the mission of living in the secular world in order to minister to it through their preaching. Gnostic influences reappeared between 1425 and 1445 in the vicinity of the town of Durango in Vizcaya under a heretical Franciscan friar named Alfonso de Mella, until the group was broken up.

Some suspect that the Knights Templars were influenced by Gnostic thought. A seal of the Knights Templar preserved in the National Archives in Paris bears the words *Secretum Templi* (Secret of the Temple), surrounded by a person with snake heads for feet and a rooster head, a Gnostic symbol known as the Abraxas. After the Knights Templar were condemned by the church in 1312 on charges of heresy and idolatry, England outlawed the order. In contrast the Council of Salamanca in 1310 found the Knights Templar innocent of the charges, and the order was never condemned in Spain.

The Gnostic idea that the physical world is evil and must be mortified surfaced again in the late Middle Ages in the Spanish *penitente* movement. Penitential *cofradías* (exclusively male confraternities or brotherhoods) appeared concurrently under ecclesiastical direction in various Spanish towns and cities, beginning in fifteenth-century Seville. Their purpose was mainly to guide the members in penance. They also organized religious festivals, helped the poor, sick, and pilgrims, and sometimes played a role in local politics. Members marched in their *cofradía* as brotherhoods, each member carrying a cross and a candle (the length of which indicated the extent of the man's sins) through the streets of Seville during Holy Week, doing penance and carrying his organization's patron image of the Virgin Mary. The *penitentes* picked up the practice of self-flagellation from groups of flagellants who spread out from Italy after the plague of 1259. Pope Clemente VI in 1349 condemned flagellant doctrine as verging on the Gnostic-linked Manichean heresy, which taught that everything physical is evil. As a result the flagellants of Seville introduced the custom of wearing pointed hoods to cover the face, with holes for the eyes, to prevent recognition of the participants by the clergy.

Their love of individual liberty inclined the peoples of Britain to two controversial Christian doctrines of a very different sort. At the end of the fourth century, the British priest Pelagius (meaning, in Greek, the Islander) asserted his belief in the free will of each person to work out his or her own fate, unhindered by any burden of original sin. For him, children were in a state of innocence until they were corrupted by the evil in the world. He argued that people can remain good and work their way to heaven by their own merits by living moral lives. He also challenged the papal claim of apostolic succession from Peter. St. Augustine of Hippo attacked Pelagianism, and the Church Council of Carthage together with Pope Zosimus condemned Pelagian teachings in 418. Nonetheless, the vortigern or high king of Britain and many of his subjects supported Pelagius. When in 425 Emperor Honorius cracked down on all Pelagian bishops of France, Britain was outside his control, but Pope Celestino I sent St. Germain, the bishop of Auxerre, to join a military effort under Ambrosius Aurelianus that defeated the forces of Pelagianism. The Anglo-Saxons showed the same anti-papal and individualistic leanings as the Britons they had conquered. For a time it was uncertain whether the Anglo-Saxons would accept papal authority. In 663 Oswy, King of Northumbria and *bretwald,* called the Council of Whitby to decide the issue. Oswy chose papal Christianity, remarking that St. Peter, in his view the first pope, kept the keys to Heaven, and he wanted to be sure to be admitted.

The ongoing push for individual freedom underlay a greater freedom of thought in England in the High and Late Middle Ages, which encouraged scholarship, science, and the arts and crafts. In the twelfth century, Adelard of Bath translated Euclid, and Henry I's minstrel Rahere gave an impetus to medical research and education with the founding of St. Bartholomew's Hospital in 1123. The thirteenth-century Oxford Franciscan professor Roger Bacon challenged the rigid scholastic approach and played his part in the increasing move to trial-and-error inductive experiments, which were giving England a lead in technical advances. Bacon also investigated gunpowder, the Chinese invention that gave the Moors the ability to fire cannon on besieging Castilian Christians at Algeciras in 1342. In the early fourteenth century William of Ockham, a Franciscan teaching at Oxford, affirmed man's ability to use reason in approaching God, arguing that people are able to grasp the essentials in religion. His view that human "semi-merit" was rewarded with God's grace enjoyed great popularity. Spanish (and Italian) theologians were prominent in criticizing this quasi-Pelagian view of Ockham, stressing that without divine assistance people could only sin. Ockham offered each of his students a symbolic razor, to cut away obstructing fuzz from their thought processes. They were to use it by posing the simple question of whether any particular line of thought or action advanced the thinker directly toward his goal. If not, it should be eliminated as an undesirable detour. Ockham's razor laid the foundations for the Protestant movement. Church statuary, clerical vestments and surplices, the priesthood, and eventually even the pope himself would be cut away as nonessential in the relationship between the Christian and his God (since Paul in I Timothy 2:5 wrote that Jesus is the only mediator between man and God). Ockham was called to trial for his views before the pope at Avignon and was thrown into the papal prison. Helped to escape, he found refuge in Germany with the Kaiser, who was having his own conflict with the papacy. The dissemination of Ockham's writings throughout England and Germany laid the foundation for Lollardism and the future Reformation. Laymen now began to assert their own opinions in religion, writing such vernacular guides to piety as *Le Livre des seyntz medicines* in 1354 by Henry of Grosmont, first duke of Lancaster, and *The Two Ways* in 1399 by Sir John Clanvowe.

In the English jingoism stirred by the Hundred Years War between England and France, anti-papal sentiment was championed by the people and protected by the crown as a way to combat papal support for France. Oxford professor John Wycliffe denied that a priest hearing confessions could know other people's spiritual states (arguing for the elimination of confession to a priest in favor of going directly to God). He questioned the propriety of religious statuary, pilgrimages, and church property. He argued that the "church" was nothing more than the saved, the clergy deserving respect only if they exhibited moral behavior.

Wycliffe also rejected the concept of transubstantiation (which holds that the essence of the bread and wine change to Christ's flesh and blood, even though the perceptible "accidents" do not) in favor of consubstantiation, which held that Christ's blood and body were in the Communion wine and wafer only in a mystical form. He also called for the congregation to drink the wine of the mass as well as to eat the wafer, thereby denying to the priests the exclusive right to the elements of the mass. Medieval English tradition had prefigured this development in the attention it gave to the legend of the Grail, which in the British tradition refers to the cup from which Jesus and the disciples drank at the Last Supper. The fourth century *Vindicta salvatoris* had claimed that Joseph founded a church in the far north after A.D. 70, and in the High Middle Ages it was claimed that he had brought the cup with him and buried it at Glastonbury. In 1249 the monks of Glastonbury declared that the Grail had been found at a nearby holy spring with red water stained by iron in the soil. The spot is still marked by a medieval plate. The story of the rediscovery of the Grail was added by the monks of Glastonbury to a revised version of William of Malmesbury's 1130 history, *De antiquitate glastoniesis ecclesiae.* The lost

Latin prose version of French romance *Lancelot du lac* (which itself claims to be a French translation of a Latin original by Walter Map, archdeacon of Oxford) and Sir Thomas Malory's *Morte d'Arthur* in the fifteenth century popularized the Holy Grail in literature. This emphasis on the importance of the mystical cup of the Last Supper doubtless played a role at the subconscious level in the English Lollard insistence that the entire congregation share in drinking the wine as the shed blood of Christ during the Communion service, which would deliver supernatural powers to the participant. This became a part of the fabric of Borderlands Anglo-Protestant heritage.

A special concern for Bible study among the English can be seen already at the end of the twelfth century; the division of the Old and New Testaments into the traditional chapters was the work of Stephen Langton of Lincolnshire, who went on to become the archbishop of Canterbury under King John. Wycliffe accepted the Bible as the sole basis of doctrinal authority, and tried to make it accessible to the average Englishman by producing the first English translation of the Bible. In 1382 Wycliffe was forbidden to continue teaching. However, he continued to exert an influence through his pamphlets and disciples, who were called Lollards (from the Middle Dutch word *lollen* meaning to mumble, perhaps because they mumbled their prayers to hide their controversial content). By the year 1400 translations of various Old Testament books had also been made (from Hebrew) into Castilian. Initially made by Spanish Jews for Jewish readers, such vernacular versions had been accepted in Castile. When the Spanish Inquisition tried to suppress Bibles in Castilian in 1498, the outcry from the Christian community was so great that the Inquisition dropped its demand. However, the issue was far less sensitive in Castile, because its Bible readers were not inclined to use the vernacular Bible to challenge authority.

In England John of Gaunt protected Wycliffe, whose call for the disendowment of the church could have brought Gaunt new revenue. So instead of being rooted out, Lollard anti-clericalism penetrated English thought. Chaucer came down hard on the clergy in *The Canterbury Tales*. His monk Piers has a passion mainly for hunting and eating, neither concordant with his Christian mission. Several of Chaucer's characters are satirized clerics and minor church officials, presenting themselves as, at the least, worldly show-offs and, at the worst, deceitful and scurrilous social parasites. John Gower in his *Vox Clamantis* likewise attacks the vices of the clergy, citing the gluttony of the prelates, the priests' neglect of their parishioners, and the lust of the mendicant friars.

The Lollard movement ran afoul of the English government at the end of the fourteenth century. A Lollard priest named John Ball became the ideological head of the Peasant's Revolt of 1381, posing the egalitarian question, "When Adam delved, and Eve span, who was then the gentleman?" Archbishop Sudbury was murdered in the uprising, but at its conclusion John Ball was beheaded, his head displayed on London Bridge. In 1395 a petition calling for an end to church wealth, idolatry, priestly celibacy, and confession was presented to Parliament and nailed to the doors of St. Paul's Cathedral. In 1401 Parliament's statute *De heretico comburendo* (on burning a heretic) empowered the English bishops to imprison and fine heretics and to burn those who relapsed. After one group plotted to murder the Lancastrian royal family by disguising themselves as actors in a twelfth-night play in 1414, forty-five Lollards were executed. In Henry VI's reign Bishop Reginald Pecock of Chichester, despite his writing an English-language refutation of the Lollard faith in Scripture, was imprisoned for agreeing that the church fathers are not always the best guides to doctrinal truths. The Lollard call for a vernacular service directly linking worshipper and God was thus making rapid inroads in English thought.

The Impact of Differing Views of Church Leadership and Doctrinal Leanings on the Borderlands

There has traditionally been a fairly close correlation of Catholicism with Hispanic parishioners, of Protestantism with Anglo congregations in the Borderlands, despite the preponderance of such non-Hispanic groups as the French and the Irish in the Catholic clergy. This dichotomy goes back to the 1820s, during Mexican control of the area, when Anglo settlers held to a Protestant tradition despite the required oaths that they be Catholics. The Castilian religious heritage has given the Borderlands a greater emphasis on hierarchy, less inhibitions regarding the enjoyment of pleasures, and a greater inclination to accept claims of supernatural phenomena. Many border nature sites are marked by Hispanic shrines in honor of the miraculous properties attributed to them.

The concern of the medieval friars to build churches, teach schools, operate hospitals, settle legal disputes, farm, ranch, and produce craft goods, especially in the depopulated zones created by the advance of the Christian frontier, prepared the Franciscans for their similar work in civilizing the region from Texas through California. Those early concerns are perpetuated in the Catholic Church's commitment to help poor and desperate immigrants coming into the Borderlands from the south. The Catholic Church in the Borderlands has continued the Hispanic emphasis on compassion, providing welfare services to the needy. The church set up an office in El Paso in 1922 to give aid to Mexican immigrants pouring into the region to escape the economic dislocation caused by the Mexican Revolution. The Bishop's Committee for the Spanish-Speaking, formed in 1945, provided funds in Los Angeles, Santa Fe, Denver, and San Antonio for such social welfare programs as clinics, settlement houses, community centers, help for migrant workers, and child care. The church called for better wages for farm workers and asked that water, lighting, and sewers be provided for poor neighborhoods. In 1968 Cesar Chavez called on Mexican Americans to appeal to the power of the church to help the poor and to promote justice, social change, and brotherly love. When an organization called Católicos Por La Raza demanded that the church become more responsive to social and economic needs of the Hispanic poor, some priests joined the efforts of the United Farm Workers. In the 1970s the Bishops' Committee on Farm Labor supported the lettuce and grape boycotts of Chavez's United Farm Workers. In the same decade, the church's Campaign for Human Development gave support to programs designed to improve the economic, political, legal, and educational standing of Mexican Americans. When war and political repression forced large numbers of Nicaraguans, Salvadorans, and Guatemalans to flee to the Borderlands in the 1980s, a grass-roots Catholic action to help the desperate illegal immigrants resulted. Bishop John Fitzpatrick of Brownsville backed the Casa Oscar Romero, a shelter caring for as many as five hundred refugees at a time; Bishop Raymundo Peña of El Paso provided a similar shelter, called Annunciation House, in that city; and Father Luis Olivares of Los Angeles let the illegals sleep in church pews at night. These actions did not go without some of the leaders being tried for lending support to illegal immigrants.

Reverence for Mary still marks the Hispanic heritage of the Borderlands. Images of Mary the Virgin Queen and of the crucified Jesus are in great evidence. An outline of the Virgin Mary was seen by many in a pattern formed by the bark of a tree on St. Francis Street in Brownsville in the early 1990s. The phenomenon attracted so many people, some bringing flowers, that for a time police had to be assigned to the area to manage traffic. Countless other local miraculous appearances of the Virgin have appeared on Borderlands objects, from windows to cars to tortillas. The idea that the Virgin Mary joined in the battles of the *Reconquista* alongside her Christian champions is incorporated into the *danzas de los Moros y Cristianos,* dances representing the battles of the *Reconquista,* transplanted to Mexico and still occasionally presented in front of some churches in the Borderlands, most notably on Guadalupe Day.

Depictions of the Virgin of Guadalupe are ubiquitous along the border. She was the most famous medieval Castilian manifestation of Mary. Alfonso XI announced that she had fought with the Christians at the battle of the Rio Salado in 1340, bringing them victory. Her statue had been rediscovered in 1326 by a cowherd named Gil Cordero, buried in an iron chest found sticking out of the ground. It was proclaimed the statue of Mary, said to have been fashioned by St. Luke at Ephesus, lent to Pope Gregory the Great in A.D. 600 to end a plague in Rome, and then purportedly passed on to Bishop Leandro of Seville to provide the same service in Spain. The Spaniards claimed that it had been buried in the early eighth century out of fear that the Muslims might destroy it. Alfonso XI built a grand basilica for the statue at Guadalupe in Extremadura, and she became the main patron saint of Spain.

The fact that Mary's statue at Guadalupe is dark complexioned brought American natives to identify with her in the sixteenth century. Although the image of the Virgin of Guadalupe that appeared on Juan Diego's *tilma* (cloak) at Tepeyac in the early sixteenth century is not that of the statue of the Virgin at the Franciscan Monastery of Guadalupe in Spain, there is an indisputable connection between the two. The Spanish monastery is Franciscan, as was Bishop Zumárraga, who reportedly gave his approval to Juan Diego's story about his vision of the Virgin, which included roses blooming out of season and the miraculous appearance of the painting of the Virgin on his *tilma.* The Tepeyac painting is close in mood, though still not in detail, to another statue of the Virgin of the Spanish monastery of Guadalupe believed to have been carved in 1499 and now known as the "Guadalupe de México." While this Spanish statue has Mary holding the baby Jesus, and looking to the left rather than to the right, it shares with the Mexican painting the wavy rays of light around the figure and the crescent moon over a cherub's head at the base. One effect of this greater reverence shown to Mary may be the idea, common among border Hispanics, that women are morally and spiritually superior to men.

The medieval Castilian tradition of religious confraternities or *cofradías* reappeared in the *penitente* confraternities of New Mexico. The New Mexican brothers likewise concern themselves with welfare, burials, and the maintenance of morality, law, and order. The heretical Flagellants of the Late Middle Ages may have influenced the self-flagellation practiced by these New Mexican *penitentes*. Juan de Oñate, founder and first governor of New Mexico in 1598, whipped himself, and the New Mexican *penitentes* launched the Good Friday custom of holding a simulated crucifixion, with a man wearing a loincloth taking the role of Jesus. In the 1850s Bishop Lamy of Santa Fe withdrew church recognition from the *penitentes*, but they won the status of benevolent societies from the territorial legislature as they were needed in many rural areas neglected by the official church. In 1960 New Mexico had as many as three thousand *penitentes*, grouped into 135 *moradas* or units. The Hispanic emphasis on penance was reinforced throughout the Borderlands Catholic community in the late 1950s by the *cursillo* (course) movement. Launched in Spain in 1947 as a one-time weekend course in spiritual renewal, the *cursillo* taught the need for confession, penance, sacrifice, and social sensitivity.

Early Protestants in the Borderlands, for their part, were known especially for their dedication to Bible study and a direct, simple relationship of each worshiper with God. Many of the early Anglo settlers of the Borderlands harbored an Ockham-based prejudice against music and especially dancing as unnecessary, sensual, and therefore diabolical. The use of the term *Bohemian* for an unconventional lifestyle dates back to English moral disapproval of the frivolous lifestyle of the Czech retinue of Richard II's first queen, Anne of Bohemia.

As in the secular aspects of the Hispanic-Anglo cultural interchange, the Hispanic Catholic and Anglo Protestant approaches to Christianity have intermingled. An ecumenical tone was set in New Mexico by its first American Governor, Gen. Stephen Kearny, who (although himself an Episcopalian) made it his practice in 1846 to attend mass along with his staff at Santa Fe's San Francisco Catholic Church. The entry of Anglo influences into the Borderlands Catholic churches was smoothed by the fact that the clergy in the late nineteenth century and early twentieth century was rarely Spanish. While first French and later Irish clergy prevailed, their tendency to be rapidly assimilated into the Anglo-American population brought an Anglicization of Borderlands Catholicism. Thaddeus Amat, bishop of Monterey, California, attacked unorthodox Hispanic religious traditions in a pastoral letter of 1853, an attitude in which he was joined by his contemporary, Bishop Lamy of Santa Fe, New Mexico. However, when Protestant proselytizing increased along with the Anglicization, the Catholic leadership began to call for an emphasis on teaching knowledge of Christianity as a way to combat conversion to Protestantism. The Protestant call for a personal relationship with God inspired the Charismatic movement, which swept through Borderlands Catholicism in the 1970s. Marilyn Kramer, a minister in the Assembly of God, converted to Catholicism and founded an organization called Charisma in Missions. Sixty thousand Catholics, mainly Hispanics, joined in the Archdiocese of Los Angeles alone. The church encouraged participation as a means of holding the loyalty of Catholics who might otherwise have been tempted to become Protestants.

Hispanic influences for their part reshaped Borderlands Protestantism. Although officially against Mexican law, Protestant worship by Anglo-American immigrants was tolerated by the Mexican authorities in the first half of the nineteenth century. While Borderlands Protestants were initially entirely Anglos, they soon began to win a few Hispanic converts, mostly from the lower class. Presbyterian Sumner Bacon and Methodist David Ayres led the way in the 1830s by supplying Bibles in Spanish to eager Mexican Texans. Methodist Alejo Hernandez continued the missionary work to Texas Hispanics, working out of Corpus Christi in the 1870s. In the second half of the nineteenth century, quite a few New Mexican *Penitentes* became Presbyterian in reaction to the Catholic Church's opposition to their movement. Although many Mexican Americans perceived their Catholicism as a dominant factor in maintaining their Hispanic identity, by the 1980s about 60,000 Hispanics were switching from the Catholic to Protestant churches, so that by 1990 20 percent of the twenty million Hispanics in the United States were Protestant. Under the impact of Hispanic views, a greater emphasis on compassion for the needy was evidenced. In the 1960s the movement to re-win lost land grants in northern New Mexico was led by the Pentecostal minister Reies Lopez Tijerina, while Presbyterian Rodolfo "Corky" Gonzales spearheaded a call for help to the poor urban Hispanics in Denver. Protestant ministers along the Rio Grande joined the National Council of Churches in support of Cesar Chavez's United Farm Workers. Protestant clergy and church members and

Jewish congregations joined with Catholics in providing shelter and food for the desperate illegal immigrants fleeing from Central America in the 1980s. Hispanics found an outlet in Pentecostal churches for their inclinations toward public religious fervor (often shown as manifestations of the presence of the Holy Spirit), toward communal fellowship (given an outlet in nightly worship with singing and shared testimony), and toward a nondemocratic choice of leaders (in this case by manifestation of the Holy Spirit).

For much of the twentieth century, Borderlands social structures encouraged Hispanics and Anglos to worship in separate congregations. This approach proved untenable after World War II, when various court decisions prohibited segregation. In 1970 the first Mexican American bishop was appointed, when Patricio Flores became the bishop of San Antonio. However, when Hispanics were first merged into Anglo congregations, they were expected to Anglicize. By the end of the century, an opposite trend was growing, with many Catholic and Protestant bilingual Spanish-English congregations taking shape in the Borderlands. The Southern Baptists are believed to have the largest Hispanic membership of the traditional Protestant denominations. The Pentecostal church has been especially successful in winning Hispanic members. Hispanic members are taking leadership positions alongside their Anglo brothers and sisters, services and Sunday schools are being held in both Spanish and English, sermons are in some cases being preached in one language with interpreters giving versions in the other to worshipers wearing earphones. Many congregations have sermons, singing, and social intercourse alternating constantly between Spanish and English. Various Borderlands *converso* families have been rediscovering their Jewish roots, feeding the Messianic Jewish movement of the 1990s. The interchange of all of these influences has given the Borderlands an especially active and rich religious life.

Concluding Remark

Borderlands religion recalls the medieval past in its doctrinal leanings, holidays, church organization, folk literature, and cultural details. Ultimately, a society's spiritual life is the most important aspect of all, determining whether a region will give a boost of hope to its residents or leave them mired in confusion or despair. One of the most positive aspects of Borderlands life is its mood of optimism and friendliness, surprisingly productive of smiles in spite of dire but never defeatist poverty. This hope for tomorrow is rooted in a strong faith. Religion has definitely added a further dimension to the Borderlands cultural mix, contributing to the distinctions between the cultural creativity of Hispanic and Anglo societies, the topic to be examined in the following chapter.

FIVE

Creative Influences

An important part of a society's identity lies in its creative life, and the collective fancies cultivated by Hispanic and Anglo Borderlands traditions form some of the most telling bonds and distinctions between them. The Spanish- and English-speaking worlds experienced much of the same cultural movements down to the start of the sixteenth century but elaborated them in different ways. Many of the Borderlands characteristics that strike Yankees as distinctive come from the Moors and other Semitic influences, while Mexicans remark on aspects of the region deriving from northern European influences.

The high points of Castilian and English creativity down to 1500 were attained in five distinct periods, each of which ushered in a new and distinct social era. These periods can be roughly defined as antiquity (with its height in the second millennium B.C.), the Dark Ages (centering on the seventh and eighth centuries), the High Middle Ages (particularly the late eleventh and twelfth centuries), the Late Middle Ages (with its most productive period in the fourteenth century), and, as the end stage of the Late Middle Ages, the age of the New Style monarchy with the spread of Renaissance influences from Italy (at the end of the fifteenth century). The original culture was formed in antiquity in the first excitement over self-expression. The Germanic conquests called for a new definition of cultural identity in the seventh and eighth centuries. The late eleventh and twelfth centuries saw the rise of a feudal society calling for its own self-expression. The crisis of the fourteenth century created a troubled era in need of explaining itself. The impact of the New Style monarchy at the end of the fifteenth century again propelled rethinking of the social identity. Castilian and English expressions of creativity down to the start of the sixteenth century would have been much more alike had it not been for the impact of Moorish culture on Castile. The similarities between Spanish and English traditions will be considered first within each category of creativity, followed by the Moorish (and general Semitic) imprint, which distinguished the Hispanic development. The chapter will conclude with a brief survey of each creative category's medieval elaboration and, then, with an examination of how Borderlands culture has been influenced by each category of Medieval creativity.

Literature

The literary activity of ancient Spain and Britain was expressed in oral forms that have survived as folktales and nursery rhymes, as well as through references in Latin-language literary works by authors of Iberian origin. The Dark Age literature of the seventh century was inspired by the pious enthusiasm of the newly converted Germanic conquerors, Visigoths from heretical to nonheretical Christianity and the Anglo-Saxons from paganism to Christianity. Historical writings documented this Christian triumph. San Isidro of Seville wrote a history of the Goths who had conquered Spain, and "the Venerable" Bede penned a history of the Anglo-Saxon people and church. Knowledge was preserved in the face of barbarian rule; for instance, Isidro wrote the *Etymologies,* which was used as a source of encyclopedic information. Moralizing literature included *Beowulf* and the poems of Caedmon and Cynewulf. Style was determined not only by the nature of the oral predecessors of many works but also by monastic writers and bards.

In the twelfth century, creative writing was stirred by the rise of Europe, with its growing towns, its crusades against the infidels, and its glittering courts. Crusading leaders inspired depictions of such fighting heroes as Rodrigo Díaz de Vivar in the anonymous *Poema del Cid* and King Arthur in Geoffrey of Monmouth's *Historia regum Britaniae*. Queen Eleanor of Aquitaine in England and her daughter Leonor in Castile acted as patronesses of courtly literature. In England works questioning inherited values ranged from Walter Map's impious goliardic student drinking songs and flippant tales to Marie de France's oppressed heroines, while in Castile the *mester de clerecía* verse directed praise to the mother of Jesus. Style was now shaped by the study of Latin in the universities and by aristocratic troubadours and trouvères in the castles.

The social and economic crisis of the fourteenth century found expression in the production of literature lamenting human shortcomings, encouraging revolt, or championing a particular social class. *Sir Gawain* tells of a hero who fails to show perfect courage, and *Pearl* describes a man's bereavement for his departed child. Ballads celebrated rebels against authority. A jaundiced view of commoners is drawn in Juan Manuel's *El conde Lucanor* and Geoffrey Chaucer's *The Canterbury Tales,* while a disrespectful presentation of nobles is presented by the English Cycle Plays. A continued defiance of traditional values is found in Juan Ruiz's *Libro de buen amor*. Educated literati, traveling minstrels, and (in England) town guildsmen now took the lead in shaping the literary style.

In the fifteenth century, Castilian literature was stimulated by the New Style monarchy and by humanist Renaissance influences coming out of Italy. Juan del Encina and Fernando de Rojas launched secular Castilian theater in the reign of Isabel la Católica. After his education at the University of Salamanca, Encina became master of ceremonies for the duke of Alba, for whom he wrote pastoral plays called *representaciones*. Isabel la Católica's son Juan watched these productions. The plays of Encina and Rojas expressed the somber mood accompanying the introduction of the Spanish Inquisition as an instrument of the emerging power of the monarchy. Italian Renaissance influences helped to shape the style. Christian humanist figures in the reign of Henry VII in England included scholar and theologian John Colet, writer and statesman Thomas More, and their friend and mentor Desiderius Erasmus, a Dutchman who studied and taught at both Oxford and Cambridge and was probably the most widely known humanist of Renaissance Europe. A rapid spread of books from such printing centers as William Caxton's Westminster Press, established in 1476, disseminated their ideas.

Impact on Borderlands Literature

Medieval literary activity is echoed in the creative writing of the Mexican-American Borderlands, rich in both novels and plays, with contributions from both of its linguistic groups. Medieval Castilian material was passed down in Mexican American folklore. The first Spanish-language play in the Borderlands was performed in April 1598 in the region later to be known as El Paso, Texas. Written by Marcos Farfán de los Godos, a captain accompanying Juan de Oñate's expedition, the play enacted the Franciscan's missionary work among the local Indians. A second play, this time a comedy, was performed in San Juan, New Mexico, in September of the same year, followed by various other plays penned in Colonial times. The more recent advent of the Anglos to the Borderlands, and their continuing drift into the region, is reflected in the backgrounds of the main Anglo writers of the region, who are often only associated with the region briefly or marginally. Both the Anglo and Hispanic Borderlands authors have tended to emphasize the Hispanic influence, although the Anglo view of that heritage has many times been colored by a Puritan work ethic and the long-standing negative stereotyping of Hispanics.

In 1859 the publishing house of Beadle & Adams marketed the first dime novel, a popular nationalistic literature that flooded America for three decades. Many of these adventure stories focus on rugged pioneer spirit and on U.S.-Mexican border conflicts. The editor of the dime novels series was Orville J. Victor, who proclaimed that his publications were accurate and consistent in their portrayals of pioneer people and incidents. Among the writers were former mountain men and those with military experience who had served in the border area, including "Buffalo Bill" Cody, Joseph Badger, Major Sam Hall, known as "Buckskin Sam," J. B. Omodkundroo, known as "Texas Jack," and Captain Jack Crawford, known as the "poet scout." Although they knew the West, most were poor writers who wrote stock melodramatic Victorian plots that bore little resemblance to the actual frontier experience, despite the announced standards of the editor. Texas romances, which also appeared in the second half of the nineteenth century, were better written, and their accounts of the early Texas cattle ranchers were more realistic. Samuel E. Chamberlain, George Wilkins Kendall, James Ohio Pattie, and John W. Audubon were among the many who published their personal recollections. Two types of novels were written: the western included stories about law and order, cattle empires, outlaws, ranches, cavalry against Indians, and revenge; in conquest fiction one ethnic group was displaced, destroyed, or defeated by another.

In some ways Borderlands fiction writers are reminiscent of certain medieval antecedents, especially in their exploration of similar themes. Pairing medieval creative treatment with its modern Borderlands counterpart points again to the richness of the Borderlands' interlaced heritage. In the Hispanic tradition, the medieval *Poema del Cid* and the modern ballad *Corrido de Gregorio Cortez* are both protests against injustice. Just like the exiled Cid, who is forced to leave home, family, and country for having opposed the will of the king, Gregorio Cortez is obliged to flee from his home and family after having killed a law enforcement officer due to a misunderstanding and makes an (unsuccessful) attempt to leave his country.

Playwrights Fernando de Rojas (author of the late fifteenth-century *Celestina*) and Luis Valdez (author of *Zoot Suit*) both wrote dark plays dealing with corruption in the social system. In *Celestina* (1499) a youth named Calisto hires the services of the witch Celestina to help him seduce the maiden Melibea. Celestina fulfills her part of the bargain and receives her reward. However, Calisto's servants kill Celestina in order to steal her wages. Celestina's gang then kills the servants in revenge and comes to Melibea's garden to murder Calisto as well. Trying to make a fast escape over the wall, Calisto falls from the ladder and is killed. Melibea runs to the top of the tower of her house and throws herself off to her death. The play ends with Melibea's father mourning the death of his daughter. Valdez's play *Zoot Suit,* which premiered in 1977, presents the murder of a young man resulting from racial prejudice in Los Angeles in the Zoot Suit riots during World War II. Both of these authors had a specific political grievance to air. Fernando de Rojas was a *converso* mayor of the town of Talavera, near Toledo. His father had been condemned and probably burned as a Judaizer in 1488; his five cousins had been obliged to reconcile with the Catholic Church; and his father-in-law had been arrested by the Inquisition. Luis Valdez was the founder in 1965 of the Teatro Campesino, providing literary support for Cesar Chavez's United Farm Workers.

In the Anglo tradition William Langland's *Piers Plowman* and John Steinbeck's *Tortilla Flat* are both works depicting the problems of the poor. Both authors knew the plight of the lower class first hand.

A moving call for reform was made about 1380 by William Langland in his lengthy alliterative poem *Piers Plowman*. A compassionate and involved observer, Langland was a West Midlander who earned a meager living as a clerk in London. The poem refers to the humble conditions in which the author and his family lived in London, concentrating mainly on the plight of the peasants but also painting a picture of the squalid life of the urban poor. The poem urges king and subjects alike to hold to the laws of Christ. A warning is given regarding the sins of envy, anger, lechery, avarice, gluttony, and laziness. Langland dreams about humble Piers Plowman, who leads pilgrims along the pathway to truth and warns them against the evils of rebellion against authority. Waking, Langland looks for Do-well, and is told by Clergy to keep the Ten Commandments and keep from sin. In a later dream, Langland sees Piers Plowman (whose power to absolve people of their sins shows him to be Christ himself) planting the seeds of prudence, temperance, fortitude, and justice. In a final dream, Langland sees Antichrist winning people to his side. Conscience looks for Piers Plowman in the spiritual struggle that will only end at Judgment Day.

Born in Salinas, near Monterey, California, Steinbeck (1902–68) worked as a fruit picker and as a ranch hand in his youth. His 1935 novel *Tortilla Flat,* set in the area of his home town, depicts the problems of a poverty-haunted Mexican American circle. Its protagonist, Danny, steals to help friends like the promiscuous Teresina and her mother, who often goes to confession and burns candles to the Virgin. It was actually medieval lore, and specifically Thomas Malory's *Morte d'Arthur,* that inspired this novel, according to Steinbeck. Danny is described as having a house not unlike the Round Table, with friends not unlike its knights. His friends, for their part, sacrifice by taking temporary jobs to throw him a party when he is dispirited, but their ragged clothes oblige them to watch his funeral from a distance when he dies.

Rolando Hinojosa Smith (who published *Estampas del Valle* in 1973), like the medieval writer Jorge Manrique (author of "Coplas por la muerte de su padre") before him, pondered the inescapable reality of death. Manrique's "Coplas" (couplets for the death of his father) are filled with a sense of the rapid passage of time and of resignation before death. He speaks of lives as rivers rushing to the sea of death and asks what has become of the noise and struggle, jousts and finery of earlier days. Manrique cautions:

> Recuerde el alma dormida,
> avive el seso y despierte,
> contemplando

cómo se pasa la vida,
cómo se viene
la muerte tan callando.

(Remind the sleeping spirit,
wake up the understanding,
Call the thought round,
how life passes in a minute,
and then comes silencing
Death without a sound.)

The poem ends:

Assí, con tal entender,
todos sentidos humanos
conservados
cercado de su mujer,
y de sus hijos y hermanos
y criados,
dio el alma a quien se la dio,
(el cual la ponga en el cielo
en su gloria),
que, aunque la vida perdi,
dexónos harto consuelo
u memoria.

(Thus departing from this life,
in command of all his senses,
surrounded by his wife,
his sons, his brothers, and his servants,
he gave his life to his Creator,
Who takes him to heaven in His glory,
and although he went to meet his Maker,
we're consoled by his memory.)

Rolando Hinojosa Smith was born in Mercedes, Texas, in 1929 and went on to be a professor at the University of Texas at Austin. Death is a constant presence in his bilingual Spanish and English collection of short stories entitled *Estampas del valle*. For example, in "Otra Vez la Muerte/Death Once Again," he laments the passing of don Victor Peláez, crying as he had done when his own mother died and feeling like an orphan once again. In "Por Esas Cosas Que Pasan/One Of Those Things," a murderer explains that he has stabbed a man to death in a cantina because he had stolen one of his women. "Beto Castañeda" tells of Beto's early death from cancer at age thirty.

Juan Ruiz (author of *Libro de buen amor*) and Jose Antonio Villarreal (author of *Pocho*) both question the validity of Christianity and of its clergy. Juan Ruiz's *El libro de buen amor,* penned in prison in 1343 by a reprobate archpriest of Hita (near Guadalajara, Spain), tells details of bad love, purportedly so that the reader will avoid them, but claims to provide those who seek carnal love with useful techniques. The autobiographical stories in verse include the attempted seduction of married women and a nun with the help of a procuress named Trotaconventos (frequenter of convents). Christ is blasphemed, as in an obscene sexual explanation of why a prostitute is called La Cruz (the Cross). In Villarreal's 1959 novel *Pocho,* the character Richard Rubio turns from both the mass and Church authority.

Juan del Encina (who wrote the *Égloga de Cristiano y Febea*) and Rudolfo Anaya (author of *Bless Me Ultima*) both comment on the power of witchcraft. The late medieval obsession with witchcraft is reflected in Juan del Encina's plays written in the reign of Isabella I. As chaplain to the duke of Alba, Encina wrote plays to be performed in the Duke's palace. They soon became so popular with the people that they were also performed in the plazas and markets. He was the founder of secular theater in Spain. His play *Égloga de Cristiano y Febea* (the eclogue of Christian and Febea) proclaims the power of the sinful world. The shepherd Cristiano becomes a holy hermit, renouncing the temptations of this world until Love appears to him in the guise of an owl (a symbol of witchcraft). Love sends the nymph Febea to Cristiano to seduce him, and Febea succeeds in driving Cristiano away from his holy vows to his damnation. At the end, Cristiano, too late, regrets his choice:

> Donde está la gran tristura . . .
> Who could suffer such attack
> of sadness
> as me in my fall from grace?
> Its hard to keep a cheerful face.
> No color exists blacker than black.
>   With churning thoughts my soul is rife.

Instead of winning eternal life,
I've thrown it over for illicit love:
To deepest hell from heaven above
I've fallen into grievous strife.

Likewise, Ultima, the *curandera* of Rudolfo Anaya's 1972 novel *Blesss Me Ultima,* obviates the authority of the church, in her case by promising help from magic. Not only is this woman more successful in offering solutions than is the clergy, but she also proves to be morally superior to the priest, who out of pure ill will leaves one of his congregation to die in a pit.

Geoffrey Chaucer *(The Canterbury Tales)* and Katherine Ann Porter *(Ship of Fools)* both ruminated on the wide variety of humanity by placing various types together on a journey. Chaucer's *Canterbury Tales* presents thirty-one companions who accompany him on a pilgrimage to Thomas Becket's tomb at Canterbury. Porter was born in Indian Creek, near San Antonio. Her 1962 novel *Ship of Fools* presents a group of passengers on a cruise to Europe. The protagonists include a man from Brownsville, who is presented as a type of fool because, despite living in a town with a majority of Spanish speakers, he knows no Spanish and because he speaks of the rarity of a hot day in December, which is actually not uncommon in his hometown. Thomas Malory *(Morte d'Arthur)* and Willa Cather *(Death Comes for the Archbishop)* looked nostalgically to past glories. Thomas Malory's *Morte d'Arthur* (published in 1485) reflects on the halcyon days of the medieval knight when chivalry was in flower. The interest centers on the role of the once dominant feudal nobility with its warring and panoply, and emphasis is placed on the social superiority of the nobility. In one story, Sir Kay and Lynet both berate Gareth, whom they mistakenly take to be a commoner, until his identity as the brother of Sir Gawain is disclosed. The author realizes that he is championing a dying culture, concluding the work with the nostalgic observation that the forces that create civilizations bring them eventually to their end. Willa Cather's 1927 novel *Death Comes for the Archbishop* evokes the history and mood of New Mexico, telling the stories of two French priests sent to the region in the mid-nineteenth century. Just as Malory longs for the days when chivalry was in flower, so also does Cather have Father Latour mournfully acknowledge the passing of his Indian culture. The defeated Navajo chieftain Manuelito is shown to be as noble as Malory's hero knights.

Many other Anglo writers of the region, including J. Frank Dobie and

Bret Harte, have drawn inspiration from the area's Hispanic roots. Yet, unlike the Hispanic authors of the Borderlands, who are personally rooted in the area, most of the outstanding Anglo writers have tended to write about the area from a distance, or after a temporary stay in the area. Richard Henry Dana's *Two Years before the Mast* was written in 1841 as a journal of his sea voyage around the tip of South America to California. Its descriptions of Southern California are based on fleeting impressions of his stay in 1835 and 1836. Bret Harte's stories set in Hispanic California were based on an enthusiasm derived as much from reading Dana's book as from his own temporary stay in California. Helen Hunt Jackson, author of the sentimental novel *Ramona* in the late nineteenth century, wrote about the conflicts between Hispanics, Anglos, and Indians in Southern California without bothering to learn Spanish. Willa Cather (1873–1947) was a Nebraskan who discovered the Borderlands in an initial stay in Arizona from 1912 to 1915 and in New Mexico in 1915, although she later made several other trips to the area. The Borderlands setting was secondary and at times coincidental to defending the cause of the downtrodden, the goal of such authors as Helen Hunt Jackson and John Steinbeck.

Hispanic writers of the Borderlands share this love of the area's heritage but from an insider's perspective. Nash Candelaria's 1977 novel *Memories of the Alhambra* tells about a Mexican American who dies in Spain on a search for his genealogy. Although Rodolfo Gonzales's self-defining *I Am Joaquin: An Epic Poem* identifies more with the Indian heritage, the Spanish and Christian aspect of his heritage is acknowledged. A local Anglo readiness to find identity in the Borderlands and a Hispanic willingness to assume a bilingual role are moving Borderlands literary output toward an increasing amalgamation of the two traditions. Publications are common both in Spanish and in English, as well as in a combination of the two, either side by side or intermixed in "flip-flop" code-switching. History writing has also carried on from its strong start in medieval tradition, beginning with Villagra's history in verse of the founding of New Mexico.

Hispanic theater tradition in the Borderlands includes continuing performances of Colonial plays (such as *El niño perdido, Adán y Eva,* and *Los reyes magos*) and such modern works as Luis Valdés's 1977 *Zoot Suit.* Bret Harte was inspired in his recreation of Spanish legends of California by the New York tales of Washington Irving. Irving in turn had leaned partially on a medieval heritage from the British Isles. The "Legend of Sleepy Hollow" with its midnight chase of Ichabod Crane by the headless horseman to a bridge across protective water is a reworking of similar legends in Germany and Britain, the most famous version by Robert Burns in his narrative poem "Tam o' Shanter," in which Tam is pursued to the bridge over the Doon River by a witch named Nannie (whom Tam calls Cutty-sark, after her fetching chemise) and her witch associates. Similarly, Irving's tale of "Rip Van Winkle" drew its inspiration from medieval tales about a supernatural passing of time, as in Walter Map's story about King Herla. This same kind of Gothic horror informs some Mexican American jokes or stories and Spanish folktales. Examples include accounts of simpletons who misunderstand instructions and gut a child they are told to "clean" or boil an old woman they are told to put in a tub of "hot" water.

Non-literary developments influenced by works of literature can also be noted. The succession of floats presenting various scenes in parades evokes the scenes of the Cycle Plays presented from a parade of wagons in late medieval England and the processions common in the streets of medieval Castilian towns. From the late medieval fad for *novelas de caballería* came the name of the state of California, first given to Baja California by Hernán Cortés, who got it from the chivalric novel *Sergas de Esplandián.* The name, which appears as the land of *Califerne* in the eleventh-century *Chanson de Roland,* was used again in *Esplandián,* published in 1510 as a continuation of *Amadís de Gaula.* Telling the story of Amadís's son, Esplandián, it presents California as an island realm of Amazons, ruled by the amorous Queen Calafía.

Outlaw Heroes

Examples of rebel heroes abound in both Castilian and English medieval literatures. The spirit of rebellion was especially expressed in the ballads (called *romances* in Castile) that mark the late Middle Ages in both societies. These rhythmic narrative songs written in stanzas, sometimes using refrains and often relying on syncopation and mixed time, emphasize sensational action stories. Created at a time of disillusionment with government, they cheer on social rebels. They were sung by obscure minstrels, who often traveled from place to place, accompanying their singing with a harp or a fiddle.

The most enduring outlaw figures from medieval literature are the Cid and Robin Hood. It is somewhat difficult but not impossible to separate the Cid of literature from the Cid of history, and educated guesses as to the historical core of the Robin Hood story have also been attempted. The *Poema del Cid,* a *cantar de gesta* (song of deeds) written in the twelfth century, relates that Gonzalo Ansúrez of Valladolid convinced Alfonso VI to permit the marriages of Gonzalo's sons Diego and Fernando González, the so-called *Infantes de Carrión,* to the Cid's daughters Cristina and María (called Elvira and Sol in the *Poema*) in a disastrous and short-lived double match. While these *infantes* probably did exist, they never married the Cid's daughters. However, the second set of marriages reported for these sisters in the poem are confirmed by history. The younger daughter María wed Count Ramón Berenguer III of Barcelona, and Cristina wed Ramiro of Navarre. The tale that the Cid's dead body was propped on his horse to fool the Moors into believing that he was still alive was a fiction later added to the Cid's story. In actuality, it was in 1101, two years after the Cid's death, that Yusuf ibn Tashfin took Valencia.

Robin Hood is the subject of forty or more ballads. William Langland refers to the "rhymes of Robin Hood" in his *Piers Plowman,* and the saying "Many speak of Robin Hood that never bent a bow" was known already by 1400. *A Gest of Robyn Hode,* a long ballad of 456 stanzas, was written in the early 1400s and was apparently printed at the end of that century. There is evidence that the character of Robin Hood, too, was modeled on one or more historical personages, although the contradictory claims are too complex to review here.

The Cid and Robin Hood represent many of the same ideals. Both are courageous. In the *Poema del Cid,* the Cid is accurately portrayed as a superb fighter, providing extraordinarily successful leadership in battle. When a lion escapes and scatters his courtiers in Valencia, the Cid rapidly subdues the beast. Robin rescues a man about to be hanged right from under the nose of the Sheriff of Nottingham. In another tale, Robin wins an archery contest, but flees when he is recognized. Both are pious. Although the literary Cid is not without flaws, he is nonetheless presented as a Christian hero, assured of God's favor by the angel Gabriel in a dream. He humbly gives God the glory for his good fortune, both when his daughters are revenged and when a battle has been won. When Robin is losing a fight, he calls on the Virgin Mary for help, which allows him to win. Both are fair. The Cid astounds the count of Barcelona by giving him his freedom after the count has attacked him and been defeated. He divides his loot generously, giving lavish gifts of money and horses. He is so just that the conquered Moors of Alcocer weep when he leaves them. Robin Hood is credited with good deeds to the poor (although neither he nor the Cid are opposed to the rich) and lends money to a knight who has lost all his possessions. Yet both are tricky. The Cid gives moneylenders two sand-filled locked chests, which he tells them contain gold, as security for a loan. Robin Hood obliges the sheriff, who has been lured into his camp, to eat from his own stolen plate and then swear to do Robin and his band nothing but good.

Both die dramatically in the fictitious accounts. The Cid's after-death charge at the head of his troops, vanquishing the Moorish enemy one more time, is one of the great scenes of medieval heroism. His body is subsequently taken by his widow for reburial at Cardeña Monastery outside Burgos. Robin goes to Kirklees Abbey to be healed of an illness, where the prioress, his relative, bleeds him excessively and then locks him in a room to die. Robin blows his horn, bringing Little John only in time to hear his dying wish. Most of all, both are rebellious. The Cid of the *Poema del Cid* repeatedly displays defiance of his own king, fighting Garcí Ordóñez, agent of their mutual king, Alfonso VI. In the late medieval *romances,* the Cid assumes an even more defiant tone. In one *romance,* he dismounts and kisses the hand of king Fernando I only because his father asks him to do so. Robin Hood attacks and victimizes leading clergymen and the sheriff of Nottingham.

The Impact of Medieval Outlaw Heroes on the Borderlands

As the Cid and Robin Hood are the medieval heroes familiar to the Western imagination of the Borderlanders, references to them are found in Borderlands lore, and, it can be argued, have shaped the protagonists of modern *corridos* and ballads. The ability to recite fragments of a *romance* about the Cid survived into twentieth century New Mexico. The saying "Zamora was not won in an hour" is still heard in that state, as well as the description of a courageous man as a "real Ci' Campeador." The medieval admiration for rebels has translated into such Mexican-American border heroes as Juan Cortina, Solomon Pico ("El Zorro"), Joaquín Murieta, and Billy the Kid. Like Robin Hood fighting and then recruiting Little John, Juan Nepomuceno Cortina of Brownsville won over the friendship of a foe, Rip Ford, by his protection of Ford's wife at a time she was in his power in Matamoros, Mexico. Songs about Robin Hood were popularized by the Anglo-Scottish border folk who settled the Mexican-American Borderlands. Juan Cortina has been called "a genuine cultural hero and Robin Hood of Texas" and a "merciless Robin Hood." His exploits, both actual and alleged, have been recorded in both historical accounts and in corridos.

In California, Salomón Pico came from a distinguished ranching family, with brothers who were mayors of San Jose and San Luis Obispo. He took to outlawry in the 1850s after his wife was raped and fatally beaten. For eight years, he robbed people on the roads, wearing a mask and cutting an ear off each victim as a trophy. Like an episode from the *De Gestis Herwardi,* and like Robin Hood rescuing a man about to be hanged from under the nose of the Sheriff of Nottingham, Pico in 1851 broke up a trial of three fellow *Californios* in Los Angeles, by shooting the hat off the head of the Anglo judge. In 1860 he was caught and executed in Baja California. His story, set safely back in Mexican times with Mexican villains, was popularized by Johnston McCulley's book *The Curse of Capistrano* in 1919. Pico was given a new nickname, *el Zorro* (the fox), and the severed ears were replaced by the cut of a "Z" on the victim's cheeks. By this route Pico found his way into various movies and TV programs in the second half of the twentieth century, cutting his trademark "Z" more innocuously into buildings, trees, or clothing.

William Bonney Jr. of New Mexico, best known as Billy the Kid, gives an Anglo model of a Borderland Robin Hood hero. The real Billy lived a short and ruthlessly violent existence from the day he murdered his first man at age twelve in Silver City until he was hunted down as a paid gunmen of a losing faction and shot to death at age twenty-one at Fort Sumner by Sheriff Pat Garrett. Like Robin Hood, he was eulogized by admirers, despite his bloody trail of victims, being praised as polite, gentlemanly, and likable. Other points of similarity between the legends woven around Robin Hood and Billy the Kid include the claim that they championed justice for the poor and down-trodden (especially Mexican-Americans), were generous with their money, exhibited religious devotion, fought corrupt sheriffs, and were finally brought down through treachery of a onetime friend. These similarities have been seen as a use of folklore to mold the border bandit in conformity to the stereotype of Robin Hood.

Architecture

Spain and Britain developed megalithic architecture in the Neolithic period. Menhirs (meaning *long stones* in Celtic) were artificially standing stones set up vertically in holes dug in the ground. They attracted lightning, believed to have been sent by the gods, and sometimes retained a charge of static electricity, considered to be beneficial for the surrounding soil and its crops. Coronation oaths were sworn while touching (sometimes flat) royal menhirs as a sign of divine approbation. The London Stone, displayed in London's St. Swithun's Lane, is believed to have been such a stone, and the Stone of Scone placed by Edward I under the royal throne in Westminster Abbey certainly was. Dolmens (*table stones* in Celtic) were formed by setting up a horizontal stone or quoin on top of two or more vertical stones. The dolmens often marked holy spots, some of which were marked by curative waters, and chieftains were occasionally buried under or near them. The stones were sometimes transported over great distances, even though some weigh over three hundred tons. Cromlechs were circles of menhirs or dolmens. Known as fairy rings, they served as centers of worship, including sacred circle dances. Stonehenge's Gaelic name, *Chatoin Ghall,* means dance of the giants. *Leys,* alignments of megaliths, marked pilgrimage routes across the countryside.

During the Roman period, imported classic Roman architecture laid the basis for the modest architectural structures of the Dark Ages. Visigothic and Anglo-Saxon churches were small and simple. The rectangular Visigothic basilicas introduced the Visigothic horseshoe arch, together with Germanic designs and striped bands of alternating stones. Perhaps the most impressive effort of this period was the little two-story stone palace now called Santa María del Naranco, built in the 840s by King Ramiro I of Asturias in Oviedo, with a double stairway and two open balconies at each end of the second-story hall. Romanesque architecture flourished in Castile and England in the second half of the eleventh and twelfth centuries. The most famous Spanish example is the Cathedral of Santiago de Compostela, begun in 1077, with much of the work completed by Archbishop Diego Gelmírez of Compostela in the early twelfth century. The most innovative of the eleventh century Romanesque churches in England was Durham Cathedral, built by William Rufus's bishop of

Durham, Ranulf Flambard. Four hundred feet long, Durham is among the longest churches of medieval Europe, in accord with the English penchant for "string-bean" churches. It made the earliest systematic use of a ribbed vault, arching over a three-story nave, and also added concealed flying buttresses to support the walls from the outside, thus employing two of the three main features of future Gothic architecture.

Thirteenth-century construction employed the Gothic architecture that had been worked out first in France in the twelfth century, but worked in distinct styles in Castile and England under the pious zeal of their kings. The Spanish Gothic churches generally followed the French giant arcade type, first built at Bourges. The Gothic cathedrals of Burgos, León, and Toledo were constructed in San Fernando's reign. Fernando's first wife Beatriz, daughter of German King Philip of Swabia, brought architects and sculptors from Germany who built Gothic structures in Castile. Together, Fernando and Beatriz laid the cornerstone for Burgos Cathedral, on whose so-called Sarmental facade their portrait statues can be seen. The first Gothic churches in England were reworked into the E.E. (Early English) style typified by their tunnel-like great horizontal sweep from the west end to the apse, with a polygonal chapter house, large transept tower at the crossing, and screen wall of continuous sculpture at the west end of the church. Henry III took a great interest in building Gothic churches, beginning Salisbury Cathedral, and rebuilding Westminster Abbey Cathedral as a grand new royal coronation and burial church. The new direction given to English Gothic put England in the forefront of architectural experimentation in the Late Middle Ages.

Fourteenth-century architecture expressed the separate class identities of the aristocracy and the rising middle class. The upper class pursuit of elegance inspired increasingly ornate forms as monarchs built sumptuous pleasure palaces for the gratification of the nobility. Alfonso XI remodeled the Alcázar of Córdoba, and built a new palace at Tordesillas, centered in fountained patios and using the Mudéjar style (combining Gothic with Moorish influences). Edward III centered his court at Windsor Castle, spending great sums to erect the great Round Hall (in 1344) and the Saint George Chapel (in 1348) to house his two new chivalric orders, the Order of the Round Table and the Order of the Garter, respectively. In church construction, England's "Dec" (decorated) Gothic architecture presented a profusion of decoration. Vaults were ornamented with secondary and tertiary ribs called tiercerons and liernes, along with reticulation or netting decoration, and foliage tracery replaced the geometric tracery typical of the E.E. style. The choir of Gloucester Cathedral (1337–57), built as a setting for Edward II's tomb after his murder, is one of the most sumptuous examples of Dec Gothic. The more sober mood of the middle class and of the Lollard movement, with its call for a simpler approach to worship, found an architectural counterpart in the "Perp" or Perpendicular Gothic. In an architectural parallel to Ockham's razor, the lines were simplified, with an emphasis on right angles. Perp Gothic reached its height under Richard II in a rebuilt portion of Winchester Cathedral. The nave, which is the longest Gothic nave in the world, was given a single large, pointed, simple window at its west end, with smaller windows at each side.

At the end of the fifteenth century, Isabel la Católica used wealth won from the *conversos* and Jews to erect grand structures in celebration of her governmental success. Two new styles of architecture emerged, both blending Italian Renaissance elements with Gothic features. The Isabeline style was more Gothic than Renaissance. Examples include the Palace of the Duque del Infantado in Guadalajara and the Hospital de Santa Cruz in Toledo, built for Cardinal Mendoza, brother of the Duque del Infantado. The church of San Juan de los Reyes in Toledo was built by the Reyes Católicos to celebrate their victory over King Afonso V el Africano at the battle of Toro in 1476. In contrast, the Plateresque style, named for its borrowing of ornate designs from silverware and other silver work, was more Renaissance than Gothic. Examples include the Hotel of the Pilgrims of the Order of Santiago, León, and various public buildings in Valladolid, including the Colegio de Santa Cruz (founded in 1479 by Cardinal Mendoza), the Colegio de San Gregorio, and the Church of San Pablo.

However, it was Moorish influence that molded Hispanic architectural forms into a distinctly different style from the English. Spanish Moorish architecture borrowed the Visigothic arch and applied it on a grand scale. Two buildings from the early Omayyad period in Spain are especially famous. The Great Mosque of Córdoba was begun by Abd al-Rahman I in the eighth century, but was built largely under Abd al-Rahman II in the ninth century. The entire main hall is crisscrossed by nineteen rows by thirty-six rows of columns with floral capitals holding red and white voussoired Visigothic arches on porphyry and jasper columns, lit by eight hundred silver aromatic oil lamps. The geometric patterns, already favored by the Visigoths, were developed into even more intricate shapes, especially in screens and windows. In the tenth century, Abd al-Rahman III built a huge palace outside Córdoba. Named Medinat al-Zahra (city of the flower) for his favorite wife, it exhibited her statue over the entry gate, in violation of the Islamic injunction against the representation of the human form. Its main building is a rectangular structure entered through a portico of horseshoe arches. It was built on three terrace levels, the lowest supporting a mosque and the quarters of the servants and slaves. The middle terrace had a botanical garden and a game park. The upper terrace contained the Caliph's reception room, living chamber, and harem. The throne room, built of gold and multi-colored marbles, centered around a mercury-filled pool, which when stirred created a moving reflection which made the room appear to spin. After the discouragement of creativity under the Almoravids in the late eleventh and early twelfth centuries, the less barbaric Almohads allowed cultural and intellectual expression to reemerge. Seville benefited from a beautification program using Moroccan architects working in their native style, encouraged by Muhammed ibn-Tumart's son, Caliph Abu Yakub Yusuf (1163–84). Most famously, the minaret of Seville's main mosque, later called the Giralda (for its weather vane), was built in 1197 to commemorate Yakub's victory at Alarcos. Seville's Torre del Oro, a graceful tower, was built in the same period to guard the bank of the Guadalquivir River.

In the early fourteenth century, Emir Yusuf I of Granada redesigned the famous Alhambra (red) Castle into a fabulously beautiful palace, divided into four main sections. The administrative section features the Hall of the Blessings, where the Emir received less important visitors. The *Serai* or public living section of the palace, where male guests were housed and entertained, centers around the Court of the Myrtles, with a pool surrounded by arches on two levels. The Comares Tower of the *Serai* houses the Hall of the Ambassadors and the Hall of the Kings, the latter being a dining hall with a ceiling showing the first ten Nasrid emirs. The *Harem* (taboo area) housed the emir's private living quarters, which were forbidden to other men. This section is arranged around the Court of the Lions, with a fountain resting on twelve stone lions. The Hall of the Two Sisters (named for two huge slabs of marble at the entrance) has myriad artificial stalactites hanging from its ceiling. Baths with brightly colored tiles are included. The *Generalife* summer palace was built farther up the slope, with rooms looking out on gardens and fountains.

Impact on Borderlands Architecture

The megalithic tradition of associating big stones with supernatural forces lives on in the Borderlands only in folklore. "The Devil's Rock" links the presence of a huge black stone in Olmito, Texas, with Satan. According to the tale, in 1866 the Devil was carrying this rock to destroy the newly built Cathedral of the Immaculate Conception in Brownsville. It was a heavy burden, so when the Devil met an old woman with two baskets of used shoes to sell, he asked her how much farther he had to go. Although he was almost there, the woman replied that it was so far that she had worn out all of those shoes walking from Brownsville. Fooled by her answer, the Devil gave up the effort, threw down the rock, and disappeared.

The architecture of the Borderlands is a felicitous blend of Hispanic and Anglo elements, sometimes in intimate conjunction. Hispanic Moorish influences are much in evidence among architectural motifs of the Borderlands. Two forms of architecture have particularly drawn on this tradition. The Pueblo-Spanish Style, first developed in Colonial Santa Fe, New Mexico, adds Spanish Moorish molding, sun-dried bricks, fireplaces, doors, windows, stairs, and other features to the Indian adobe construction. The style is simple, as its originators lacked the rich detail of geometric forms found in richer parts of the Spanish-speaking world. In the 1880s, the Mission Revival or Spanish Revival style of architecture was shaped in California and spread through the U.S. Southwest and beyond. The style was popularized through San Francisco's Panama-Pacific Exposition in 1914, with its "Cloister" pavilion, and San Diego's Panama-California Exposition in 1915, with its Spanish Colonial city. Many elements were drawn upon. The romantic impulses of the movement inspired a reworking into grand forms of such medieval Spanish motifs as stucco walls, arched porticoes, and bell towers. The Spanish Revival style also perpetuated such Arabic architectural elements as the red terra-cotta-tiled sloping roof, the inner patio with a monumental fountain, flowers, and other plants, the *zaguán* or vestibule between the street and patio, arched galleries, balconies, window grates, and tiled floors.

Surviving influences of the Mudéjar style (the reworkings of Moorish motifs in Christian Spain) on the Mexican-American Borderlands include carved ceilings, geometrical tracery on facades, jalousies, ivory inlays, and the *alfiz* or ornamental rectangular wooden frames surrounding doors. Other Spanish Moorish architectural motifs passed along include square columns supporting corridor roofs, traces of the horseshoe arch, a plain, unpretentious exterior, marble and plaster plaques, brilliant colors, and ingenious designs. To these elements was added a Romanesque ground plan, massive walls, and rounded arches. Religious architectural examples include the missions of San Diego, San Luis Rey, San Juan Capistrano, and San Fernando in California, San Xavier del Bac in Arizona, the San Ildefonso presbytery and San Miguel and Córdoba sanctuaries in New Mexico, and the Mission of San Antonio de Valero (the Alamo) in Texas. Many of these buildings were restored. Notable secular buildings of Spanish architecture in the Borderlands include such Colonial structures as the Presidio in Monterey, the governor's palace in Santa Fe, and the houses of the La Villita section of San Antonio, and campus structures of the University of Texas in Austin and of the University of California at Los Angeles. The town most affected is Santa Barbara, California, which—by a city ordinance promulgated after the extensive earthquake damage to the town in 1925—required all new buildings to be constructed in the "California" or Spanish Revival style.

The common wooden A-frame structure seen throughout the area traces back to the Celtic and Germanic long halls but without their wattle-and-daub siding and thatched roofs. The far colder winters, greater temperature fluctuations, and heavier rains of New England obliged the English settlers there to abandon thatched roofs as too prone to catch fire from the large fires required for warmth and to use shingles instead. They replaced wattle-and-daub with clapboard siding to prevent cracks from appearing in the walls. Doors and windows were constructed flush with the walls so that water would not seep inside. As in the case of Spanish Colonial architecture, the poverty of the society necessitated a simpler construction void of trim and fancy details. From the Anglo-Scottish border tradition of cabin construction came the placing of a breezeway through the middle of a house for ventilation, once popular in south Texas, and the name *cabin* itself. The Anglo-style yard with lawns and flower trim has precedents in medieval England, as can be seen in the writing of Alexander Neckham. This scholar, who had helped to foster the study of science at Oxford in the early thirteenth century, gave a description of how to lay out a garden in his *De naturis rerum* (on the nature of things). At least two of the plants he recommended are popular in the Borderlands, sage and roses. Medieval Europe also had a tradition of mixed gardens; Neckham suggested cultivating food plants like cucumbers, onions, lettuce, garlic, and fruit trees, as well as herbs for medical problems, alongside the flowers. Such a combination of decorative, nutritional, and medicinal plants can be found in many Hispanic Borderland gardens.

Curiously, most Hispanic Borderlanders live in Anglo-tradition A-frame houses, while most Spanish Revival homes house Anglos, a cultural exchange determined by economic status and building costs. However, a combination of Hispanic and Anglo characteristics has created several mixed styles. Examples of the Monterey Territorial style first appeared in the San Francisco Bay area with a house built by the Yankee merchant Thomas Larkin in 1836 to 1840. The Hispanic-Anglo mix can also be seen in the Craftsman Style, a fashion in furniture making and interior decoration introduced as part of the Arts and Craft Movement during the height of the Spanish Revival movement in the early twentieth century. This Craftsman Style worked Spanish and Moorish decorative designs into English approaches to the working of wood, leather, and wicker. A blending of Anglo and Hispanic styles in Santa Fe, New Mexico, combined American forms and colors to Spanish brick cornices, lime plaster, painted shutters, iron grills, and tiles. Along many Borderlands streets one sees Anglo wooden A-frame houses with a shingle roof and a front yard alternating with Hispanic brick houses built right on the street, with an interior patio and sometimes a balcony. In Brownsville, the Anglo-style front yard is often combined with a Spanish-style patio, which is placed in the back of the house rather than in the middle of it. Some Brownsville houses, including Henry Miller's "White Cottage," were built in the Anglo style but of brick instead of wood.

The many Gothic churches in the Borderlands might also be noted. Late nineteenth-century examples built in Brownsville, Roma, and Laredo were built by Padre Keralum, a French Catholic missionary architect trained in Paris as a follower of Violet-le-Duc's neo-Gothic movement.

Art

The hunter-gatherers of the Paleolithic period in Spain left behind a reputation for artistic talent that has echoed through many generations of Hispanic mural artists. The paintings at Altamira Cave overlooking the Bay of Biscay in Santander are especially renowned. Red ochre and black charcoal mixed in fat were used to outline bison and other animals, as well as people and boats. In Britain these early folk are remembered especially for their mazes. Maze patterns have been found carved and painted on the walls of early-inhabited caves, sometimes associated with a spiral pattern, the symbol of eternity. The tradition has been preserved to the present day in turf and hedge mazes. The concept of intricate patterns was echoed in rope knotting with the development of macramé, which was imitated in manuscript illumination designs in the Dark Ages.

The seventh century produced *cloisonné* ceramic objects, with wide interstices left for the enamel or gems, in such shapes as a Visigothic bronze and garnet eagle. The Visigoths hung dedicatory crowns and crosses, studded with gem stones, from hooks in the churches as gifts of the kings. The English carved stone graveyard crosses. The carvings on the Ruthwell Cross illustrate the Old English poem *The Dream of the Rood* and bears an inscription cut in runes over the cross that quotes a passage in the poem telling about a comforting vision of the cross. Visigothic manuscript illuminations, such as Beatus de Liébana's *Apocalypse,* are closer to the more realistic Byzantine representations, while Anglo-Saxon manuscript illuminations were influenced by Irish macramé-type designs.

Decorative sculpture received special attention in the second half of the eleventh and the twelfth centuries. The wealth Castile gleaned from tribute given by Muslim *taifa* states of the south in the eleventh century helped to build the Church of San Isidoro in León in 1063. The remains of San Isidro of Seville, obtained as part of Seville's tribute to Fernando I, were reburied in this new pantheon church. The church featured portal sculpture (in the form of a few scattered figures of biblical personages, fish, and animals), as well as mural paintings (using the bright colors and shapes of the manuscript tradition). In 1100 a figure portal was built at the cloisters of the Monastery of Santo Domingo de Silos in Burgos. The figures were elongated and highly stylized, with small heads and feet placed pointing downward as if dancing. About 1188 a figure portal was added in the *Pórtico de la Gloria* of the Church of Santiago at Compostela. Both the door jams and the tympanum over the door are richly covered with stone saints, clustered around a figure of Jesus with his hand lifted in greeting. Each saint is individualized. Daniel is still the smiling youth of Nebuchadnezzar's court, placed between the serious elders Jeremiah and Isaiah. Saint James rides on crusade over another entry to the church.

Ferrer Bassa of Barcelona developed oil painting in the late thirteenth century using a now-lost ingredient to retard cracking and fading. The use of oils spread across the Iberian Peninsula to Portugal, from where in the early fifteenth century Jan Van Eyck, in Lisbon on an ambassadorial mission, brought the new medium to his native Flanders. From there the invention spread on to England and elsewhere.

In the fourteenth and fifteenth centuries, Italian Renaissance art exerted an influence on both Spanish and English creativity. Jaume Huguet of Barcelona, who painted for Fernando the Catholic, combined Renaissance elements with Gothic touches in religious paintings that included depictions of saints. The same combination can be seen in the works of his contemporary Bartolomé Bermejo, who came from Andalucía to Barcelona and was praised for the three-dimensional depth conveyed in his landscapes. He, too, did religious scenes, such as his *Pietà* and *The Arrest of Santa Engracia*. Pedro Berruguete's *St. Dominic and the Albigensians* shows books being burned, and his *Heretics Being Burned in an Auto da Fe* critically shows an inquisitor dozing off from boredom while heretics are executed. In England Richard II patronized the Renaissance-Italian-touched International Style, based on Giotto's paintings with their emphasis on landscapes and three-dimensional effects. On the 1390 Wilton Diptych, Richard is shown kneeling, while Richard's badge of a white deer is depicted on the back. Renaissance influences were patronized in the fifteenth century by Humphrey of Gloucester, regent for the boy King Henry VI.

Impact on Borderlands Art

Some art historians see a thread of artistic influences through the Hispanic tradition from Altamira to the late twentieth century murals of East Los Angeles. European techniques such as the use of the fresco have been the language used to convey Mexican American artistic expression and content. The most basic medieval Spanish influence on later art is the use of oil painting, although this was launched in Cataluña rather than Castile. Popular wood-carving of doors, tables, chairs, benches, and reredos, particularly in New Mexico, was influenced by Spanish sculptural tradition. The carving of sacred images *(santos)* in the Dark Ages was one skill passed down to the Mexican-American Borderlands, where New Mexican *santeros* (*santos* carvers) produced both *retablos* (two-dimensional images) and *bultos* (three- dimensional). The production reached a creative height in the eighteenth and nineteenth centuries, when *santos* were in demand for homes and churches. Borderlands shrines like that at San Juan, Texas, exhibit metal reproductions of body parts that were healed, given in gratitude to God, at times with ex voto paintings showing how God answered a prayer.

The Chicano movement of the 1960s stimulated an artistic (and literary) outpouring called the Chicano Renaissance. Murals were painted on buildings and highway overpasses, and special attention was given to the Virgin of Guadalupe (a theme tracing back to fourteenth-century Castile), along with strictly New World themes like Pre-Columbian Indians, the Mexican Revolution, and Chicano experiences.

Music

Down to the fifteenth century, significant differences separated Castilian and English music. Spanish music followed the system originally laid down by Pythagoras, resting on his theory of the divine numbers underlying nature. Pythagoras felt that humans can come closer to divinity by surrounding themselves with the numbers and proportions favored in the creation of the universe. He argued that there are only five "regular" shapes, those which can move around evenly inside a sphere. These five shapes were the four-sided tetrahedron or pyramid, the six-sided hexahedron or cube, the eight-sided octahedron, the twelve-sided dodecahedron, and the twenty-sided icosahedron. Of these five forms, Pythagoras believed that the cube was the ideal mystic shape, with its proportions of six (faces), eight (angles), and twelve (edges). Pythagoras extended these numbers to music. He maintained that the ideal musical tones, each determined by a string's length at a given tension, and harmonies were achieved by use of the octave, the fourth, and the fifth. The Pythagorian preference for intervals of fourths and fifths was passed on to the medieval music of Continental western Europe. San Isidro of Seville in His *Libri sententiarum* follows Pythagoras's argument, claiming that the liturgical chants were an effective means whereby people could associate with the angels. With the acceptance of the Roman ritual in late eleventh century Castile, schools of Gregorian chant were established in San Millán de la Cogolla, Toledo, and elsewhere.

The British Isles, in contrast, held to its own ancient musical system, based on intervals of thirds and sixths. In eleventh-century England, music began to detach itself from religious ceremony to become an art form in its own right, achieving a high degree of elaboration. By the early thirteenth century, the English were masters of the principles of composition, as can be seen in the song "Sumer is icumen in." At the end of the Middle Ages, the British system displaced the Pythagorian approach in Spain (as elsewhere in continental Europe). This switch was partly a case of music following politics. The prestige of Henry V at the height of his success in the Hundred Years War extended to a momentary fad for the music of his court musician, John Dunstable. Dunstable's *Mass in Commemoration of the Battle of Agincourt* became especially popular in France, and his music was widely imitated.

The earliest Spanish musical compositions that can be dated with certainty are Dark Age plain chant, which had no set time values assigned to the notes. The Spaniard Prudentius in the late fourth century set a model for the writing of hymns with his *Cathemerion* or daily hymnal. In the Visigothic period, Seville's two brother bishops San Isidro and San Leandro both composed and performed music. In Toledo San Isidro's disciple San Ildefonso wrote hymns, alleluiahs, and masses. San Julian and San Eugenio, Archbishop of Toledo, also composed. San Eugenio was so prolific that Visigothic music is often called Eugenian chant. His works include musical laments for the deaths of King Chindasvinto and his Queen Reciberga. San Eugenio's teacher had been Archbishop Brauli of Zaragoza, which was the third major center of Visigothic music. The Visigothic or Mozarabic ritual, which incorporated melodies from before the Moorish invasion of Spain, spread from Seville to three other centers of musical study: Zaragoza, Toledo, and Palencia. The Christian tradition in music retained sufficient energy under the Moorish occupation to produce the Mozarabic "Song of the Sibyl," whose earliest surviving version dates from the mid-tenth century. It is based on the Sibylline Prophecies of ancient Rome, which had spoken of Apollo born as a human baby to a virgin mother, coming to restore the lost Golden Age. The lines form an acrostic spelling out *Ichthus* (fish) the Christian symbol and acronym of the Greek words ἰχθύς (Jesus Christ God's Son Savior).

Harmony appeared by the start of the tenth century in the form of the *organum,* where the same tune was sung by two voices at two different pitches. At the beginning of the twelfth century, John Cotton of England described how to put different sequences of notes together in changing sets of harmony. Mensural or measured music, setting the duration of each note, appears to have started in Islam in the tenth century. The practice was spread from Spain to England in the twelfth century by Adelard of Bath and other English translators in Toledo. John of Garland, a product of Oxford University in the early thirteenth century, wrote a treatise on musical time-value notation. Polyphony appeared in the twelfth century, the Latin pilgrim songs in Santiago de Compostela's *Codex calixtinus* being among the earliest surviving manifestations. Professional minstrels (called *juglares* in Castile) provided musical entertainment, along with juggling and verse recitations, in courts and market places. Minstrels were especially favored at the courts of Alfonso VIII and his Queen Leonor and of their grandson Fernando III and his Queen Beatriz. In the second half of the thirteenth century, *mester de clerecía* verse praising Mary was collected by Alfonso X into a book entitled *Las Cantigas de Santa María,* as mentioned above. Some of the 430 songs are by Alfonso himself, and most of the hymns are in the Galician dialect, popularized by the pilgrimage to Santiago de Compostela. The distinction between singer and poet remained blurred in the Renaissance-influenced compositions of the fifteenth century (mainly in the Castilian language). Juan del Encina composed sixty-eight of the songs included in the *Cancionero de palacio.* One of his songs, entitled "Qué es de tí, desconsolado," gives a sympathetic description of Emir Boabdil's loss of the kingdom of Granada, which Encina witnessed first hand.

As in other fields of medieval creativity, the Moorish element adds a distinguishing mark to the Hispanic heritage in music. Abd al-Rahman's main court musician, Ziryab, founded the Hispano-Arabic musical school in ninth century Córdoba. The Arab love of song reached an all-time height in the *taifa* states of southern Spain in the eleventh century, with two main types of verse forms: the *muwashshah* (with an AA/BBBAA/CCCAA rhyme scheme, a long poem sung in Arabic, with a final *jarchya* strophe sung in the local proto-Spanish of that period) and the *zajal* (with an AA/BBBA/CCCA rhyme scheme, a short verse song danced and sung in the eleventh century Spanish of al-Andalus). The *villancico, copla,* and *estribote* stem from the *zajal.* A *villancico* was originally a song of a village dweller *(villano).* It shared some characteristics with the madrigal, which came into popularity in England but not Castile at the end of the Middle Ages, but was simpler and placed more emphasis on the words, rhythm, and chords than on the melody. Moorish music exerted a strong influence on Christian Spain, despite a decree of the Council of Valladolid in 1322 forbidding the introduction of Moorish or Jewish elements into Christian religious elements.

Impact on Borderlands Music

The early Castilian and British influences on Borderlands music are important and varied. Ancient elements are said to have survived in medieval church music, and they may have been transmitted in folk songs as well. The influence of Gregorian chant can still be detected in New Mexican *penitente* songs and *romances* about Christ's Passion. Eight Gregorian modes have survived: Eolio (Aeolian), Mixolidio (Mixolydian), Lidio (Lydian), Dorio (Dorian), Hypolidio (Hypolydian), Hypofragio (Hypophrygian), Jonio (Ionian), Hypojonio (Hypoionian), One of Prudentius's fourth century hymns, set to a melody of 1715, is still sung as "Earth Has Many a Noble City." Prudentius's *Divinum Mysterium* is sung in the U.S. Southwest as both *"Fruto del amor divino"* and "By the Father's Love Begotten," set to a musical trope of the eleventh century:

> . . . corde patris genita est sapientia, filius ipse est,
> sanctus ab aeterno subsistit spiritus ore,
> tempore nec senior pater est nec numine maior. . . .

The sweetness of the early Latin hymns has influenced Mexican American popular song, including the *alabados,* songs of praise sung during Holy Week from Texas to Arizona. The *alabados* of New Mexico contain elements of old Spanish church modes, and employ the eight-syllable verse quatrain with second and fourth lines rhymed or assonant, as is common in Spanish folk poetry. The Christmas music generated from the schools of Gregorian chant established by the eleventh century in Spain has proven to be especially durable. The Mexican American Christmas tradition includes the English carols (originally sung while doing a circle dance) and the Spanish *villancicos.* Carols, written for Easter, Whitsunday, and May Day as well as for Christmas, were popularized in the religious revival of the thirteenth century and continued strong through the late Middle Ages. Surviving English medieval Christmas carols range from "God Rest Ye Merry, Gentlemen" through "The Holly and the Ivy," " A Virgin Unspotted," "The Cherry Tree Carol," "The First Noel," "The Seven Joys of Mary," "The Boar's Head Carol," "The Coventry Carol,"

"Here We Come Awassailing," "Venite Adoremus," "The Golden Carol," and "I Saw Three Ships" to "Greensleeves." Christmas carols are still at times accompanied by hand-bell ringers, a tradition first established around 1300 by Sir Thomas de Sotthill, in expiation of a murder he had perpetrated. Surviving Spanish *villancicos,* which were being sung regularly in Spanish churches in the late Middle Ages, include *"En el frío invernal"* from Catalunya. Religious *milagros* and *gozos* with earlier counterparts found in Alfonso el Sabio's *Libro de las cantigas* are still sung in New Mexico. Music sung on the feasts of saint's days includes *alboradas* sung at dawn, *salutaciones* to greet the saint's statue, *alabanzas* to praise it, *Ave Marías, salves,* and *cuandos* to be sung through the day, and *despedidas* to bid good-bye to the image at the end of the celebration. Two other categories of traditional songs are laments for the dead, called *sufragios,* and prayer requests called *rogativas.* Various Mexican children's songs trace back to Asturias.

The guitar, the most popular Borderlands musical instrument, was common already in early Spain. It is disputed whether it derived from the Roman *cithara* (itself taken from the Greeks) or was first introduced to Spain by the Arabs, who called it the *quitara.* The popularity of the guitar caused the Castilians to reject the lute, which was preferred in Renaissance England. One famous Borderlands use of the guitar is for the serenade, a nocturnal concert performed outside a house to surprise and honor somebody inside, listening from a window or door. The name comes from the troubadour song called a *serena,* which was likewise performed at night. Most typically, the border serenading is done for a birthday. The term *trovador* is still used, being applied to song leaders in churches. The medieval jongleur who sang the ballads has been replaced by the street-corner guitarist and the popular mariachi groups, who perpetuate the corridos from Texas to California. In a *mariachi,* guitars are frequently accompanied by violins and voices. The term *mariachi* comes from the French *mariage,* since it was used to play for weddings in the period of the French occupation of Mexico.

The *romance* (ballad), typical of late medieval Castile, was once sung from Texas to California, and continued to flourish in New Mexico until recently. *Coplas* and *décimas* were once also known in California and New Mexico. Phrases and names popularized in Castile by the medieval *romances* are also still in current use by Mexican Americans. Two California ballads have protagonists with the Visigothic names of Gerineldo and

Meregildo. The South Texas border has also developed (and perhaps even invented) a new form stemming from the medieval *romance,* called the *corrido.* The Andalusian peasants already called their *romances corridos,* and many of the Mexican *corridos* are mere variants of Iberian *romances* with medieval versions. The *corrido's* name (from *correr,* to run) comes from the way the song "ran" from mouth to mouth. The simple and repetitive melodies for this narrative lyrical composition, its octosyllabic lines, its syncopated meter of thirty-two basic notes with four principal accents, and its narration of contemporary events are especially reminiscent of the medieval Andalusian *romance.* Themes common to both the *romance* and the *corrido* include conflict against unjust authority, the battle between the sexes, the importance of family, and love of the home area. Both forms place an emphasis on the hero's horse and weapons. The beard is used in the *romance* and the mustache in the *corrido* as a symbol of manhood. The poetic convention of the hero's battle cry beginning with the words *"Yo soy"* is found in both forms. Ballads dealing with the Cid particularly anticipate the *corrido* in its poetic form, including the placement of a farewell at the end of the work and in its theme of conflict. The *corrido's* four-linc stanza balances lines one and two with lines three and four, and the song ends in a conventional farewell called a *despedida.*

The Texas-Mexican band called the *conjunto,* born at the turn of the nineteenth to twentieth century in Monterrey, Mexico, has been a musical vehicle for popularizing ballad music or *corridos* along the Texas-Mexican border. Beginning with an accordion and a *bajo sexto* (twelve-string guitar) as its foundation, the *conjunto* later added the *tambora* (drum) and a second guitar. Among the early pioneers of *conjunto* recording in Texas were Narciso Martinez and Santiago Jimenez. At first performing almost exclusively instrumental music, lyrics began to be added in the mid-1940s. *Corridos* were used by *conjunto* bands and also by the later *tejano* ensembles, which reintroduced the accordion and added a synthesizer, keyboard, and other electric instruments. *Tejano* groups have included Selena y los Dinos, Joe Lopez and Mazz, David Lee Garza y Los Musicales, Emilio Navaria and Rio, La Mafia, and Roberto and Bobby Pulido.

The Borderlands' romantic songs in Spanish look back to Moorish precedents. Moorish-style rhythms still typify Texano music. Moorish men expressed romantic love through their songs. Abd al-Rahman II, who had eighty-four children, wrote poems about his love for his many harem girls. One song asks, "Did Allah among his wonders create anything more pleasing to the eye than the beauty of a young woman?" To one woman he gave a fabulously expensive so-called dragon necklace, with this verse: "She who wears this necklace is herself a more precious jewel." Ibn Hazm of Valencia's *Taur al-Hammama* ("The Dove's Neck Ring," referring to the dove's extra neck rings in mating season), in which the man is devoted to his lady's slightest wish, was non-adulterous. Yehuda Halevi of Toledo wrote Hebrew-language love poems to his wife, as the one and only woman of his life. Emir al-Mutamid of Seville placed a premium on poetry, making a street poet his prime minister and addressing love songs to a poet slave-girl named Rumaikiya. Rumaikiya had been in the street during a popular festival where al-Mutamid was present in disguise, singing verses for his prime minister to complete. When at one point this official hesitated, Rumaikiya intervened and tossed verses back and forth with al-Mutamid. Intrigued, al-Mutamid bought her and took her back to the palace, where he soon married her. She gave him sons and a daughter, and al-Mutamid could not do enough for Rumaikiya. According to literary tradition, Al-Mutamid added the beautiful *Patio de las Doncellas* ("of the Maidens") for her in the Alcázar at Sevilla. When she expressed nostalgia for the snows of her native North, he planted the fields outside her window in their palace at the Alcázar at Córdoba (which he had by then conquered) with almond trees, to cover the ground with their white blossoms to look like snow. And when ex-slave girl Rumaikiya joined some peasant women treading red clay for bricks, al-Mutamid had the clay saturated with expensive perfume to make it worthy of her feet. Brownsville's Joe Lopez of MAZZ in his song "No te Olvidaré" gave a similar example of a man's love in his song "No te olvidaré."

Moorish women also expressed their love in song. Wallada, a princess of Córdoba, sang her love for a man named Ibn Zaydun, even though he was just a commoner. However, she later dumped him, to his distress. A more lasting love was shown by Rumaikiya for her husband, the same Emir al-Mutamid of Seville mentioned earlier, who wrote love songs for her. The "Tale of the Wise Wife" included in Juan Manuel's *El conde Lucanor* tells how Rumaikiya (here spelled Ramaiquía) cleverly demonstrates her loyalty to al-Mutammid (called Abenabet). At one point, when the couple has fallen out, the emir banishes Rumaikiya from the palace but allows her to take with her whatever possession she most prizes. He also grants her a farewell drink together. Overcome by fatigue, al-Mutamid falls asleep. When he awakes, he finds himself sitting beside Rumaikiya far from the palace. She has drugged him and taken him with her as her most precious possession. Moved, al-Mutamid returns to the palace with her. Such a romantic view on the part of a woman for a man is echoed in Borderlands songs like "Fotos y Recuerdos," sung by Selena of Corpus Christi. The song tells how a lonely woman kisses the photo of her beloved each night before falling asleep—all that remains of her love being the photos and the memories. Like Rumaikiya, who was exiled and sent with her deposed husband as a prisoner of state to Morocco, the murdered Selena's fate has added a lasting sadness to her lyrics.

English ballads and songs crossed the Atlantic with the early settlers and spread west. "Greensleeves" has proven to be the most durable of the lot. The now largely forgotten but once popular "Columbia, the Gem of the Ocean" is sung to a twelfth-century tune believed to have been written by Thomas Becket, doubtless in his youthful soldiering days. Francis Scott Key's "The Star Spangled Banner" follows to the tune of an old English drinking song.

Dance

Ancient Britain and Spain shared holy circle dances, at times held in cromlechs, including a deer-hunting dance. To insure success in a coming hunt, dancers would circle a man representing a deer, with muddied face and wearing a deer pelt and antlers, and shoot arrows at him. In the twelfth century, Spaniards Christianized the dance, so that the victim now represented a Moorish Muslim, attacked and, after a hard struggle, overcome by Christians in the *Reconquista*. Sung or chanted verses and a few dance steps were added. The Moors are usually converted at the end. The resulting Dance of the Moors and Christians *(danza de los moros y cristianos)* is first known to have been performed in 1150. The English were soon imitating this Christianized version and still perform it under the distorted name of the Morris dances. Ritual fertility dances performed in the Iron Age temples of Tanit in Gades (Cádiz) to the accompaniment of the *castañeta* and tambourine laid an early foundation for the flamenco music and dances of Andalucía, as mentioned earlier in chapter 1. The focus of these performances, as in ancient Spain, has continued to be the temptress beguiling a lover. Circular folk dancing was performed by the upper class in the castle halls and by the lower class on the village greens in the High and Late Middle Ages. Only at the close of the Middle Ages did a more genteel and polished, specifically court style of dancing develop in Italy and spread via France.

Impact on Borderlands Dance

The Borderlands tradition in dance has been touched by the Paleolithic period. There are many latter-day survivals of the Neolithic circle dances. Hispanic versions, called *corros,* and likewise sung while holding hands in a circle, are preserved in Borderland Spanish-language children's games, including "Rueda, Rueda de San Miguel," "Doña Blanca," "Mate Rile, Rile Lo," and "La Víbora, Víbora del Mar." One of the earliest Mexican versions of the last-named *corro* even mentions Count Roland, whose death in Spain was sung in the *Chanson de Roland.* "La Viudita" has children singing while standing in a circle around a girl designated as the "widow," until she is able to choose another girl to take her place. English-language border children's games include "Here We Go Round the Mulberry Bush," "Drop the Handkerchief," and "Go In and Out the Window." The Moorish dance was brought from Spain to Mexico in the sixteenth century. There it was both performed in its original version and also reworked into a song with dance representing Hernán Cortéz's conquest of Mexico. In this final form it has passed into Mexican American tradition, being presented on such occasions as the Virgin of Guadalupe Day in front of Borderlands churches. The *danza del venado* or "dance of the deer" is still performed locally. The *cante flamenco,* including malagueñas and sevillanas, left a distinct mark on Mexican music, and flamenco dances are still fostered by dance groups in the Mexican-American Borderlands. Arizona's dance of the *matachines,* performed to a monotonous rhythm, stems from the love of buffoons as entertainers in medieval Castile. The *matachines* (from the Arabic *matauchihin,* meaning masked man) were originally buffoons who danced in motley costumes with bells attached.

Medieval English folk dancing formed the basis for the square dance, which became so much a part of Anglo-American culture, outside and inside the Borderlands. Square dancing is now often organized for winter visitors to border communities. The influence came to the Borderlands by way of a circuitous route of development. In the England of the 1650s ruled by Oliver Cromwell and his Puritans, the aristocratic dances emphasizing status, so popular at the court of the deposed Stuart Dynasty, were no longer acceptable. The search for a more egalitarian dance was led by John Playford, whose 1651 *English Dancing-Master* repopularized the simpler steps of the medieval folk dance. No rank dictated who would dance with whom; everyone danced together without regard for status. Of the variations presented, it was the "longway" (with couples in two lines facing each other) that caught the popular imagination. In the Anglo-American colonies, the Virginia Reel gained particular fame. However, during the War of 1812 the longway fell out of favor in the United States, as it was a dance associated with the British enemy. In its place Americans turned to the French Quadrille of friendly France. This dance, composed of squares formed by four couples each, was actually another English folk dance. Thought of as quaintly Arcadian or rustic, it was popularized at Versailles in the later seventeenth century under the name of a *cotillon* (petticoat). Borrowing the square dance via this French route, the Americans incorporated the French terms that had come to be attached to it, including the "alaman" (*à la main* or take the hand), the "do-si-do" (*dos-à-dos* or back to back), and the "promenade." The square dance continued to be popular in the hard-working West, thanks to the introduction of calls by the fiddler. This innovation allowed dancers to join in after a brief introduction to only six or eight basic calls, without having to go to dancing school or to practice extensively before the dance. The dance was roughened by the fact that on the frontier, and most notably in the California Forty-niner Gold Rush, women were in short supply. A new convention called for those men (a not inconsiderable number) who were wearing patched pants to dance the part of the ladies. This gave the dance an extra speed and athleticism in swinging the partners, encouraged the prompter or caller to weave in rude rhymes and personal comments on the dancers into the calls, and added the call at the end of a dance to "promenade to the bar and treat your partners."

Cooking

Food preparation, a basic part of everyday living, can also be thought of as a culinary art, a part of Borderland creativity. Since Mexican recipes have left the biggest impress on border cooking, its origins derive only in small part from medieval Castile and England. Rice soups and paella actually stem from Valencia in Cataluña. The omelet so beloved in Castile (and which they call a *tortilla*) takes second place in the Borderlands to scrambled eggs mixed with cheese and peppers.[1] The medieval cooks enjoyed combining lamb offal, medium onions, bread crumbs, vinegar, and eggs into a stew. Borderlanders make a similar mixture but prepare the beef liver as a cold loaf liver pâté. Gazpacho, originally a cold soup using mashed oil, vinegar, garlic, and (often stale) bread, derives from Andalucía. After Columbus opened up the New World to trade, tomatoes, potatoes, beans, and spices were added to the recipe. It wasn't until the early sixteenth century, that the tomato was naturalized in Spain and became the dominant ingredient in gazpacho. *Menudo,* much enjoyed as a Hispanic Borderland dish, is like the medieval recipe for tripe, mixing stock, honey, salt, wine, onions, ginger, and vinegar with intestines into boiling water.

Spanish Jewish participation in trade included the transport of sugar and the production of sweets in a variety of forms. Three of their inventions are still favorites in the Mexican-American Borderlands: *pan dulce* (sweet breads), braided breads, *camotes* (candied sweet potatoes), and *calabaza* (candied squash). *Mazapán,* a local candy made of peanut base in imitation of the original almond-paste marzipan of Castile, is a typical Sephardic sales product. Marzipán itself was first developed at San Clemente Monastery in Toledo at the time of a famine in 1212, when the monks turned the local almond crop into a tasty candy.

Crypto-Jewish *converso* influence has been detected in a one-time widespread border Hispanic disinclination to eat pork, although this distaste has now largely disappeared. While this preference lasted, local Hispanics were inclined to mock their Anglo neighbors as ham-eaters. Northern Mexicans typically avoid eating any kind of meat with milk, a characteristic shared by a number of Mexican Americans as well. Some supposedly non-Jewish Borderlands Hispanics still avoid putting pork and other foods on the same plate and will not drink milk with meat.[2] Goats and chickens are sometimes slaughtered in the Hebrew ritual manner in the Borderlands. The throat is cut with one stroke, holding the body so that the blood does not touch it, and the blood is drained from the body before placing it in salt or salt water.

Such ongoing border dishes as hunter's stew, pancakes, fritters, mulled (spiced) wine, meat pies, fruit tarts, and *menudo* were all included in the recipe book of Richard II of England. Our expression "to eat humble pie" resulted from its being thought of as a peasant's meal. The shared love of hunting in medieval England and the Borderlands is reflected in the venison or hunter's stew, in which bread crumbs and deer blood are used for taste. The only differences between the medieval English recipe and the border version are the modern substitution of bay leaves and cloves instead of ginger, and the option of crackers instead of bread crumbs for thickening. Borderlands beer batters for fritters compare closely with the old English fruit batter—composed of flour, salt, eggs, ale, and saffron—which was used especially with apples. Today beer substitutes for ale, the saffron is omitted, and fish, meats, or any type of fried food stand in place of fruit. To help in speeding consumption of wine, a concern of medieval England due to limited storage capacities, a hippocras or mulled wine was created of red wine, sugar, cinnamon, ginger, cloves, grains of paradise, and orange or lemon peel, to be served warm. A Borderlands recipe for mulled wine uses almost the same ingredients, but less heavily spiced—a trait of medieval cooking. The English-Scottish border settlers in the Mexican-American Borderlands brought their medieval love of the pancake, and their preference for boiling and frying.

Concluding Remark

As the above survey of creativity suggests, one of the strongest points of appeal of the Mexican-American Borderlands is its interwoven cultural flavor. From fountained patios behind A-frame homes through mariachis' strumming chords of third and sixth intervals to the literary *bandidos* to rodeo cowboys doing the do-si-do, the medieval component of that heritage is central. The distinct Hispanic and Anglo cultures, born out of political, economic, social, religious, intercultural, religious, and creative developments in the Middle Ages, have shaped a particularly rich blend of medieval heritages along the Mexican-American border. Yet despite a harmonization of Hispanic and Anglo influences in the Borderlands today, in the Middle Ages the disparate economic, social-class, and religious structures of Castile and England led to the rise of hostility in Anglo-Hispanic relations. The history of this clash will be the subject of the following chapter.

SIX

The Development of Anglo-Hispanic Conflict

Hispanics and Anglos brought hostile stereotypes of each other with them when they first came into contact with each other in what are now the Mexican-American Borderlands. Many of the first Anglo-Americans to settle in the area when it was still under Mexican rule in the first half of the nineteenth century recorded disapproval of the Hispanic inhabitants in letters written back home. These stereotypes are usually traced back to the sixteenth century and to the start of the so-called Black Legend, which disparaged Spaniards as cruel and fanatical exploiters. The Black Legend ironically drew material from the humanitarian campaign of Friar Bartolomé de las Casas to convince Carlos V to protect the natives of America from exploitation. In his concern to protect the American natives from mistreatment, las Casas vividly depicted cases of cruelty on the part of certain Spanish *conquistadores*. English colonizers used these opinions as a convenient justification for their incursion into the Spanish spheres of interest and quoted such incidents depicted by Las Casas as typical of Spaniards. However, the roots of Anglo-Hispanic hostility reach back earlier than the Black Legend. Anglo-Hispanic relations had already been jaundiced by medieval English intervention in the Iberian Peninsula, intended either to frustrate Castilian expansionism or to dominate the Castilian economy. When the Castilians responded to this English aggression with a naval buildup in British waters and by supporting Irish liberation efforts, they hit a particularly sensitive English nerve, the matter of security in what were deemed English waters. Thus, by the end of the Middle Ages, Hispanics and Anglos had begun to form negative impressions of each other. This final chapter focuses on how such problems first arose in Europe and will hopefully dispel some of the clouds of resentment overshadowing both societies in the Borderlands.

Move toward Anglo-Hispanic Interaction

Separated as they were by France and the Bay of Biscay, Castile and England avoided conflict with each other throughout antiquity and the Dark Ages. Early on, the northwestern Spanish Christians, being preoccupied with the land threat from Moorish al-Andalus, had no fleet. The Saxon kings of England, starting with Alfred the Great, had maintained fleets that by the mid-tenth century were active in all waters around the British Isles. However, they were too concerned with blocking Viking threats to consider naval or maritime involvement against Spain. The Norman Conquest paradoxically did away with any official English fleet (the best instrument for adventuring in Spain) and simultaneously ended the Viking threat (freeing England for exactly such ventures). Just as Julius Caesar centuries earlier had destroyed the Celtic fleet at the battle of Quiberon Bay to cow the Britons, William the Conqueror similarly may have distrusted the loyalty of Saxon sailors. The Norman kings, like Edward the Confessor, depended on the Cinque Ports, the five major ports of the English south coast, to provide ships in time of emergency, and in exchange gave tax relief to those towns. The absence of a permanent navy meant that these kings had to bribe the Danes not to attack and to depend mainly on their feudal armies to meet any threat. It was the collapse of Scandinavia into a period of weakness and civil war after 1066 that allowed the English to turn to overseas initiatives.

The First Plan for English Domination of Castile

The new strength of England under William the Conqueror attracted offers of alliance from Spain. Soon after the Norman Conquest, the sons of the late Fernando I of Castile (Sancho II, Alfonso VI, and García), each of whom had inherited his own rival kingdom, tried to bolster their positions seeking the hand of one or another of William's daughters. William of Poitier's *Gesta Guillelmi ducis Normannorum et regis angliae* speaks of two of the brothers seeking such a marriage, but all three of them may have done so. Sancho II seems to have married a certain Alberta, who may have been one of William's daughters. Names are given for five of William's daughters, and there were still others whose names are unknown. According to one contemporary source (the *Vita* of Count Simon of Crépy) and two early twelfth century sources (the *De gestis regum anglorum* of William of Malmesbury and the *Historia ecclesiastica* of Orderic Vitalis), a daughter of William was sent to wed Alfonso VI but died en route. Orderic Vitalis gives her name as Agatha. García, too, reportedly sought William as a father-in-law.

If the plot of a group of Spanish conspirators had materialized, William the Conqueror and Alfonso VI would have pitted their strength against each other. Following the murder of Sancho II and the imprisonment of García, the triumphant Alfonso planned to hand Galicia as a fief to his daughter Urraca and her bridegroom Raymond of Burgundy. The rebels, still attached to the deposed García, opposed this plan and plotted Alfonso's demise. Culturally, Galicia was a detached piece of Portugal and lacked the link of a common language with Castile and León. In 1087 the rebels launched a revolt against Alfonso VI, taking advantage of his recent defeat by the Almoravids at the battle of Sagrajas (or Zalaca). The two main leaders of the plot were Count Rodrigo Ovéquiz (who had shared the Cid's exile in Zaragoza) and Bishop Diego Peláez of Santiago de Compostela (a follower of García, who had appointed him to his post, and also once attached to Sancho II). According to a French cleric attached to the episcopal court of Peláez, Ovéquiz and Peláez offered to hand Galicia over to William the Conqueror. During that time the aggressive Normans were attracted to Galicia by the large number of French who were settling in northern Spain along the route to Santiago. At the battle of Hastings, William the Conqueror's minstrel Taillefer had sung the *Chanson de Roland* extolling a military invasion of Spain. The plot might have worked had not William, in 1087, suffered a fatal injury when his horse stumbled, throwing him with great violence against his saddle pommel. Alfonso reimposed his authority in Galicia, and Peláez was deposed from his bishopric.

This attempt to draw England into Iberian politics was the start of an ongoing problem for Castile. The fact that William had made the English government the most powerful in Europe at that time created a potential for economic growth, and London moved to profit from the opportunity of overseas commerce. The call of the Crusades to joint military and naval action in the Mediterranean gave the English experience with sailing in Iberian waters. English ships sailed through the Straits of Gibraltar to support the First Crusade in the Levant. Edgar the Aetheling, the rightful king of England pushed aside as a boy first by Harold of Wessex and then William the Conqueror in 1066, led the effort as a Saxon prince with Saxon sailors. He headed about thirty apparently private ships and in 1097 supplied the crusader army at the siege of Antioch, capturing Syrian coastal fortresses. It was an English ship that saved the life of Baudouin I of the Latin Kingdom of Jerusalem after his defeat in the battle of Ramleh, by carrying him from Arsuf to safety in Jaffa. Sailing into the Mediterranean proved to be impractical for the English at this early date. They were not able to contend with the continual eastward push of wind and current through the Straits of Gibraltar to return to the Atlantic, and after 1107 an Almoravid naval buildup made it too dangerous to navigate the Straits in either direction for a generation. In the meantime, English commerce had followed the crusaders (and pilgrims) into Spain. In the 1100s and in response to the previous developments, Archbishop Diego Gelmírez of Compostela built a fleet based in Galicia and invested in maritime trade. The new English naval strength in the Atlantic waters soon became a frustration for Castilian commerce as English pirates carried out frequent raids on the Castilian coast in the early twelfth century, keeping sea passages insecure and retarding the Castilian economy.

English Consolidation of Portuguese Independence from Castile

Since the plan to win a point of entry for English influence into the Iberian Peninsula by supporting the independence of Galicia was blocked, the English repeated the attempt in Portugal, this time with success. A Portuguese revolt led by Afonso Henriques, seeking independence from Castile, was consolidated thanks to English help. Afonso was crowned Afonso I, first king of Portugal, in 1143, but with the rich port city of Lisbon still in Muslim hands, the new Portuguese kingdom was too tiny to be viable.

The Portuguese effort was saved by an expedition of 13,000 Englishmen, Normans, Flemings, and Germans, which in 1147 left Dartmouth for the Holy Land in over 160 ships to help the Second Crusade. (Civil war prevented England's King Stephen from participating.) On their way to the Holy Land, the expedition stopped in Portugal, where Herveo of Glanvil, one of the commanders of the English troops, convinced the other commanders to help Afonso conquer Lisbon. Staging a four-month siege together with the new Portuguese military order of Évora (or Talavera), the English helped to capture Lisbon from the Moors in October 1148, giving the new kingdom of Portugal a viable size and a major city as its capital. The expedition then abandoned its original goal of fighting in the Levant and sailed back to England. Anglo-Portuguese ties continued to bolster the new Kingdom of Portugal. The first bishop of Lisbon, appointed by Afonso Henriques, was the Englishman Gilbert of Hastings. In 1151 Bishop Gilbert recruited another army in England for a further crusade against the Moors on Portugal's southern border. This force captured the town of Alcácer the following year. Using Lisbon as a new port of call, the English ships returned to the Mediterranean later in the twelfth century.

English leverage on Castile increased after Eleanor of Aquitaine, Castile's near neighbor on the Bay of Biscay, became queen of England (at the succession to the English throne of her husband Henry II in 1154). Under Henry II, the English naval force still consisted only of the king's personal galley, the Southampton-based *Esnecca* (sea snake) and fifty-seven transports that the five main ports on the English Channel (the *Cinque Ports*) were obliged to provide for forty days each year. In recognition of England's growing importance, twelve-year-old Alfonso VIII of Castile was married in 1170 to nine-year-old Leonor, daughter of Henry and Eleanor, and in 1190 Leonor's older brother, Richard the Lionhearted, married Berengaria of Navarre. At the same time, the English continued their support of the breakaway Portuguese kingdom in its expansion south into Moorish territory. In 1188 or 1189 an Anglo-Flemish force helped Sancho I of Portugal to capture Albor Castle from the Moors, and in 1189 an Anglo-Flemish-German army sailing from Sandwich and Dartmouth also took Silves for Portugal. In 1195, when the Almohad Sultan crossed from Morocco into Spain, defeated Alfonso VIII in a battle fought near Ciudad Real, and laid siege to Toledo, Richard momentarily considered sending help to Castile before the Almohad threat receded. However, Richard the Lionhearted also continued to strengthen Portugal. A fleet of 110 ships with

English crusaders sailing from Dartmouth in support of Richard's Third Crusade in 1190 stopped in Portugal on the way and helped to push the Moors into the Alentejo. These English ships, like those in the First Crusade, proved unable to return west through the Straits of Gibraltar.

After Alfonso VIII's conquest of Alava and Guipúzcoa in 1199 and 1200, which gave Castile a common border with Aquitaine's southernmost region of Gascony, the Castilians found a new way to counter English power by threatening Aquitaine. The presence of unruly Basques on both sides of the western Pyrenees had long created an uncertain border, causing military problems between Spain and its northern neighbor, and some of the Gascon nobles urged Alfonso to be their overlord. Furthermore, the Castilian and French royal families were drawn closer together when in 1200 Eleanor of Aquitaine (as part of a settlement between France and England) brought Leonor's daughter Blanca to marry the heir to King Philippe Auguste of France. The medieval alliance system would henceforth pit the Germanic areas (England, the Lowlands, and Germany) against France and Spain.

The strains between Castile and England became more apparent under King John. When Eleanor's death left Aquitaine to John in 1204, Alfonso laid claim to Gascony. Alfonso made the unlikely argument that at the time of his marriage his father-in-law, Henry II, had pledged Gascony as security for the payment of Leanor's dowry. Maintaining that the dowry had never been fully paid, Alfonso invaded Gascony and besieged Bayonne in 1205 and 1206, at the same time that French troops were taking Anjou and Normandy from John. Meanwhile, John was creating a new Portsmouth-based English navy. This naval force was at first placed under two officials who were simultaneously responsible for collecting taxes on French goods. William Longsword, Earl of Salisbury and John's illegitimate half-brother, was subsequently given authority over the fleet and over the newly created office of Keeper of the King's Ports and Galleys, with responsibility for naval administration. The ships built were mainly galleys (with oars and sails) but also included *naves* (square-sailed merchantmen) and busses (heavy transports), with wooden "castles" at bow (forecastle) and stern (the poop). As a result England rapidly became a maritime power. By 1204 forty-five galleys were patrolling the English coasts, with five in Irish waters. In 1210 Geoffrey Lacey led the fleet in a search for pirates. In 1213 the English navy under the direction of the earl of Salisbury prevented a French invasion of England by winning a naval victory off Damme. In 1217 under the leadership of Hubert de Burgh, England's navy once again defeated a French fleet, at the battle of Sandwich (or Dover). The Gascons merchants, dependent on English purchase of their wine exports, held loyal to England, and Alfonso's invasion failed. A new Moorish invasion of Castile's southern border was the final factor convincing Alfonso to drop his claim to Gascony.

Relations improved again under the next set of kings, the cousins Henry III and Fernando III. Since both kings aspired to a holy reputation, and Henry admired Fernando's military campaigns against the Moors, the two engaged in frequent positive diplomatic exchanges. After Alfonso X became the next king of Castile, the Basques caused problems again. In 1253 the Gascons rebelled against Henry III's lieutenant in Gascony, his brother-in-law Simon de Montfort. The young Alfonso the Wise, who despite his epithet had a penchant for making unlikely hereditary claims, resurrected his grandfather's supposed right to Gascony. Alfonso asserted this claim as supposed heir of Arthur of Brittany, who had been captured and murdered by his uncle King John. Because a claim to England itself was at least implied, Henry III came to believe that Alfonso was planning to invade his island kingdom. When the Gascons once again held to their English allegiance with its wine profits, Henry turned to diplomacy to soothe relations with Castile. A treaty was arranged in 1254 and was sealed by the marriage of Henry's son, the future Edward I, to Alfonso's half-sister Eleanor of Castile. Alfonso resigned his claim to Gascony in return for various concessions, including English participation in Louis IX's planned crusade against the Maghreb. The wedding was held in Burgos, where Alfonso knighted the young bridegroom. Edward also made gestures of good will to the Castilians. Although in 1270 Edward and Eleanor had included a visit with Alfonso the Wise on their itinerary to join Louis IX's crusade against Tunis, it is not clear whether this rendezvous materialized.

One of the happiest personal conjunctions of the Hispanic and Anglo worlds in the Middle Ages was in the love shared between Edward and Eleanor. When Edward on crusade in the Holy Land was stabbed by an Arab assassin with a poisoned knife, Eleanor's tireless care nursed him back to health. Edward was equally devoted to Eleanor and was eager to satisfy her every whim. When she admired a particular English castle, Edward gave it to her as a gift, and it has been known as Queen's Castle ever since. When Eleanor died, while in the north of England with her husband, Edward ordered a series of elaborate crosses erected wherever her funeral cortege halted for the night on its route to burial in Westminster Abbey. The last of these elaborate "Eleanor Crosses" was put up only blocks from Westminster Abbey. A modern reworking of the cross now stands on the spot, off Trafalgar Square, designated *Charing Cross,* a corruption of the French *chère reine* (dear queen). Trade between Castile and England grew during this time. In 1297 Edward granted privileges to Spanish merchants in England. Manufactured English implements and cloth were exchanged for such Castilian raw materials as iron, leather, wine, oil, and even wool. England was the major beneficiary of the trading system, its favorable import-export ratio spurring a new peak of prosperity and living standard under Edward I.

However, even in this period Anglo-Castilian relations remained strained. Alfonso continued for a time to patronize certain Gascon lords and was angered when in 1255 Alfonso's rebellious younger brother Enrique was given refuge at the English court. Eleanor of Castile's mother, who disliked her stepson Alfonso the Wise and had left Castile even before her daughter's wedding to live in Abbéville, sympathized with her other stepson, Enrique, so much that she was even linked to him romantically by gossip. Antagonism was also generated by the vainglorious competition in 1257 between Alfonso and Henry III's brother Richard of Cornwall for the titles of king of Germany and Holy Roman Emperor. Thanks to heavy bribes, Alfonso received four, and Richard three, of the votes of the seven German electors, and Germany was burdened with two titular emperors. The claims to the rights of the imperial title could have acted as a pretext for English intervention in Castile and, so, were important for the Castilians to counteract. Edward III would be offered the title of Holy Roman Emperor by the German electors, and at the end of the fourteenth century Richard II would entertain the idea of trying for it. In an attempt to protect Castile from such Holy Roman imperial claims to universal dominion, the Castilian kings looked to the argument of the late Vicente of Spain, to the effect that Castile had its own separate empire with hegemony over the various kingdoms of the Iberian Peninsula. Furthermore, the steadily growing trade ties between England and Portugal continued to bolster Portuguese independence from Castile. By the mid-thirteenth century, the items being imported from England into Portugal included grains, copper, and tin, as well as wool, linen, and silk cloth. Mutual safe-conducts and privileges were granted to each other's merchants by Edward I and Portugal's King Denis. But Alfonso was determined to assert Castile's position on the high seas. With the help of Genoese and other foreign sailors, he took the first steps in establishing a Castilian navy consisting of eighteen galleys based at Seville. Seeds of the coming Anglo-Castilian wars of the Late Middle Ages were sown through the eleventh, twelfth, and thirteenth centuries through all of these developments.

Castilian trade competition with England soon led to military confrontation. In return for King Philippe IV of France's help in securing papal recognition of Sancho's claim to the throne, Sancho IV formed an anti-English alliance with France, sending land and makeshift sea forces to help France fight the English in 1294. Two years later, in 1296, Santander, Sebastián, and Bilbao formed the Brotherhood of the Coast *(Hermandad de la Marisma)* to protect the joint interests of the northern ports. In 1303 these towns began regular shipments of wool north. At about the same time, Spanish pirates based in Santander began to prey on English merchant ships. The English pirates for their part continued to attack Spanish shipping. In 1321 Hugh Despenser the Younger, Edward II's right-hand man, was making a profitable side business of piracy on foreign shipping in the English Channel. As England moved into the Hundred Years War with France, the Castilian fleet became an important factor in the struggle for control of the English Channel. In 1335 a diplomatic mission was sent to Castile by Edward III but failed to prevent Castile from renewing its alliance with France the next year. An English naval victory over France off the coast of Sluys in 1340 gave England control of the English Channel and free passage for its army to France. After Edward's great victory at Crécy in 1346, he managed in 1348 to arrange for his second daughter, Joan, to marry Alfonso XI's son and heir, Pedro. However, Joan died of the Black Death in Bordeaux en route to Castile. Alarmed, the French persuaded the Castilians to marry Pedro to their own candidate, Blanche of Bourbon, and Castilian ships continued to show hostility to the English.

In the summer of 1350 trade competition between Castilian and English wool caused a major naval confrontation. Forty-four Castilian warships sailing in the English Channel en route to Bruges encountered a group of English ships returning home from Bordeaux with a cargo of wine, sinking ten of the English ships and killing all the crews. Hoping to punish the Castilians on their return trip, Edward III gathered a makeshift fleet (the regular English navy having been discontinued) of fifty vessels, mostly merchant ships, at Sandwich. In August he intercepted the Castilians in the battle of Winchelsea. The Castilian ships were larger, specifically outfitted as fighting vessels, provided with crossbowmen, and reinforced with mercenaries hired in Flanders. The English balanced those odds with the speed of their longbowmen and by their incredibly reckless courage. Edward III crashed his ship into the lead Castilian ship with such force that the mast of the Spanish ship broke off, while Edward's own ship began to take on water. As the lead Spanish ship managed to move on, King Edward ordered his own ship lashed to a nearby enemy vessel and, in hand-to-hand fighting between the crews, took it over. During the heavy fighting twenty-year-old Edward, the Black Prince (so called for his black armor), commanded a ship with his ten-year-old brother, John of Gaunt, aboard, and his ship likewise sprang a leak and began to sink rapidly. The Black Prince imitated what his father had just done in the same predicament, by trying to board and capture an enemy ship. Seeing him failing in that effort, Henry of Lancaster, Earl of Derby, attacked that same Castilian ship from the opposite side, captured it, and pulled the Black Prince and his men aboard just before the Prince's deck disappeared under the waves. By sundown the English had won a great victory, with twenty-four ships taken and the rest of the enemy having fled. Edward III dubbed himself the "king of the sea."

The Black Prince's Plan to Dominate Castile

The alliance system shifted after Pedro the Cruel murdered Blanche, his French queen, souring Franco-Castilian relations. Blanche's cousin King Charles the Wise of France subsequently joined Aragon in backing Enrique de Trastamara's attempt to grab the throne. Meanwhile, Edward III's armies continued to win smashing victories over France in the Hundred Years War, now led by Edward III's son Edward, the Black Prince. In 1356 the Black Prince left Bordeaux on a raid into French territory and was trapped near Poitiers by a French army under King Jean II. The battle was a rough repetition of the experience at Crécy. Despite the French army's seven-to-one numerical advantage in trained fighting men, the Black Prince pushed them back with combined frontal and flank attacks, while the English archers showered them with arrows. The Black Prince was named Prince of Aquitaine and was given responsibility for winning cooperation from Castile. Thus Pedro the Cruel turned to England to bolster his position, signing an Anglo-Castilian alliance in 1362. By this pact Pedro also hoped to win English acceptance of the growing Castilian wool sales to Bruges. The stakes were high for all concerned, for if Enrique could win the Castilian throne, a joint effort by the combined French and Castilian fleets might take control of the English Channel away from England and thereby end England's ongoing Hundred Years War against France. King Charles V of France therefore sent Bertrand du Guesclin with mercenary troops to help Enrique in Castile. In 1366 the rebel force took Pedro by surprise, sweeping rapidly from one end of Castile to the other. Pedro fled to Seville, whose clergy (particularly strong in the south of Castile due to their role as protector of Christianity from lingering Islamic elements) stirred the town to revolt against him. So Pedro fled on to the court of his uncle, Pedro the Severe of Portugal, and then on to La Coruña in Galicia, while Enrique occupied Seville.

The English, comprehending the danger posed to their naval control by Enrique de Trastamara's success, rallied to redeem Pedro's cause. Pedro was brought from La Coruña to Bordeaux in an English ship. However, upon his arrival Edward, the Black Prince, took advantage of Pedro's dilemma to extract from him more than he could reasonably fulfill.

In the Treaty of Libourne, signed in September 1366, Pedro agreed to pay vast sums to the English and to surrender to them Vizcaya with its Basque ports (as guarantee of the payment). He also had to give Guipúzcoa and various castles on the Ebro River to King Charles II of Navarre; and to allow the English kings to hold a perpetual right to intervene militarily in Castile. In addition, Pedro had to grant the English merchants important trading privileges and to exempt Englishmen in Castile from taxation.

In February 1367 the Black Prince and his younger brother, John of Gaunt, Duke of Lancaster, accompanied Pedro at the head of an English army that invaded Castile from Bordeaux. This force met Enrique and his French allies at the battle of Nájera on April 3. At midnight before the day of the battle, the Black Prince positioned his men to attack the Castilian flank. John of Gaunt, eager to prove his fighting worth to his hero brother, led the vanguard. Some of Enrique's Castilian cavalry deserted at the onset of the fight, foiling du Guesclin's plan of attack. The English longbow once again decimated the French chivalry, cutting du Guesclin's vanguard off from the rest of the Trastamara army. When du Guesclin was thereby obliged to surrender, Enrique fled, leaving as many as six thousand of his men dead, compared to only sixty-four losses for the Black Prince. Victorious Pedro and the Black Prince then occupied Burgos.

Yet, following the victory, Pedro could hardly honor the unreasonable terms of the agreement the English had forced on him. He did try, without success, to raise money to pay them, but he balked at letting the English garrison twenty castles in Vizcaya as security for repayment on their loans. Pedro knew that to allow the English to hold these castles was contrary to Castilian interests and would make it difficult for him to reestablish his authority.

Frustrated, the Black Prince moved on to an even bolder scheme to try to strengthen England's position in Castile. He decided to orchestrate a multiple attack on Castile in order to divide it up between England, Portugal, Aragon, and Navarre. The main chunk of territory was to go to the Black Prince himself, as king of a greatly reduced Kingdom of Castile. Both Pedro the Cruel and Enrique of Trastamara were to be eliminated. The Black Prince pulled back to Aquitaine in August 1367 to prepare for this joint campaign, but he found himself beset by other problems. He was hard-pressed to pay the Gascon and mercenary troops of his recent venture. More importantly, by the start of 1369 he was fatally ill. Showing symptoms of liver cirrhosis, he had fits of dizziness, hallucinations, memory loss, and uncontrollable rages.

Naval Warfare

Enrique de Trastamara's subsequent murder of his brother Pedro and his ascent to power as Enrique II, described in a previous chapter, shifted Castile's alliance from England back to its traditional ally, France. The English merchant community that had been established in Seville was massacred on Enrique's order. Castile hoped to use the French alliance to guarantee the lucrative Flemish market for Castilian wool, in competition with wool from England. In 1371 Charles V of France had granted special privileges to Castilian merchants exporting to Harfleur and Rouen. Enrique II did his part with naval action against England. In 1372 he personally went to Santander to supervise the strengthening of the Castilian fleet. He made sure that it was a first-class fleet, constructed under the direction of Genoese shipbuilders and composed of swift, highly maneuverable galleys under professional admirals and sea captains. Its main port was at Seville, where special dockyards had been built for it. In contrast, the English naval effort was suffering from neglect by the elderly and lecherous Edward III and the ailing Black Prince. The former English policy of maintaining a fleet was obstructed by ongoing quarrels between Parliament and the king over who should finance it. Fleets were formed ad hoc in emergencies, were composed largely of impressed transport ships, and were in no sense a true navy. The merchants received no encouragement to invest in the sea trade, which was left unprotected.

Furthermore, just as England had weakened Castile by its support of Portugal, so Castile discovered in Ireland a British counterpart to play off against England. In 1361 Edward III had commissioned his son Lionel, Duke of Clarence, as lord lieutenant of Ireland with a large army to try to prop up the teetering English control. In 1366 Clarence had convened an Irish Parliament that proclaimed the severe Statute of Kilkenny, forbidding marriage between Englishmen and Irish, the use of the Irish language or dress, or the pasturing of Irish-owned animals on English-owned land. The Irish were to live apart from the English, and in all the English-held towns they were ordered to live in their own ghettos. However, the Statute of Kilkenny was widely ignored, and Clarence had left Ireland that same year, resigning his justiciar office in frustration. Rebel Irish ships now joined in the effort to take the seas away from the English, while Spanish merchants settled in Ireland, where their descendants still bear the family name of Spain—called Kathleen Spain, Sean Spain, Patrick Spain, etc.

In June 1372 a forty-eight-ship Castilian fleet commanded by Ambrosio Bocanegra blockaded English-held La Rochelle to aid Charles V's siege of that port. A smaller English fleet under Sir John Hastings, Earl of Pembroke, tried to break the blockade, but Castile's cannon-armed ships barred the way. At dawn on June 22, Bocanegra tied oil-filled row boats to the heavier English ships, then set them on fire, so that the flames spread to the other English ships. Most of the English ships sank, and the rest scattered. Before the English ships could regroup, Bocanegra attacked and defeated them. The Earl of Pembroke was taken as a prisoner back to Santander, where he and the other captives were thrown into a dungeon chained together two-by-two. Du Guesclin gave some of his lands in Castile in exchange for their freedom, but Pembroke's health was so undermined that he died before reaching home. This naval battle of La Rochelle established Castilian naval superiority for some time, and La Rochelle's trade became a virtual Basque monopoly. Their combined force allowed Spain and its allies to grab control of the English Channel and the Bay of Biscay, thereby holding English armies out of France and bringing a temporary halt to the Hundred Years War.

John of Gaunt's Plan to Dominate Castile

The English tried to break this naval stranglehold by a new dynastic marriage. In 1371 John of Gaunt, Duke of Lancaster, recently widowed of his first wife, married the murdered Pedro I's eldest surviving daughter, the exiled Constanza, which allowed John to claim the Castilian throne in her name. The next year, Constanza's younger sister Isabel, also in exile from Castile, was married to Edmund, Earl of Cambridge, John of Gaunt's younger brother. Gaunt then formed a court of expatriate Castilians in England, in the hope of making himself king of Castile, picking up on the uncompleted schemes of his moribund brother, the Black Prince. He tried to mobilize the coalition of England, Portugal, and Aragon earlier planned by the Black Prince for a joint attack on Castile. Pere III of Aragon expressed interest but in the end did nothing. However, Fernão I of Portugal, whose merchants felt elbowed out of the Atlantic trade by the Cantabrian and Basque success, allied with Gaunt. Portugal had continued its special trading relationship with England through the fourteenth century; Lisbon and the other Portuguese ports were heavily dependent on their trade with England and Flanders.

Fernão recognized John of Gaunt as the rightful king of Castile and went to war against Enrique II. In 1372 Gaunt stirred a rebellion in Galicia in preparation for making a landing there, but Enrique quickly crushed the revolt. Twelve Castilian ships then blockaded the Portuguese coast, while Enrique captured Lisbon from the land side. Fernão, with no English help in sight, held out in the Castle of São Jorge until he was forced to sign a humiliating peace. Deprived of Portuguese support, the English (though still holding Calais, Cherbourg, Bayonne, and Bordeaux on the French coast) were left in a still more weakened naval position. Hanseatic League merchants took advantage of the situation to win a monopoly over handling England's trade with North Sea ports. For the time being, Castilian rather than English wool became Flanders's major import. In 1373 du Guesclin took Brest from the Earl of Salisbury, and the combined Castilian and French fleets sacked the Isle of Wight. In 1377, they burned Rye and Hastings and sacked Lewes, Folkstone, Portsmouth, Dartmouth, and Plymouth. In 1378 John of Gaunt, whose nephew was the new child king Richard II of England, suffered a naval defeat at St. Malo in Brittany, although the same year the private English fleet of London victualler John Philipot captured the French-linked Scottish pirate John the Mercer.

Enrique II's policy of naval confrontation continued unabated under his son Juan I. In August 1379 Cantabrian ships prevented an English fleet from entering Saint-Servan, capturing four English ships and forcing the English to withdraw. That same month the Castilians conquered the Castle of La Roche Guyon on the Breton coast. Confrontations also took place close to Brest. In July 1380 Fernán Sánchez de Tovar led a Franco-Castilian fleet from La Rochelle in an attack on Jersey and Guernsey, followed by an August raid into the Thames estuary. The raiders burned Gravesend, while the Londoners watched the flames from a distance.

To recoup English fortunes, John of Gaunt began a new rapprochement with Portugal. In June 1380 Fernão I of Portugal, Richard II, and John of Gaunt (acting as presumptive king of Castile) signed a triple alliance. This Treaty of Estremoz committed the English to send to Portugal an expedition of one thousand soldiers and one thousand archers under Gaunt's younger brother Edmund of Langley, Earl of Cambridge, to put Castile in John of Gaunt's hands. To strengthen the agreement at the personal level, the Earl of Cambridge's son Edward was engaged to marry Fernão's daughter and heir Beatriz. All foreign ships were forbidden to trade in England, although this extreme measure proved impossible to enforce.

The Peasants' Revolt, which hit England at this point, prevented the earl of Cambridge from setting out with the fleet until June 24, 1381, saving Juan I from the full impact of the planned alliance. Even then, when Cambridge sailed, it was without proper financing because Gaunt was unpopular with the latest English Parliament. Not waiting for the tardy arrival of the English force, a twenty-six ship Portuguese fleet attacked the seventeen-ship Castilian fleet off the coast of the Algarbe in southern Portugal. Fernán Sánchez de Tovar turned his Castilian ships back toward Seville, luring the Portuguese admiral, the count of Ourem, into a pursuit. Once the Portuguese ships were strung out and had lost their battle order, Tovar suddenly turned his fleet around off the coast from Saltes. Arranging them at an oblique angle to give maximum firing freedom to his crossbowmen, he dealt a total defeat to the Portuguese, bringing booty and prisoners back to Seville.

By this time Juan I's army had crossed the Portuguese border, conquering Miranda and Mogadouro in July and setting siege to Almeida Castle in August. In the fall of 1381 a body of French troops and French subsidies further strengthened Juan's campaign. The earl of Cambridge's undersupplied army finally arrived in Portugal, but an eighty-ship Castilian fleet blockaded the Tagus estuary in March. With Fernão I's health failing, Queen Leonor Téllez of Portugal and her lover Andeiro secretly negotiated peace with Castile in August. The surprised English were obliged to return home. The Castilian army withdrew from its border conquests, and Fernão's daughter and heiress Beatriz was betrothed to Juan I's second son. After the pro-English Philip van Artevelde of Ghent grabbed control of Bruges in May 1382, Juan I sent Fernán Sánchez de Tovar and Fernán Ruiz Cabeza de Vaca with a fleet to support a French attack on Flanders. On November 27, 1382, a combined French and Castilian army (including Juan I's advisor Pedro López de Ayala) defeated the pro-English Flemish rebels at the battle of Roosebeke. A French policy was imposed on Flanders, which restored close trading ties with Castile.

Since Juan I's first wife, Leonor of Aragon, had died in a miscarriage, it was twenty-four-year-old Juan himself rather than his son who married ten-year-old Beatriz of Portugal, in April 1383. According to the agreement, Juan's elder son by Leonor of Aragon was to inherit Castile, though only a son by Beatriz could inherit Portugal. Portugal was to remain free of Castilian troops. Queen Leonor Téllez hoped by this arrangement to make Juan I her protector. But when she met Juan, she was disillusioned by his soft nature and told João, Master of Avís, that she wished that "the man were more of a man." Her skepticism over Juan's ability to hold the English out of Portugal was well founded.

The Second English Guarantee of Portuguese Independence from Castile

Fernão I died half a year later, in October 1383. Although Leonor Tíllez became regent of Portugal for Beatriz, she was unpopular, and Juan I tried to take over the Portuguese government in his wife's name. Juan I's chancellor, Pedro López de Ayala, and the royal council warned the king in vain against this policy, advice Ayala repeated in his *Rimado del Palacio.*

Most of the Portuguese nobles rallied to Juan, as a result of which many of the Portuguese houses (including the Pimenteles, Pachecos, and Silvas) were transformed into Castilian noble families. However, the (partly Jewish) middle class of Lisbon was scared by the anti-bourgeois policy of the Trastamara kings of Castile. In December 1383 they created a new royal council with João the Master of Avís (an illegitimate half brother of Fernão I) as protector of the realm. In 1384 Juan besieged Lisbon, but an epidemic spread from the town to the king's camp, forcing him to retreat. Meanwhile, João sought an alliance with Richard II of England. In July the English government authorized João's agents to recruit soldiers in England for a campaign in Portugal. Most importantly, João obtained a detachment of English longbowmen. At the beginning of 1385 Juan I reinvaded Portugal with French auxiliaries and Spanish cannons. In reaction, in April, a national assembly meeting in Coimbra declared Beatriz illegitimate and João de Avís was crowned as King João I of Portugal. The issue was decided at the battle of Aljubarrota, on August 14, 1385. The English longbowmen cut down the Castilian knights, whose cannons were not yet sufficiently perfected. The more aristocratic Castilian army, loathe to place such a formidable weapon in the hands of commoners, never adopted the long bow. In England, with its collected store of popular rights and liberties and its higher standard of living, commoners were required to practice shooting the longbow on the village greens. Moreover, João had prepared the battlefield with covered pits, into which the Castilian horses toppled onto hidden stakes. As the Castilian forces faltered, Juan I escaped on the horse of Pedro González de Mendoza, who was left to be killed on the battlefield. Pedro López de Ayala, who had advised against the campaign, was captured and put in a cage until ransomed.

By overplaying his hand, Juan I had compromised Castilian control of the English Channel and its domination of the wool sales to Flanders by driving Portugal into the arms of England. The English now regained control of the English Channel, with the help of the pirate Richard of Arundel, sending much of the trade with Flanders back to the English Merchants of the Staple. The deficit budgeting of the Hundred Years War, backed by English merchants, had given rise to a capitalist class in England. The English became favored merchants in Portugal, eventually establishing such local trading families of English origin like Oporto's Sandemans, Cockburns, and Crofts, who dealt in port wine. To hold Juan I at bay, João I encouraged Richard II's uncle John of Gaunt, still married to

Pedro the Cruel's daughter Constanza, to invade Castile. Gaunt used his leverage over the government of his royal nephew Richard II to support his own claim to the Castilian throne.

John of Gaunt repeated his attempt to conquer the throne of Castile in 1386. In May of that year, England and Portugal signed the Treaty of Windsor, and the English Parliament gave ample funds for Gaunt's troops, which were transported from Plymouth in July in a fleet of over ninety ships. Gaunt's nephew Richard II gave Gaunt and his wife Constance golden crowns to wear as king and queen. Pere III of Aragon was getting on in age, and his Francophile son Joan prevented Aragon from cooperating with Gaunt's invasion plans, but Portugal was still favorable to the English overtures. On the other side, Charles VI of France sent two thousand soldiers to fight for Juan I. Gaunt landed at La Coruña in July 1386, and occupied Galicia. The quasi-Portuguese Galicians were cooperative, won over by Gaunt's lenient treatment of the natives and the boost to the local economy from sales to the English occupation forces. After Gaunt's elder daughter by his first wife, Philippa of Lancaster, was married to João I in February, Gaunt and João jointly invaded Castile via Benevente in March 1387. The Castilians resisted fiercely. Two months later, no significant town had been taken, the troops were sick and deserting, and João proposed that they give up the effort. After a good cry slumped over on his horse, Gaunt agreed and made peace. The terms included the face-saving marriage the next year of his second daughter, Catherine of Lancaster, to Juan I's son, the future Enrique III. A temporary respite in the sea conflict was brought by a treaty between England, Castile, France, and Scotland, signed at Leulingham near Boulogne on June 18, 1389. Portugal joined the peace the following January. However, the two competing alliance systems remained in place, leading to renewed warfare in the following century.

Meanwhile, Hispanic and Anglo relations had been newly exacerbated by their opposing stands over the Great Schism of 1378 to 1415, when popes supported by England were restored in Rome. In 1380, the Castilian clergy gave allegiance instead to a continuing papacy at Avignon. A strong and lasting partisan spirit divided England from Castile on this issue. Urbano VI of the Roman line egged on this conflict by sending a holy banner for John of Gaunt to carry in a crusade against the Castilian king, with special remission of sins for all who would lend financial support to the expedition. The Council of Constance, which brought an end to the Great

Schism, became the setting of another clash between Castilians and English. The Spanish kingdoms in 1417 tardily abandoned the cause of the Avignon papacy and sent representatives to the council, only to find that their position as a voting "nation" (along with the Germans, French, and Italians) had been taken from them by the English. The Spaniards were finally admitted to the voting process as a fifth nation, but even then, the English united with the German and Italian nations to block the Spanish choice for pope. Nor did agreement on the reunified papacy restore religious harmony between the two nations. In 1422 the English envoy at the court of Pope Martino V engaged in a fist fight with the Castilian ambassador right in the middle of the Easter mass being held in St. Peter's Basilica in Rome.

Anglo-Hispanic Naval Warfare in the Early Fifteenth Century

At the start of the early fifteenth century, Castilian ships moved boldly in the English Channel. The Castilians now enjoyed a virtual monopoly of trade with Flanders and carried out a naval attack on Cornwall in 1405. Nonetheless, the English naval presence was gradually restrengthened. Henry IV reorganized the English merchants, and Henry V created a new English navy. The ongoing alliance with Portugal, whose queen Philippa of Lancaster was Henry IV's full sister, helped the recovery. Henry V's cousin Henriques the Navigator was simultaneously building up the strength and expertise of the Portuguese fleet at his study centers of Coimbra University and Sagres. In 1410 the regency government of Castile signed the Treaty of Fuenterrabía with England, agreeing to end the pirate attacks that had been assailing English commerce over the previous decade. Four years later Henry V gave permission to recruit four hundred English lancers to help Henriques the Navigator capture Ceuta on the Straits of Gibraltar for Portugal. The next year, Castilian ships joined the French and Genoese in trying to block English access to the Norman coast and threatened the southern coast of England. However, the English naval victory of Harfleur over the French on August 15, 1416, fought without Castilian participation, cleared the way for safer crossings. More Englishmen were recruited for the Portuguese effort against the Moors in 1417, and new fortifications were built in 1418 to guard Portsmouth from Castilian naval threats.

However, the English navy was abandoned in the minority of Henry VI (due to the actions of his regent uncles), and England's maritime presence was allowed to deteriorate once again. Adam de Moleyns, Bishop of Chichester, in his *Libelle of Englysche Polycye* in 1437, urged the government to maintain the navy and support English trade but to no effect. England's special relationship with Portugal eroded, even though the Castilians under Juan II sided with Dauphin Charles against the English claim to France and continued to harass the English at sea. In the 1430s, Spaniards contributed to the Irish attempt to expel the English. They joined Irish troops in 1430 in attacks on the English-held town of Waterford, and by the middle of the decade they held the upper hand in the seas around Ireland. *The Libelle* specifically warned the English government to beware of the growing cooperation between Spaniards, French, Scots, and Irish. Naval attacks on England by seamen of these nations increased in the 1440s. In 1443 fear of a major Castilian naval onslaught led the English to build a series of new harbor defenses in Calais. Blockading the Gironde River in 1453, Castilian ships helped the French and Bretons force England to surrender Gascony to France and to end its Hundred Years War against France. The Castilian fleet also won the upper hand over Hanseatic League competitors in the English Channel, and the Castilians signed a treaty favorable to their trade in Flanders. In their anger over the loss of Gascony, some private Englishmen began on their own initiative to fight back against Castile. Pirate raids against Castilian shipping in the English Channel were launched from England's southwest coast. In 1458 the earl of Warwick, in charge of the garrison at Calais, captured a Spanish trading fleet loaded with goods. Warwick's loses during the six-hour battle involved none of his ships and only eighty men, while the Castilians lost seven or eight of their twenty-eight ships and over two hundred men. The battle restored the English as a major naval power.

In 1460 Edward IV grabbed the English throne and restored a stronger foreign policy. His efforts to encourage cloth production in England while Enrique IV was supporting a Castilian textile industry brought a new source of Anglo-Castilian conflict. The Castilians produced cloth in Segovia, Zamora, Ávila, and Soria but had problems competing with cloth made from the thicker English wool; even richer Castilians preferred imported cloth. Further bedeviling Anglo-Castilian relations, Margaret of Anjou, wife of the deposed Henry VI of England, tried in the 1460s to rally support from Enrique IV (as the grandson of Henry's aunt Catalina of

Lancaster). In 1462 a false alarm of an imminent Franco-Castilian attack disconcerted the English, and Edward IV sought acceptance from foreign powers in exchange for trading concessions. He granted trading privileges to the German Hanseatic League in exchange for naval aid in the English Channel, exempting Hanseatic merchants from duties on the export of English goods. Hanseatic merchants for a time became a prominent presence in London. Burgundian merchants, too, were given trading concessions in the North Sea area. Edward also came to an understanding with Castile. In 1466 he exempted Castilian merchants from paying duties on the export of English goods, stimulating the start of a significant Castilian participation in trade with England. A treaty was signed between the two kingdoms in 1467, but two years later Enrique IV moved back to a pro-French policy in 1469.

Steps toward the Overseas Competition of Early Modern Times

As we have noted, Portugal had long lived in fear of domination from Castile. Its alliance with England and its trade with the Lowlands and England had helped Portugal to maintain its independence. The Wars of the Roses had toppled the house of Lancaster along with its close dynastic link with Portugal, which the houses of York and Tudor had not renewed. The attempt of Portuguese King Afonso V, the African, to conquer Castile in the name of his expected bride Juana la Beltraneja failed at the battle of Toro in 1475. Portugal was now encouraged to cooperate with Spain by the formation of new ties between Spain and England. In 1475 England agreed to pay Castile a considerable amount of compensation for the damage done its ships by English pirates. From 1475 Edward IV seems to have been patrolling English waters with small squadrons, keeping them safer for merchant vessels. Afonso V's first reaction was to break the longstanding Portuguese treaty with England in favor of a Franco-Portuguese alliance. However, the combined economic strength of England and Castile was too powerful for Portugal to defy for long, and Edward IV renewed the traditional English alliance with Portugal in 1482.

The Anglo-Castilian accord prevailing after 1475 allowed Isabel la Católica and Henry VII to turn their attention in the 1490s to supporting exploration across the Atlantic Ocean. The Castilian economy at the end of the Middle Ages was dangerously weakened by the Spanish Inquisition's attack on its middle class. Castile would surely have faded from great power status, despite its unification with Aragon into the new kingdom of Spain, had not the wealth of the New World strengthened its coffers at this point. Spain used its geographic proximity to Portugal and its superior military power to elbow in on the bonanza that smaller but healthier Portugal was creating through its explorations and colonies in the Atlantic. Isabel and Fernando's hope of using England in its struggle against France brought on Spain's last major interaction with England in the Middle Ages, but the resulting shift of English ties from Portugal to Spain was a significant side effect. Isabel offered three main incentives to Henry VII. First, Castilian recognition of Henry's right to be king offered considerable prestige. As a usurper king, Henry needed to solidify his dynasty by winning recognition from the major powers. England's northern mercantile rivals were lending aid to overthrow Henry, the Hanseatic League supporting Lambert Simnel in 1487 and Burgundy backing Perkin Warbek in 1496. In the face of these rebellions, Henry was trying to bolster his status in any way possible. He tried to compensate for his weak position in the English royal clan by insisting on a claim that he was a descendant of Welsh royalty. To underline this dubious identity, he named his eldest son Arthur, after the fabled Celtic king, and arranged for the boy to be born at Winchester, the city supposedly built by King Arthur.

Secondly, Isabel satisfied the long-standing English eagerness for increased participation in Castilian trade. Despite the long-standing rivalry between Castilians and Englishmen for the Atlantic hauling business, the exchange of Castilian raw materials for English manufactured products was increasingly lively. Henry was giving major attention to supporting England's position on the seas, using diplomacy to expand English markets abroad. His Navigation Acts gave a boost to English shipping. In March 1489 England and Spain signed the Treaty of Medina del Campo, which conceded considerable trading advantages to the English. Customs duties on both sides were set at the rates of 1459, ending the favorable rates won by the Castilians from Edward IV. The Castilians balanced this loss in part by their own navigation act of 1494, which prohibited the use of foreign ships for the export of Spanish goods when Spanish ships were available.

A third inducement was added when Castile entered into a marriage alliance with the Habsburg rulers of the Lowlands, as it was important for Henry VII to assure the continuation of England's vital trade link with

Flanders. Isabel won an alliance with the duke of Burgundy, ruler of the Lowlands, by offering diplomatic support against France. In 1496 Isabel's daughter Juana, later to be dubbed *la Loca* (the mad), was wed to the young duke of Burgundy, Philip el Hermoso (the handsome), followed the next year by the marriage of Isabel's son Juan to Philip's sister Margaret. The new Anglo-Spanish trade understanding was sealed by a marriage alliance between Spain and England. In 1501 Isabel and Fernando's youngest daughter, Catherine of Aragon, was married to Henry VII's son Arthur, Prince of Wales. Arthur died soon after, and the troubled reign of Juana la Loca that followed Isabel's death complicated arrangements for a new marriage for Catherine. However, in 1509 Arthur's brother, the new king Henry VIII, picked up the bride and the alliance. Thus, the country that had provided Portugal its main support since the battle of Aljubarrota in 1385 drifted away from that commitment. Although Henry VII renewed the Anglo-Portuguese alliance in 1489 and again in 1499, the special relationship was compromised and would not be restored until the mid-seventeenth century.

At the same time, Isabel drew Portugal closer to her own sphere of influence by continuing the traditional marriage alliances between the Castilian and Portuguese royal families. In 1496 the Portuguese King Manoel the Fortunate obliged Isabel by expelling the Jews from Portugal in preparation for his marriage to Queen Isabel's eldest daughter Isabel in 1497. When she died the next year, Manoel wed her sister María and after María's death married Isabel's and María's niece Leonor. The main reward from these alliances would not be attained until later. In the reign of Isabel's grandson Charles I (of Spain, also Holy Roman Emperor Charles V), Portugal would begin to allow an overmighty Spain to dominate its policy. Then, in 1580, the ongoing intermarriage between the Spanish and Portuguese houses would lead to the succession of King Philip II of Spain to the throne of the Portuguese Empire as well.

The new allies Castile and England made parallel moves at almost the same time to establish their positions on the world seas. First, Isabel, while renouncing Castilian navigation rights south of the Canary Islands in return for Portuguese recognition in 1479, at the same time brought Portugal to abandon its claims to the Canaries, Castile's subsequent point of departure for exploration to the west. She then made use of the services of a renegade navigator with a marginal share in Portuguese maritime secrets, Cristóbal Colón (Christopher Columbus). Perhaps a Genoese of

Catalan extraction (since he wrote letters in Catalan), Colón had entered the circle of Portuguese navigators by marrying the daughter of one of them. He had wanted to persuade the Portuguese to reach India by sailing west but had been rebuffed by João II. Lacking a formal education, Colón had found it difficult to distinguish between reliable and unreliable sources. All educated people throughout the Middle Ages had realized that the world was round; Adelard of Bath had remeasured its circumference in the twelfth century with reasonable accuracy. It was Washington Irving who invented the story that Colón had to fight against a general conviction that the Earth is flat. Colón also argued that the Earth is two-thirds the size it really is, but João had been warned by his navigators not to buy the argument.

Isabel herself was skeptical. However, she wanted to cut in on the Portuguese success overseas and therefore gave Colón minimal backing in 1492. Colón was lucky enough to discover gold in Hispaniola, and he never stated that the land to which he had sailed was not Asia. A Spanish colony grew up on that island, and Spanish exploration of the Caribbean continued. Isabel and Fernando induced the Spanish Pope Alessandro VI in 1493 to mediate a division of the globe into two spheres of colonization rights between Spain and Portugal, in return for making Alessandro's son Juan the duke of Gandía. Spain was granted the area west of a line one hundred leagues west of the Azores and Cape Verde Islands. The Portuguese felt too weak to contest this decision and in 1494 contented themselves with arranging the Treaty of Tordesillas, which shifted the Line of Demarcation 270 leagues farther west and thus brought Brazil into the Portuguese sphere.

Henry VII, unintimidated by the Treaty of Tordesillas, was quick to establish England's own claims across the Atlantic. On his authorization John Cabot sailed west from Bristol in 1497, in a ship called the *Matthew*. A counterpart to Cristóbal Colón, and perhaps his exact age, Cabot may also have been born in Genoa. In 1476 he had become a Venetian citizen but in the early 1480s had moved to Bristol. He, too, received support from wealthy backers for his scheme to reach India by sailing west. As Colón did for Spain, Cabot gave England its first claim to American territory. His probe along the coasts of Labrador, Newfoundland, and New England brought him a pension from Henry and in 1498 a larger expedition of four or five ships, one personally equipped by Henry. On that second voyage, he explored farther south, perhaps as far as Chesapeake Bay. Like Colón,

Cabot had a son who followed his father's footsteps to the New World, Sebastian Cabot, a cartographer who received patronage from Henry VII. In 1508 Sebastian led an expedition that pushed farther north along the coast of North America, going perhaps as far as Hudson's Bay.

Henry VII's Plan to Intervene in Castile

There was one final scheme for English intervention in Castile, which (like that of William the Conqueror four centuries earlier) never advanced beyond the planning stage. After the death of Philip I of Castile in September 1506, Henry VII entertained the notion of marrying his widow, Queen Juana la Loca. He knew her personally from a visit she had made to England and seemed to like her. Henry's suit was encouraged by Catherine of Aragon, who wrote praising him to Juana, her sister. However, Juana's confinement at Tordesillas for mental incompetence frustrated Henry's plans to become her consort. By blocking the traditional Anglo-Portuguese alliance with an Anglo-Spanish entente, Isabel's policy guaranteed that England would not link up with Portugal to block Castilian pursuit of transatlantic trade and colonies. As a result, England would not surpass Spain's position on the high seas until the Anglo-Portuguese treaty sealed by the marriage of Charles II and Catherine of Braganza in 1662.

Thus, the medieval wars between the English and the Castilians planted the first seeds of mutual hostility and negative stereotypes. A mood of Hispanic-Anglo confrontation is at least faintly reflected in the *Amadís de Gaula,* one of the Castilian *novelas de caballería,* which came into vogue in Castile in the late Middle Ages and reached their height of popularity in the sixteenth century. *Amadís* was given its present form at the end of the fifteenth century, an edition of 1508 being the oldest to have survived. However, it was already extant in some form in the fourteenth century, as is shown by references in López de Ayala's *Rimado de palacio,* the *Cancionero de Baena,* and other works of that century. Amadís is a military hero during an unspecified ancient time fighting for an alliance system—composed of Spain, France, Scotland, and Ireland—pitted against England and the Roman Empire, which was the actual alliance system of the late fourteenth century involving the German-based Holy Roman Empire. However, the story concludes on a tone of reconciliation, with Amadís defending the British King Lisuarte.

The English view of Hispanics was more insistently disapproving. In a poem by Laurence Minot, written to celebrate the English naval victory of Winchelsea, the Spaniards are described as haughty and arrogant robbers. John of Gaunt developed a jaundiced view of Castile, shaped by his distaste for the sadism of Pedro the Cruel, his contempt for Enrique de Trastamara, and his unhappy marriage of convenience with the self-important but unimpressive Constanza of Castile. John Chandos's panegyric on the Black Prince was similarly critical of the Castilians. A Christianized Spanish Muslim character in the romance *Duke Rowland and Sir Otuel of Spayne,* written around 1390, is presented as a brave gentleman, but also as arrogant, aggressive, and mocking. In *The Canterbury Tales,* Geoffrey Chaucer puts in the mouth of the Monk a condemnation of the treachery of Enrique de Trastamara in murdering his brother, "noble . . . worthy Petro, glorie of Spayne." In the same work, in a passage accepted as having foreign policy implications, the Pardoner warns against the excessive strength of the sweet wines of Spain (Lepe being a town on the coast of Huelva):

> Now kepe yow fro the white and fro the rede,
> And namely fro the white wine of Lepe,
> That is to selle in Fysshstrete or in Chepe.
> This wyn of Spaigne crepeth subtilly
> In othere wynes, growynge faste by,
> Of which ther ryseth swich fumositee
> That whan a man hath dronken draughtes thre,
> And weneth that he be at hoom in Chepe,
> He is in Spaigne, right at the toune of Lepe. . . .

The loss of Gascony in 1453 as a result of a Castilian naval blockade set loose a wave of national shame and dejection in England. Anti-Castilian sentiments were rife in the 1450s and 1460s, when the earl of Warwick's attacks on Spanish shipping from Calais met with a mood of celebration from the English. In Thomas Malory's *Morte d'Arthur,* written by 1471, Spain is belittled and Spaniards are presented in a negative light. In the episode where King Arthur fights and kills Lucius and takes his place as Roman Emperor, Lucius is aided by troops of most of the Mediterranean countries, including Egypt, Syria, Turkey, Cyprus, Greece, and Cataluña, but Spain is made to seem merely a province of Portugal, whose king brings along many thousands of Spaniards as part of his army. In another story, Spain is mentioned in a sinister connection. Sir Urry, the "good knyght" from Hungary, at a tournament in Spain kills Sir Alpheus (i.e., Alfonso), son of a Spanish earl. Alpheus's mother is presented as a "grete sorseras" who works "her suttyle craufftis" so that Sir Urry's seven wounds from the tournament cannot heal but continue to bleed and fester. Urry's mother brings him in a horse litter to England, where at King Arthur's court on Pentecost he is healed after a prayer request for him by Sir Launcelot.

Clearly, the history of the Hispanic and Anglo relationship in the Middle Ages, tension-ridden since the days of William the Conqueror and Alfonso VI, shows that hostilities and concomitant prejudices did not begin with the Protestant Reformation and the Black Legend.

Results for Mexican-American Society

We still speak of "building castles in Spain" when referring to a farfetched undertaking, in a vague evocation of those distant attempts of the Black Prince and his brother John of Gaunt to dominate Castile. This undertaking raised specters of Anglo domination of Spanish-speakers out of which Hispanic resentment against Anglo exploitation began to take shape. The Treaty of Libourne in 1366 prefigured a long line of similar Anglo plans for developments in the Hispanic world, from the Treaty of Utrecht and its *asiento* through the machinations of Joel Poinsett, John Slidell, and Henry Lane Wilson in Mexico to NAFTA.

Despite many instances of amicable mixing and intermarriage of Anglos and Hispanics in the Borderlands from the very first, a countertradition of mutual antagonism long dogged their relations. A Borderlands Anglo tradition of violence can be traced back in part to hostilities on the English border with Scotland. The Anglo-Scottish warfare begun by Edward I's conquest of Scotland and by Robert Bruce's successful independence movement continued to rage through the rest of the Middle Ages, as Scotland joined France, Castile, and Irish rebels in an on-going challenge to England. This endemic fighting kept the border between England and Scotland insecure, allowing local clans to carry out devastating raids in the name of the feuding Scottish and English kings. The resulting instability created an English-Scottish border society whose traits, it has been argued, later helped to shape some of the characteristics of Mexican-

American border culture. Emigrants from the Anglo-Scottish border, along with their fellow Anglo-Scots who had settled in Northern Ireland in the seventeenth century, poured into the Appalachian region from 1718 to 1775. From there they spread on to Texas, New Mexico, Arizona, and Southern California, starting in the period when these regions were still under Mexican sovereignty. These English-speaking settlers brought with them their pugilistic society, which added to Mexican-American border violence and exacerbated Anglo-Hispanic relations in the late nineteenth and early twentieth centuries.

To some Mexicans these new Anglo arrivals were "arrogant, overbearing, aggressive, conniving, rude, unreliable and dishonest."[1] While some Mexican American terms to describe Anglos are innocuous, others reflect disapproval. *Gringo* is said to come from the first two words of the song "Green grow the rushes, O!" popular with the American soldiers who marched through Mexico in the Mexican War. *Gademe* and *sanavabiche* probably come from the excessive use of the vulgarities *God damn* and *son of a bitch* by the American soldiers in the same war. Some of the names are physical descriptions. *Güero* means fair-skinned, *colorado* red-skinned, *cristalino* no color, *ojos de gato* cat-eyed (that is light-colored), and *patón* big-footed. Some terms refer to diet. *Repollero* refers to a cabbage-eater, related to the term *Kraut* to describe a German or German-American. *Bolillo* is a hard French white bread, a term first applied to the French soldiers who invaded Mexico in the 1860s and also evoked white skin. *Jamonero* means a ham-eater. Some of the names used are more obscure in origin, including *gavacho,* first used by urban Mexican-Americans in Los Angeles. Hostile terms for Anglos include *godo* (signifying a barbarian), *cara de pan crudo* (meaning a face of unbaked bread), and *cucaracha* (cockroach).

Some of the Anglos for their part were influenced by Hispanophobic and anti-Catholic traditions, viewing Mexicans as "lazy, shiftless, jealous, cowardly, bigoted, superstitious, backward, and immoral."[2] The nineteenth century Anglo writing about the border (usually after only a brief experience with the region) conveys a feeling of moralistic, physical, and intellectual superiority over Mexican American "greasers" and "yellow bellies." At the same time they idealize *hacendados* or romanticize beautiful *señoritas* who seem out of place with their often cowardly, degenerate male counterparts.

In the mid-1800s, Anglo-Mexican relations were adversely affected by the Texas Revolution and the U.S.-Mexican War. In January 1847 a force led by Pablo Montoya, a Mexican peasant, and Tomasito Romero, a Pueblo Indian, killed Governor Charles Bent and five other Americans in Taos. Padre Antonio Jose Martínez was also rumored to have been an instigator of this rebellion. In the repression approximately 150 Mexicans were killed, and fifteen rebel survivors were sentenced to death. California's Bear Flag Revolt and the American occupation of California also included incidents of ethnic conflict and violence. Bear Flag supporters stole livestock, looted homes, and in some cases injured and murdered innocent Mexicans and Indians. Mexican resistance soon emerged. In Los Angeles, José María Flores briefly led guerrillas against the occupation forces, while Andrés Pico confronted Col. Stephen Kearny's troops near San Diego.

In the early years of American sovereignty, while some Anglo men married into prominent Mexican families, acquiring land, political clout, and esteem, other Anglos felt that former Mexican citizens, though now Americans, were still "Mexican" and of a lower social status. Local bosses or "patrons" influenced Mexican voters to vote for Anglo candidates, providing beer and food at preelection rallies or *pachangas*. American control was supported by law enforcement agencies such as the Texas Rangers or *rinches*. Although Anglos thought that the Rangers were heroically maintaining law and order, Mexican Americans considered the *rinches* cruel and unfair, killing unarmed Mexican laborers whom they accused of being horse thieves, and falsifying reports to Austin about confrontations with Mexican bandits.

As incidents of oppression of the Mexican population multiplied, bandit heroes appeared who championed both personal causes and those of the oppressed Mexican. Such was Juan Nepomucena Cortina. To the majority of Anglos, Cortina was the Red Robber of the Rio Grande, while among Mexicans and Mexican-Americans he was their protector against Anglo injustice. He had fought on the Mexican side in the U.S.-Mexican War at the battles of Palo Alto and Resaca de la Palma. Between the late 1850s and the mid-1870s, the so-called Cortina Wars resulted in the deaths of both Anglo and Mexican Texans. Cortina resented the judicial, political, and property changes that the Anglo newcomers had brought, and when he shot a Brownsville town marshal that he found pistol-whipping a drunken Mexican ranch hand, he became an outlaw. In September 1859 Cortina returned to Brownsville with about fifty followers, raising the Mexican flag but killing five people in the process, three Anglos and two

Hispanics. He later waged battles against a local militia, the Texas Rangers, and federal troops led by Robert E. Lee in February 1860. Cortina's activities and alleged activities were used as a pretext for ethnic violence by both Anglo and Mexican-Texans, with a resulting loss of life and property.

Joaquin Murieta of California is probably the best known bandit hero of the nineteenth century. He was a Mexican miner from Sonora who—after some Anglos stole his mining claim, lynched his brother, raped his wife, and whipped him—became a legendary highway man. Accused of many crimes in Calaveras County in 1852 and 1853, he was one of five "Joaquins" for whom one-thousand-dollar rewards were posted. In 1853 rangers displayed a head, preserved in a jar of whiskey, they claimed to be that of Murieta. That "proof" and most of the information about his life, however, is still disputed. The *"Corrido de Joaquín Murieta"* praises him in stanzas beginning, "Señores, soy mexicano . . . "

> Gentlemen, I am a Mexican,
> but I understand the English speech;
> Backwards and forwards I learned to read it
> from my brother, who took out time to teach.
> And I make any American
> lie in fear and trembling at my feet.

After being involved in the killing of a constable in 1852, Tiburcio Vasquez of California became a fugitive and a bandit popular among the poor. He was quoted saying that with 60, 000 dollars he could raise enough men and wagons to lead a revolt in Southern California. In the 1870s his real and alleged crimes were sensationalized in local newspapers. In 1871 he and his followers robbed a Visalia stagecoach, and in 1873 they robbed a store in Tres Pinos. Captured after avoiding arrest for over two decades, he pled that he had merely been avenging Anglo injustices committed against Hispanics. Nonetheless, he was found guilty of murder by an all-Anglo jury and was hanged in San Jose in 1875. His execution led to further violence when two of the Anglos who had captured him were killed by a Mexican named Romo, who was himself captured and lynched.

Ethnic violence continued in the Borderlands for decades after the U.S.-Mexican War. The California gold rush of 1849 dramatically affected Anglo-Hispanic relations. As competition and conflicts surfaced over mine claims and mining codes, incidents of abuse, vigilantism, and violence against Mexican immigrants became commonplace. One of the most documented incidents of California vigilantism occurred at Downiesville in 1851 and ended with the hanging of a pregnant woman named Josefa who had killed a drunken Anglo miner after he had broken into her shack and threatened her and a male friend. The Cart War of 1857 pitted Anglo-Texan freight workers against *Tejano* ox-cart *arrieros*. Some Anglos initiated a campaign to force the *Tejano arrieros,* or muleskinners, out of business, forming bands that preyed on the *Tejano* freight trains, stealing or destroying the merchandise and the ox-carts, and killing some of the *arrieros*. Federal troops were finally sent to protect the victims and to end the attacks. In 1875, violence erupted in Colfax County, New Mexico, when constable Cruz Vega was accused of murdering Rev. T. J. Tolby and lynched by vigilantes. In 1877 a confrontation between Anglos and Mexicans erupted near El Paso over control of the local salt lakes that for years had been considered communal property by the Mexican American residents. Samuel Maverick claimed a large portion of the salt beds, but Hispanics continued to use the rest of the unclaimed salt beds. In 1877 Anglo politician Charles Howard asserted his right to the area not claimed by Maverick and served notice that fees would be levied for taking salt from his property. When Howard had two Mexicans arrested for allegedly taking salt illegally, tensions turned to violence. After Howard was forced to renounce his claim, he shot Louis Cardis, a former political opponent who had supported the Mexican attempts to use the salt beds. Howard and several other Anglos were then killed by a mob of enraged *Mexicanos* who had been Cardis's followers. The lawlessness that ensued included destruction of property, looting, and lynchings. Peace was finally restored when the U.S. government sent federal investigators and in 1878 stationed troops at Fort Bliss.

The cattle boom of the 1870s and 1880s and the subsequent creation of large cattle ranches forced many small ranchers, especially Mexican Americans, out of the ranching business. On the surviving, Anglo-owned ranches, Hispanic and Anglo ranch hands usually ate in separate facilities, while most ranch foremen were Anglos. Anglo farmers coming to Texas from other southern states with plans to make profits from the expanding cotton market hired mainly Mexican migrant workers, further increasing resentment. Prejudices, hostilities, and violence continued into the twentieth century. In June 1902 Sheriff W. T. Morris and some deputies rode to the Karnes County, Texas, farm of Gregorio Cortez to inquire about some stolen horses. After a verbal altercation, the sheriff shot and wounded Gregorio's brother Romaldo, and Gregorio Cortez shot and killed Morris. Cortez fled to the Robledo Ranch in Belmont, Texas, about fifty-five miles away. When a posse led by Robert Glover arrived at the ranch, shots were exchanged, and Cortez killed Glover. Cortez once again escaped but was captured later that month. Although he was twice acquitted of the murder of Sheriff Morris, he was found guilty of murdering Glover and sentenced to life imprisonment. Nonetheless, in 1913 he was pardoned by Governor O. B. Colquitt.

The Mexican Revolution of 1910 led to renewed conflicts along the border and to Anglo-American sentiment against Mexicans and Mexican Americans. When the push of the Mexican Revolution and the pull of expanding American industry and commercial agriculture caused a dramatic increase in Mexican immigration to the United States, nativist sentiment against the new immigrants swelled. In 1912 the Mexican ambassador protested the lynchings, murders, and general mistreatment of Mexicans in Texas and California. In 1915 the controversial *Plan de San Diego,* which urged revolution against Anglo tyranny—for the founding of a new country from the territories lost by Mexico in the U.S.-Mexican War—and the execution of all white males over sixteen, led to violence in south Texas. Transportation lines were disrupted, ranch and farm properties were damaged, and innocent people lost their lives as a result of guerrilla attacks launched by supporters of the plan. Texas Rangers and federal troops were sent to restore order but not before lynching and vigilante activities had cost lives and visited terror on both the Anglo and Mexican communities. In 1916 Pancho Villa's raids on Columbus, New Mexico, and Santa Ysabel, Chihuahua, cost dozens of American lives and led to an international crisis. Subsequently, the Pershing Expedition was sent into Mexico to capture Villa, and over 100,000 members of the National Guard were sent to patrol the border.

During the 1930s labor unrest and repatriation of Mexican workers added to ethnic tensions. Mexican and Mexican American farm workers participated in strikes in the Imperial Valley, in the Santa Clara Valley and other agricultural areas throughout California. Owners relied on police powers, massive and indiscriminate arrests, excessive bails, deportations, expensive litigations, vigilante actions, and other forms of intimidation to destroy unions. As unemployment and welfare rolls increased during the Great Depression, so did anti-Mexican sentiment. Between one-fourth and one-half million Mexicans were repatriated, voluntarily and involuntarily.

During World War II, Anglo-Hispanic hostilities again erupted in Los Angeles during the Zoot-Suit race riots of June 1943. After eleven sailors had allegedly been attacked by a gang of Mexican American boys in a predominantly Mexican neighborhood, the police and two hundred sailors began a so-called "clean-up" campaign in East Los Angeles, targeting anyone wearing the broad-shouldered, oversized zoot-suit "drapes." Only nine sailors were arrested, and no charges were filed. The Los Angeles newspaper coverage virtually condemned the victims, implying that the zoot suiters would respond with violence. Sailors, joined by marines and soldiers, ordered zoot suiters to remove their clothes and in some cases stripped and beat them. The police could never find the culprits but did arrest many of the victims.

Between one-third and one-half million Mexican Americans served in the armed forces in World War II, many of whom were killed or wounded. Five *Tejano* soldiers received the Congressional Medal of Honor, and Mexican Americans developed a strong pride in being American citizens. All the same, the segregated facilities that they had known before the war continued, especially in Texas. Sergeant Macario García was refused service at a cafe in Sugarland, Texas, because he was Mexican American. When he refused to leave, a fight ensued with the owner. When the authorities arrived to restore order, those involved were told to forget the incident. Later García was arrested on assault charges. In the Rio Grande Valley, Sergeant Jose M. López was denied service at a restaurant because he was of Mexican descent. The director of the only funeral home in Three Rivers, Texas, refused to provide services for Félix Longoria, a Mexican American soldier killed during the war. The refusal gained national attention when the G.I. Forum protested. Senator Lyndon B. Johnson later arranged for Longoria's body to be buried at Arlington National Cemetery.

In the 1960s the Chicano movement brought a major upswing of political activism among Mexican Americans. Jose Angel Gutierrez was at the forefront of this movement in Texas, organizing MAYO, the Mexican American Youth Organization in 1967. MAYO attempted to publicize problems of segregated and inferior schools, harassment from law enforcement authorities, and employment issues. In November 1969 hostilities erupted in Crystal City, Texas. Although the great majority of the student population in Crystal City schools was Mexican American, many were excluded from extracurricular activities. When the school board refused to discuss this and other student grievances related to language and culture, Gutierrez, parents, and students organized a boycott of classes involving 1,700 students. Citizens managed to elect Mexican American school board members and city councilmen. From this group action emerged the Raza Unida Party, also founded by Gutierrez. Party candidates were elected at the local and county level. At the same time in northern New Mexico, Reies Lopez Tijerina attacked Anglo usurpation of lands, insisting that they be returned to their rightful owners. In 1963 Tijerina organized the *Alianza federal de mercedes* (the Federal Alliance of Land Grants) to recover the lands. The activities of their secessionists movement led to military confrontations with state authorities in the town of Tierra Amarilla and at Kit Carson National Park. Although Tijerina antagonized both the Hispanic and Anglo establishment in New Mexico, he brought national attention to the unresolved issues of the Treaty of Guadalupe Hidalgo.

Since the 1960s, Mexican Americans have moved into many positions of prominence in the Borderlands. Examples include labor leaders like Cesar Chavez, U.S. senators like Joe Montoya of New Mexico, U.S. representatives like Henry B. Gonzalez of Texas, governors like Tony Anaya of New Mexico, mayors like Henry Cisneros of San Antonio, folklorists like Dr. Américo Paredes, authors like Dr. Rolando Hinojosa-Smith of the University of Texas at Austin, university presidents like Dr. Juliet García of the University of Texas at Brownsville, singer-composers like Selena, movie actors like James Edward Olmos, and businessmen like Laredo's Tony Sanchez of the International Bank of Commerce. Sociologically, we can see the same coming of age in the many intermarriages between Hispanics and Anglos.

As a better modus vivendi has been established between Borderlands Hispanics and Anglos, an evolution from inherited prejudice to mutual appreciation has occurred. This progression can be traced in the literature of the Borderlands. In the nineteenth century, Mexican Americans and Anglo-Americans described each other in a negative light. The nineteenth-century *corridos* spread a jaundiced view of Anglo-Americans. In "El Corrido de Kiansis," about Texas *vaqueros* on cattle drives, Anglos are incompetent, unable to master a herd of steers requiring only ten Mexicans to control. In a *corrido* about Joaquín Murieta, Anglos are murderous and cowardly, trembling with fear before the Mexican American hero, whose wife and parents have been killed by them.

Anglo-Americans returned the insults, but not uniformly. On the one hand, Richard Henry Dana, who sailed to California in the early 1830s, believed that California Hispanics were cruel and violent. George Wilkins Kendall, who traveled in New Mexico in the 1840s, pitied the local Hispanics because he found them to be technologically backward and ineffective. Thomas Jefferson Farnham described Californians as an "imbecile, pusillanimous race of men and unfit to control the destinies of that beautiful country." James Ohio Pattie wrote in his narrative that the Mexicans were cowardly. James Audubon in his *Western Journals* described the Mexicans as thieves and expressed his hatred of "all things Mexican." W. T. Pritchard, who wrote "In the Backwoods of Mexico," an article in *The Overland Monthly,* argued that Mexicans were morally deficient. Sam Hall, a popular dime novelist, described the Hispanic inhabitants of the Rio Grande as the "most lawless, cowardly, and cruelest men on the American continent, assassins by trade, bandits by nature." Texas romance writers Samuel Hammett and Jeremiah Clemens were equally derogatory. At the turn of the century, literary Darwinists O. Henry and Stephen Crane described the Mexican as a cowardly, witless scoundrel. On the other hand, Walter Colton, a Congregational minister who became mayor of Monterey in 1847, described the California Mexicans not as decadent but as carefree and romantic and as yet unaffected by American materialism and corruption. Also, Brete Harte in the late nineteenth century depicted the Californios as brave and elegant, though unable to adapt to American technological ingenuity.

Such expressions of admiration for Mexican Americans on the part of Anglo-American authors have become frequent in twentieth-century literature. Post—Word War I disenchantment with American culture among American writers translated to portrayals of the Mexican as uncomplicated and uncontaminated by American materialism. Willa Cather and Katherine Anne Porter were examples of such writers, with Cather's *Death Comes to the Archbishop* becoming a model for many of the works of that era. In the next generation, John Steinbeck's Mexican characters evolve from the simple Danny in *Tortilla Flat*to the dignified and courageous Juan Chicay in *The Wayward Bus*. John Rollins Ridge in *The Life and Adventures of Joaquin Murieta,* described Murieta as intelligent, courageous, witty, and proud.

Literary characterizations of Anglos by Mexican American writers have also grown more positive, though less consistently so because of wounds left by the not-so-distant days of frequent Anglo exploitation of Hispanics. Negative depictions of Anglos include Gloria Anzaldua's description of "white" culture as ignorant, Américo Paredes's mention of "damn gringos" and their "dam [*sic*] gringo lingo," and Rolando Hinojosa's line referring to Anglos as illogical. In contrast, Saline R. Ulibarri's 1970s short story "El Relleno de Dios" (the stuffing of the lord) portrays the Anglo priest Father Benito as bringing happiness and harmony with him even though he mangles Spanish, pronouncing *reino* (kingdom) like *relleno* (stuffing). Benito's humor and kindness fill the church for every mass, and many members of his congregation weep when he is reassigned to another parish. Rodolfo Anaya's poem "Walt Whitman Strides the Llano of New Mexico" describes this transcendentalistically inclined poet as a wise old grandfather, capable of leaping between continents. Whitman's book *Leaves of Grass* is compared to a folk-healer's herbs, teaching Chicanos how to see beauty and how to choose the right words to describe it.

Concluding Remark

These two cousins, Hispanic and Anglo societies of early Europe, entered the modern period with much in common but already embroiled in conflict. When Hispanics and Anglos later met in the Borderlands, this conflict had escalated through centuries of intervening complications to the point that awareness of their many similarities and common roots were lost in the dreadful mix of contempt and ignorance. The cousins did not know that they were cousins. Runaway hatred on a national and international scale, exemplified in such countries as India, Nazi Germany, and Cambodia can destroy the best of societies. Not even the easy-going and sensible Borderlands is immune from the damage that can result from overemphasizing past wrongs and nourishing resentments. Nonetheless, thanks to enduring affinities, such antagonisms have not prevented the gradual harmonizing of heritages in the Mexican-American Borderlands.

CONCLUSION

As this study has shown, many of the foundations for the interaction of Hispanic and Anglo societies were laid by the year 1500. The Basque, Berber, Celtic, Roman, Germanic, and French contributions to the blood, history, customs, and names of both societies provided similarities and a mutuality that have facilitated their merger in the Borderlands, while the Semitic stamp on Hispanic culture has given it much of its distinctive attraction. Political and judicial liberties are enjoyed in the Borderlands today thanks to efforts in both medieval Castile and England, although the Hispanic approach has placed more emphasis on order while Anglo concerns have leaned toward individual rights. The intense clash between the upper class and the commoners in the late Middle Ages has left Hispanics with a heritage of aristocratic values such as machismo, a concern with family, and a love of display, while the same tensions gave Anglos such middle-class inclinations as a strong work ethic and a commitment to promptness and reliability. The choice of diverse paths of religious expression before 1500 molded two forms of piety (the Hispanic more concerned with compassion and respect for authority and the Anglo more devoted to Bible study), creating a duality that has enriched Borderlands worship. From science and learning through literature and music to art and architecture, medieval culture has defined many elements of Borderlands creativity. While the hostilities and negative stereotypes generated by Hispanic-Anglo warfare of the Middle Ages passed on prejudices and problems still not entirely overcome, a realization of the interlinked past can draw Hispanic and Anglo subcultures in the Borderlands together.

To anyone unacquainted with the intertwined historical roots of Spain and England, the many close parallels between medieval Castile and England must seem curious. The other major societies of medieval western Europe—French, German, and Italian—did not share many of the nation-forming experiences of Castilians and Englishmen. While the Basque and Iberian peoples who shaped early Spain and Britain also influenced France, they are absent from the German and Italian record. Nor were France, Germany, and Italy in comparable danger of succumbing to foreign conquest in the eighth through eleventh centuries. Nothing in the High Middle Ages similar to the large-scale movement of French peoples into Spanish and English territory occurred in Germany. France and Italy were not yet experiencing a movement of national unification in the ninth century as were Spain and England. Neither the French nor Germans were subjected to foreign rule in the early eleventh century as were the Spanish and the English. Neither Germany nor Italy shared Spain and England's creation of a modern state in the High and Late Middle Ages. The Anglo-Hispanic blend creating the Mexican-American Borderlands is thus not a randomly coincidental combination of any two European cultures, but rather a merger of two strongly linked cultures with a closely parallel historical experience. A deeper awareness of this dual Anglo-Hispanic, or Hispanglic, heritage reaching back through so many centuries can only be a positive step for Borderlands society. Borderlands cities might even highlight their bicultural European proto-history by choosing two official foreign sister cities each, one in Spain and one in England. Centrally located El Paso might find its best counterparts in Madrid and Oxford; pleasure-oriented Los Angeles could be paired with Seville and Bath; and traditionalist San Antonio might be matched with Santander and York.

Having completed this survey of the Anglo and Hispanic medieval heritage, we will conclude with a brief but instructive examination of the early maritime impulses that would eventually bring these influences to the Mexican-American Borderlands. A consideration of the urge to navigate the Atlantic Ocean will serve to focus the story one last time on the generating origins of Borderlands culture.

Even though most Borderlanders do not live close to the sea, their very existence as a bilingual society has resulted from the naval orientation of early Castilians and Englishmen. This early taking to the sea is understandable as both the Iberian Peninsula and the British Isles are surrounded by water and have many good ports. As Europe's western-most projections they invited adventurers to sail west.

Many English words having to do with the sea offer evidence of early

English maritime interest. A few of the many Anglo-Saxon words relating to the sea are *sea* itself, *afloat, boat, fleet, gangway* (once an Anglo-Saxon word for a road) *mast, neap, oar, sail, ship, steer, strand, and fore* and *aft. Starboard* for the right side of the ship (as opposed to *port* for the left) comes from *steer board,* referring to the steering paddle used to guide a ship before the invention of the rudder in the course of the Middle Ages. Since the steer board was always attached on the right side of a ship, the ship was obliged to tie to a dock from its left side, which thus became the port side. The Vikings who settled in England at the end of the Dark Ages added their own maritime vocabulary to English, including the words *billow,* (homeward) *bound* (meaning headed and having nothing to do with the Anglo-Saxon word *to bind*), *keel, raft, stern, tug, wake,* and *windlass.* The wake of a ship originally referred to the breaking up of the ice in a frozen body of water. The English language is studded with sea-based idioms and sayings. A short list of these includes to be *all in the same boat, at sea, in ship shape, in the wake of, left stranded, out of one's depth, over one's head, taken aback* (originally referring to square sails suddenly pressed by a head wind against the mast); *clear the decks, clutch at straws, desert a sinking ship, a lump sum* (originally used in nautical vocabulary), *on the rocks, smooth sailing, have a ship come in, head above water, launch into, make a splash, pour oil on troubled waters, ride out a storm, on the brink, show one's true colors, sink or swim, steer clear of, stem the tide, swim against the current, take the helm, take the wind out of someone's sails, tide yourself over, turn adrift,* and *touch bottom.* The saying "still waters run deep" is another example. Many phrases hearken back to fishing in particular, including *a big fish in a little pond, a fish out of water, a pretty barrel of fish, a red herring, as slippery as an eel, drink like a fish, fish for compliments, fish in troubled waters, other fish to fry,* and *jump at the bait.*

Ancient voyages are commemorated in art and legend. A temple near Cádiz built in the eighth century B.C. honored Melkart, Phoenician protector of sea travelers, and depicted his deeds. A Roman source (Pomponius Mela) tells how Albion of Britain joined "his brother" Atlas of Spain in a vain naval effort to hold Hercules out of the Atlantic area when he sought to retrieve the golden apples of the Hesperides. The fruit, apparently a lucrative trading item, seems to have been the orange, for in Hebrew an orange is called a *tapuach zahav* (golden apple), while in Greek and Arabic an orange is called a *portokalion* and a *portugali* (fruit of Portugal) respectively. In Greek, furthermore, citrus fruit is called *hesperides* (western). Arausio, a town north of Greek Marseilles where oranges were introduced, was later repronounced to give us the name of an "orange" in French and English. This conflict over possession of the golden apple therefore recalls an early determination of Spaniards and British to guard their interests in Atlantic trade.

Many Spanish-language riddles also testify to the importance of the sea in the Hispanic psyche. Answers to these riddles range from fish, swordfish, sharks, and whales to sand and islands. Two examples might be given: "En mí mueren los ríos . . .":

> The rivers find their death in me
> and the boats go over me;
> my name is very short:
> It has only three letters. [Answer: *el mar,* the sea]

Another goes, "Ayer vinieron . . .":

> Yesterday they came,
> they have come today,
> they will come tomorrow:
> always with noise. [Answer: *las olas,* the waves]

Dark Age literature likewise reminds us of the Anglo-Saxon love of the sea. This attachment is most hauntingly stated in the anonymous Anglo-Saxon poem "The Seafarer," a dialogue between an old and a young sailor. Unable to dissuade the young man from a maritime calling by reminding him of the risks and hardships involved, the old man at the end concurs on the pleasures of a life at sea, singing:

> My heart beats in my breast again,
> My feelings call the flood of the sea
> over the whale's way wind returning;
> Over the corners of the earth comes again to me,
> Greedy and gluttonous, the gull's voice.
> My heart demands the deep whale road
> Over the broad sea.[1]

Thus from the earliest times both Spanish and English culture imparted to their sailors a fascination with the Atlantic Ocean. A vibrant Mexican-American Borderlands future awaited their cultural descendants across that "broad sea."

SOURCES

Introduction

The principal works dealing with the question of the pertinence of the Middle Ages to modern America, or the lack of it, are Lynn White Jr., "The Legacy of the Middle Ages in the American Wild West," *Speculum* 40 (April 1965): 73–79, 95; Luis Weckman, *The Medieval Heritage of Mexico* (New York: Fordham University Press, 1992); and Owen Ulph, "The Legacy of the American Wild West in Medieval Scholarship," *American West* 3, no. 4 (1966): 50–52, 88–91. A discussion of the issue can also be found in Norman F. Cantor, *Inventing the Middle Ages: The Lives, Works, and Ideas of the Great Medievalists of the Twentieth Century* (New York: William Morrow, 1991). All of these sources were of use throughout the book.

A treatment of the link between language, culture, and the construction of reality can be found in Zdenek Salmann, *Language, Culture, and Society: An Introduction to Linguistic Anthropology* (Bolder, Co.: Westview, 1993); M. A. K. Halliday, *Language As Social Semiotic: The Social Interpretation of Language and Meaning* (London: Edward Arnold, 1979); and George W. Kelling, *Language: Mirror, Tool, and Weapon* (Chicago: Nelson-Hall, 1975).

For the views of Hispanic-Anglo relations in the United States Southwest, one might read Rodolfo Acuña, *Occupied America, A History of Chicanos* (New York: HarperCollins, 1988); *Bolton and the Spanish Borderlands,* ed. John Francis Bannon (Norman: University of Oklahoma Press, 1964); Antonio S. Blanco, *La Lengua Española en la Historia de California* (Madrid: Ediciones Cultura Hispánica, 1971); Carlos M. Fernández-Shaw, *The Hispanic Presence in North America from 1492 to Today,* trans. Alfonso Bertodano Stourton et al. (New York: Facts On File, 1987); L. H. Gann and Peter J. Duignan, *The Hispanics in the United States: A History* (Bolder, Co.: Westview, 1986); Carey McWilliams, *North from Mexico: The Spanish-Speaking People of the United States* (New York: Praeger, 1990); Stanley R. Ross, *Views Across the Border: The United States and Mexico* (Albuquerque: University of New Mexico Press, 1978); James Diego Vigil, *From Indians to Chicanos: The Dynamics of Mexican American Culture* (Prospect Heights, Ill.: Waveland Press, Inc., 1980); Walter Prescott Webb, *The Great Frontier* (Austin: University of Texas Press, 1964); David J. Weber, *Foreigners in their Native Land* (Albuquerque: University of New

Mexico Press, 1973); David J. Weber, *The Spanish Frontier in North America* (New Haven, Conn.: Yale University Press, 1992); David J. Weber, "The Spanish Legacy in North America and the Historical Imagination," *The Western Historical Quarterly* 23 (1992): 16–22; and Carolyn Zeleny, *Relations between the Spanish-Americans and Anglo-Americans in New Mexico* (New York: Arno, 1974). Most of the above sources are drawn on throughout the book.

Rolf Johannsmeier, *Spielmann, Schalk und Scharlatan, die Welt als Karneval: Volkskultur im Späten Mittelalter* (Reinbek bei Hamburg: Rowohlt, 1984) was a source for the survival of ancient northern European influences into medieval culture. Henry Osburn Taylor, *The Classical Heritage of the Middle Ages* (New York: Frederick Ungar, 1957) deals with the survival of classical ancient influences into the Middle Ages.

Chapter One: Linguistic Influences

1. These and all subsequent nursery rhymes follow the text as rendered in William S. Baring-Gould and Ceil Baring-Gould, *The Annotated Mother Goose* (New York: Bramhall House, 1962).

2. This information was provided by Isabel de la Torre of Brownsville and is quoted with her permission.

3. A whole book of such comparable English and Spanish proverbs has been compiled by Luis Isgla, S.J.: *English Proverbs and Their Near Equivalents in Spanish, French, Italian, and Latin* (New York: Peter Lang, 1995).

For the linguistic considerations considered at the outset of this chapter, see John Bissell Carroll, *Language and Thought* (Englewood Cliffs, N.J.: Prentice-Hall, 1964); E. H. Lennenberg and J. M. Roberts, *Publications in Anthropology and Linguistics,* memoir 13 (Bloomington,: Indiana University, 1956); and M. Stanley Whitley, *Spanish/English Contrasts: A Course in Spanish Linguistics* (Washington, D. C.: Georgetown University Press, 1986).

The section on the various linguistic heritages and their ethnic roots in antiquity draws on Jorge Alonso, *Tartessos: tres mil años de enigma* (Granada: Roasa, 1983); Helen Cam, *England before Elizabeth* (New York: Harper & Brothers, 1960); Roger Collins, *The Basques* (Cambridge, Mass.: Blackwell, 1990); *Hispanos en los Estados Unidos,* ed. Rodolfo J. Cortina and Alberto Moncada (Madrid: Ediciones de Cultura Hispánica, 1988); Germán Delibes, Julio Fernández Manzano, Fernando Romero Carnicero, and Ricardo Martín Valls, *La prehistoria del valle del vuero* (Valladolid, Spain: Ambito Ediciones, 1985); Pedro González Blanco, *Contribución de los Judíos Españoles a la cultura universal* (México: Editorial José M. Cajica Jr., 1958); Richard J. Harrison, *Spain at the Dawn of History: Iberians, Phoenicians, and Greeks* (London: Thames & Hudson, 1988); Robert J. Littman, *The Greek Experiment: Imperialism and Social Conflict 800–400 B.C.* (New York: Harcourt Brace Jovanovich, 1974); Livy, *The War with Hannibal,* trans. Aubrey de Sélincourt (Harmondsworth [England]: Penguin, 1972); W. E. Lunt, *History of England* (New York: Harper & Brothers, 1957); Jean Mazel, *Avec les Phéneciens: à la poursuite du soleil sur la route de l'or et de l'étain* (Paris: Robert Laffont, 1968); William McNeill, *A World History* (New York: Oxford University Press, 1999); Stanley G. Payne, *A History of Spain and Portugal* (Madison: University of Wisconsin Press, 1973)—an ongoing source through the book; Guy Ragland Phillips, *Brigantia* (London: Routledge & Kegan Paul, 1976); Clayton Roberts and David Roberts, *A History of England* (Englewood Cliffs, N.J.: Prentice-Hall, 1985); Robert K. Spaulding, *How Spanish Grew* (Berkeley: University of California Press, 1971); Luis G. de Valdeavellano, *Historia de España Antigua y Medieval* (Madrid: Alianza Editorial, 1988); and David Harris Wilson and Stuart E. Prall, *A History of England* (New York: Holt, Rinehart & Winston, 1984).

The section on the various linguistic heritages and their ethnic roots in the Dark Ages draws on Leslie Alcock, *Arthur, Britain: History and Archeology A.D. 367–634* (Harmondsworth, England: Penguin, 1971); Peter Hunter Blair, *Roman Britain and Early England* (New York: Norton, 1963)—a source for other chapters as well; Alice E. Lasater, *Spain to England* (Jackson: University Press of Mississippi, 1964)—another repeated source; Alf J. Mapp Jr., *The Golden Dragon: Alfred the Great and His Times* (LaSalle, Ill.: Open Court, 1974); *The Reign of Cnut: King of England, Denmark and Norway,* ed. Alexander R. Rumble (London: Leicester University Press, 1994); Claudio Sánchez-Albornoz, *España y el Islám* (Buenos Aires: Editorial Sudamericana, 1943); E. A. Thompson, "The Conversion of the Spanish Suevi to Catholicism," in *Visigothic Spain: New Approaches,* ed. Edward James (Oxford: Clarendon, 1980); Luis G. De Valeavellano, *Orígenes de la Burguesía en la España medieval* (Madrid: Espasa-Calpe, 1975); and Herwig Wolfram, *Geschichte der Goten: Von den Anfängen bis zur Mitte des sechsten Jahrhunderts* (Munich: C. H. Beck, 1980).

The section on the various linguistic heritages and their ethnic roots in the Middle Ages proper draws on Poul Borchsenius's *The Three Rings: The History of the Spanish Jews* (London: George Allen & Unwin, 1963); Adriaan H. Bredero, *Christendom and Christianity in the Middle Ages: The Relations between Religion, Church, and Society,* trans. Reinder Bruinsma (Grand Rapids, Mich.: William B. Eerdmans, 1994); J. P. Clébert, *Los Gitanos,* trans. Carmen Alcalde and María Rosa Prats (Barcelona: Aymá Editora, 1965); Marcelin Defourneaux, *Les Français en Espagne aux XIe et XII siècles* (Paris: Presses Universitaires de France, 1949); Max I. Dimont, *Jews, God, and History* (New York: Signet Book of the New American Library, 1962); Angus Fraser, *The Gypsies* (Oxford: Blackwell, 1992); *Medieval Latin,* ed. K. P. Harrington (Chicago: University of Chicago Press, 1972); *Music for Everyone, No. 21: The World's Best Collection of Folk Songs and Ballads of All Nations,* ed. Herbert Haufrecht (New York: Remick Music, 1958); J. N. Hillgarth, *The Spanish Kingdoms: 1250–1516* (Oxford: Clarendon, 1976)—a principal source drawn on throughout the book; Paulino Iradiel, Salustiano Moreta, and Esteban Sarasa, *Historia Medieval de la España Cristiana* (Madrid: Catedra, 1989); Jacques Lafaye, "Le Messie dans le Monde Ibérique: Aperçu," in *Mélanges de la Casa de Velázquez,* vol. 7 (Paris: Éditions E. De Boccard, 1971); É. Lévi-Provençal, *La Civilización Árabe en España Cristiana* (Madrid: Catedra, 1989); Judah Nadich, *The Legends of the Rabbis: Jewish Legends of the Second Commonwealth* (Northvale, N.J.: Jason Aronson,

1994); Joseph O'Callaghan, *A History of Medieval Spain* (Ithaca, N.Y.: Cornell University Press, 1975); Michael Prestwich, *Edward I* (Berkeley: University of California Press, 1988); and *Biblioteca de autores Españoles desde la formación del lenguaje hasta nuestros días: poetas Castellanos anteriores al siglo XV,* ed. Tomás Antonio Sánchez, Pedro José Pidal, and Florencio Janer (Madrid: Ediciones Atlas, 1966).

Sources drawn on for the impact of early linguistic groups on Borderlands customs include Poul Borchsenius, *The Three Rings: The History of the Spanish Jews* (London: George Allen & Unwin, 1963); Eldon Cagle Jr., *The History of Fort Sam Houston* (n.p., n.d.); Louise A. K. S. Clappe, *The Shirley Letters from the California Mines in 1851–1854* (San Francisco: n.p., 1922); Ricardo Elizondo Elizondo, *Los Sefarditas en Nuevo León: Reminiscencias en el Folklore,* Cuadernos del Archivo, no. 11 (Monterrey, Nuevo León: Gobierno del Estado de Nuevo León, Secretaria de Administración, Archivo General del Estado, 1987); John Edwin Fagg, "The Iberian Background," *Introduction to Chicano Studies: A Reader,* ed. Livie Isauro Duran and H. Russell Bernard (New York: Macmillan, 1973); Floyd S. Fierman, *Roots and Boots: From Crypto-Jew in New Spain to Community Leader in the American Southwest* (Hoboken, N.J.: KTAV Publishing, 1987); David Hackett Fischer, *Albion, Seed: Four British Folkways in America* (New York: Oxford University Press, 1989); Sylvia Raquel Flores García, *Nogales: Un siglo en la historia* (Hermosillo, Sonora, Mexico: Editorial Reprográfica, 1987); Carlos Fuentes, *The Buried Mirror: Reflections on Spain and the New World* (Boston: Houghton Mifflin, 1992); L. H. Gann and Peter J. Duignan, *The Hispanics in the United States: A History* (Boulder, Col.: Westview Press, 1986); François Ganshof, *Histoire des Relations Internationales* (Paris: Hachette, 1953); Leo Grebler et al., *The Mexican-American People: The Nation, Second Largest Minority* (New York: Free Press, 1970); Christopher Hibbert, *The English: A Social History* (London: Grafton, 1987); Michael Holmes, *King Arthur: A Military History* (London: Blandford, 1996); Alice E. Lasater, *Spain to England* (Jackson: University Press of Mississippi, 1964); Patricia Nelson Limerick, *The Legacy of Conquest* (New York: Norton, 1987); Luce López-Baralt, "The Legacy of Islam in Spanish Literature," in *The Legacy of Muslim Spain,* ed. Salma Khadra Juyyusi (Leiden: E. J. Brill, 1992); Gabriel Marcella, "Spanish-Mexican Contributions to the Southwest," *The Journal of Mexican American History* 1 (fall 1970); Carey McWilliams, *North from Mexico: The Spanish-Speaking People of the United States* (New York: Praeger, 1990); Leon C. Metz, *Border: The U.S.-Mexican Line* (El Paso: Texas Western Press, University of Texas at El Paso, 1990); Joseph O'Callaghan, *A History of Medieval Spain* (Ithaca, N.Y.: Cornell University Press, 1975); Alwyn Rees and Brinley Rees, *Celtic Heritage: Ancient Tradition in Ireland and Wales* (London: Thames & Hudson, 1973); *America, Frontier History, A Documentary History of Westward Expansion,* ed. Martin Ridge and Ray Allen Billington (New York: Holt, Rinehart & Winston, 1969); Robert K. Spaulding, *How Spanish Grew* (Berkeley: University of California Press, 1971); James H. Sweet, "The Iberian Roots of American Racist Thought," *The William and Mary Quarterly,* 3d series, 54, no. 1 (January 1997); W. L. Warren, *King John, 1167–1216* (New York: Barnes & Noble, 1996); Lynn

White Jr., "The Legacy of the Middle Ages in the American Wild West," *Speculum* 40, no. 2 (April 1965); and Otis E. Young, "The Spanish Tradition in Gold and Silver mining," in *Arizona and the West* 7, no. 4 (winter 1965).

The section considering the impact of early linguistic groups on speech drew on *The Sephardic Heritage: Essays on the History and Cultural Contributions of the Jews of Spain and Portugal* (New York: KTAV Publishing, 1971); Margaret Bryant, *Modern English and Its Heritage* (New York: Macmillan, 1962); Charles E. Chapman, *A History of Spain* (New York: Free Press, 1965); Ricardo Elizondo Elizondo, *Los Sefarditas en Nuevo León: reminiscencias en el folklore,* Cuadernos del Archivo, no. 11 (Monterrey, Nuevo León: Gobierno del Estado de Nuevo León, Secretaria de Administración, Archivo General del Estado, 1987); Rex Weldon Finn, *The English Heritage* (London: MacDonald, 1948); David Hackett Fischer, *Albion, Seed: Four British Folkways in America* (New York: Oxford University Press, 1989); Pedro González Blanco, *Contribución de los Judíos Españoles a la cultura universal* (México: Editorial José M. Cajica, Jr., 1958); *New Larousse Encyclopedia of Mythology* (London: Hamlyn, 1959); J. N. Hillgarth, *The Spanish Kingdoms: 1250–1516* (Oxford: Clarendon, 1976); Alice E. Lasater, *Spain to England: A Comparative Study of Arabic, European, and English Literature of the Middle Ages* (Jackson: University Press of Mississippi, 1974); Julio Mangas Manjarrés and José María Solana Sáinz, *Romanización y Germanización de la meseta norte* (Valladolid: Ámbito Ediciones, 1985); *The Legacy of Muslim Spain,* ed. Salma Khadra Jayyusi (Leiden: E. J. Brill, 1992); Américo Paredes, *Folklore and Culture on the Texas-Mexican Border* (Austin: Center for Mexican American Studies of the University of Texas at Austin, 1993); Barbara Softly, *The Queens of England* (New York: Stein & Day, 1976); Robert K. Spaulding, *How Spanish Grew* (Berkeley: University of California Press, 1971); and Luis Weckmann, *The Medieval Heritage of Mexico* (New York: Fordham University Press, 1992).

The main sources for the section concerning the impact of early liguistic groups on names are Grace de Jesús C. Álvarez, *Topónimos en Apellidos Hispanos* (Garden City, N.Y.: Estudios de Hispanófila, Adelphi University, 1968); Rex Weldon Finn, *The English Heritage* (London: MacDonald, 1948); Alice E. Lasater, *Spain to England* (Jackson: University Press of Mississippi, 1964); Haim Levi, *Tratado de nombres Sefardis* (Tampa: International Federation of Messianic Jews, 1997); Herbert Lockyear, *All the Men of the Bible* (Grand Rapids, Mich.: Zondervan, 1958); Herbert Lockyear, *All the Women of the Bible* (Grand Rapids, Mich.: Zondervan, 1958); Jean Mazel, *Avec les Phéniciens: á la poursuite du soleil sur la route de l'or et de l'étain* (Paris: Robert Laffont, 1968); *Diccionario de apellidos Vascos,* ed. N. Narbate Iraola (San Sebastián: Editorial Txertoa, 1989); Yvonne Navarro, *First Name Reverse Dictionary: Given Names Listed by Meaning* (Jefferson, N.C.: McFarland, 1993); and Robert Spaulding, *How Spanish Grew* (Berkeley: University of California Press, 1971).

Among the sources for general medieval influences on the Borderlands via the Hispanic route the following might be mentioned: Alfonso X, Rey de Castilla, *Lapidario* (Madrid: Editorial Castalia, 1982); *Hispanos en los Estados Unidos,* ed.

Rodolfo J. Cortina and Alberto Moncada (Madrid: Ediciones de Cultura Hispánica, 1988); Carlos M. Fernández-Shaw, *The Hispanic Presence in North America from 1492 to Today,* trans. Alfonso Bertasdano Stourton et al. (New York: Facts On File, 1987); and Luis Weckmann, *The Medieval Heritage of Mexico* (New York: Fordham University Press, 1992).

The section on the general medieval influences on the Borderlands via the Anglo route drew on Louis Charpentier, *Los gigantes y su origen* (Buenos Aires: Bruguera, 1975); Rex Weldon Finn, *The English Heritage* (London: MacDonald, 1948); James Frazier, *The Illustrated Golden Bough* (Garden City, N.Y.: Doubleday, 1978); Robert Graves, *The White Goddess* (New York: Farrar, Straus, & Giroux, 1966); Christina Hole, *English Traditional Customs* (Totowa, N.J.: Rowman & Littlefield, 1975)—a source used throughout the book; *A Celtic Miscellany,* trans. Kenneth Hurlstone Jackson (Harmondsworth, England: Penguin, 1973); Paul Murray Kendall, *The Yorkist Age: Daily Life During the Wars of the Roses* (New York: Norton, 1970); James Lydon, *Ireland in the Later Middle Ages* (Dublin: Gill & Macmillan, 1973); Snorri Sturluson, *Heimskringla: History of the Kings of Norway,* trans. Lee M. Hollander (Austin: University of Texas Press, n.p.); W. L. Warren, *King John, 1167–1216* (New York: Barnes & Noble, 1978); and Lynn White Jr., "The Legacy of the Middle Ages in the American Wild West," *Speculum* 40 (April 1965): 73–79 and 95.

Among the sources for general medieval influences on the Borderlands via both the Hispanic and Anglo routes, the following should be mentioned: Grace de Jesús C. Álvarez, *Topónimos en apellidos Hispanos* (Garden City, N.Y.: Estudios de Hispanófila, Adelphi University, 1968); James Burke, *Connections* (Boston: Little, Brown, 1978); John Mack Faragher, *Daniel Boone: The Life and Legend of an American Pioneer* (New York: Henry Holt, 1992); Carlos M. Fernández-Shaw, *The Hispanic Presence in North America from 1492 to Today,* trans. Alfonso Bertodano Stourton et al. (New York: Facts On File, 1987); Rex Weldon Finn, *The English Heritage* (London: MacDonald, 1948); A. Daniel Frankforter, *The Medieval Millenium: An Introduction* (Upper Saddle River, N.J.: Prentice-Hall, 1999); Robert Graves, *The White Goddess* (New York: Farrar, Straus & Giroux, 1966); Jacques Heers, *L'Occident aux XIVe et XVe siècles, Aspects économiques et sociaux* (Paris: Presses Universitaires, 1963); Christopher Hibbert, *The English: A Social History* (London: Grafton, 1987); Christina Hole, *English Traditional Customs* (Totowa, N.J.: Rowman & Littlefield, 1975); Luis Isgla, S.J., *English Proverbs and Their Near Equivalents in Spanish, French, Italian, and Latin* (New York: Peter Lang, 1995); Gerald Johnson, *Our English Heritage* (Westport, Conn.: Greenwood, 1949); Gabriel Marcella, "Spanish-Mexican Contributions to the Southwest," *The Journal of Mexican American History* 1 (fall 1970); Gonzalo Martínez Díez, *Alfonso VIII, Rey de Castilla y Toledo* (Burgos, Spain: Editorial La Olmeda, 1995); Marvin H. Pakula, *Heraldry and Armor of the Middle Ages* (South Brunswick, England: A. S. Barnes, 1972); Kristin E. White, *A Guide to the Saints* (New York: Ivy Books, 1991); Luis Weckmann, *The Medieval Heritage of Mexico* (New York: Fordham University Press, 1992).

A number of observations on the importance of the Jewish community in the

Borderlands derive from the participation by Milo Kearney and his wife Vivan in Brownsville's Baruch ha-Shem Messianic Synagogue and its contacts to other Borderlands messianic synagogues. This movement attracts Hispanic families with a *converso* background and an interest in researching their Spanish roots.

Chapter Two: Political and Legal Influences

1. This is a childhood recollection of both René Vásquez, Jr., and Isabel de la Torre of Brownsville and is quoted with their permission.

Many works in addition to those sources mentioned above were utilized for preparing this section. Some of the sources used for discussing the general political and legal developments of the High Middle Ages are Marc Bloch, *La Société Féodale* (Paris: Éditions Albin Michel, 1968); Norman F. Cantor, *Inventing the Midle Ages: The Lives, Works, and Ideas of the Great Medievalists of the Twentieth Century* (New York: William Morrow, 1991); Bryce Lyon, *A Constitutional and Legal History of Medieval England* (New York: Harper & Row, 1960); and Joseph R. Strayer, *On the Medieval Origins of the Modern State* (Princeton: Princeton University Press, 1970).

Sources used for the Hispanic political developments in this period include *Emperor of Culture: Alfonso X the Learned of Castile and His Thirteenth-Century Renaissance*, ed. Robert I. Burns (Philadelphia: University of Pennsylvania Press, 1990); Carlos Estepa Díez, *El Nacimiento de León y Castilla (Siglos VIII–X)* (Valladolid: Ambito Ediciones, 1985); Richard Fletcher, *The Quest for El Cid* (Oxford: Oxford University Press, 1989); Carlos Fuentes, *The Buried Mirror: Reflections on Spain and the New World* (Boston: Houghton Mifflin, 1992); José Angel García de Cortázar, *La Época Medieval* (Madrid: Alianza Editorial, 1988); J. N. Hillgarth, *The Spanish Kingdoms: 1250–1516* (Oxford: Clarendon, 1976); Gabriel Jackson, *The Making of Medieval Spain* (Norwich, England: Harcourt Brace Jovanovich, 1972); Gonzalo Martínez Díez, *Alfonso VIII, Rey de Castilla y Toledo* (Burgos, Spain: Editorial La Olmeda, 1995); José María de Mena, *Entre la cruz y la espada: San Fernando* (Sevilla: Editorial J. R. Castillejo, 1990); José Miranda Calvo, *La Reconquista de Toledo por Alfonso VI* (Toledo: Instituto de Estudios Visigótico-Mozárabes de San Eugenio, 1980); Joseph O'Callaghan, *A History of Medieval Spain* (Ithaca, N.Y.: Cornell University Press, 1975); Joseph O'Callaghan, *The Learned King: The Reign of Alfonso X of Castile* (Philadelphia: University of Pennsylvania Press, 1993); Fray Justo Pérez de Urbel, *España Cristiana: comienzo de la Reconquista (711–1038)* (Madrid: Espasa-Calpe, 1964); Bernard F. Reilly, *The Kingdom of León-Castilla under King Alfonso VI, 1065–1109* (Princeton, N.J.: Princeton University Press, 1988); Bernard F. Reilly, *The Kingdom of León-Castilla under Queen Urraca, 1109–1126* (Princeton. N.J.: Princeton University Press, 1982); Bernard F. Reilly, *The Medieval Spains* (Cambridge: Cambridge University Press, 1993); José-Manuel Ruiz Asencio, Amando Represa Rodríguez, Julio Valdeón Baruque, and Luis Suárez Fernández, *Valladolid Medieval* (Valladolid, Spain: Editorial Sever-Cuesta, 1980); Cristóbal Taltabull, *25 Canciones Españoles del Renacimiento* (Barcelona: Ediciones Armónica, n.d.); Enrique de Tapia Ozcariz, *Las Cortes de Castilla: 1188–1833* (Madrid: Editorial Revista de Derecho Privado, 1964); and Luis G. de Valdeavellano, *Orígenes de la Burguesía en la España medieval* (Madrid: Espasa-Calpe, 1975).

Among the sources tapped for Anglo political developments in this age are Salimbene de Adam, *The Chronicle of Salimbene de Adam,* Medieval and Renaissance Texts and Studies, vol. 40, ed. Joseph L. Baird, Giuseppe Baglivi, and John Robert Kane, (Binghamton, N.Y.: Medieval and Renaissance Texts and Studies, 1986); Maurice Ashley, *The Life and Times of William I* (London: Weidenfeld & Nicolson, 1973); Richard Barber, *Henry Plantagenet: A Biography* (New York: Barnes & Noble, 1964); Frank Barlow, *William I and the Norman Conquest* (New York: Collier, 1965); Michel de Boüard, *Guillaume le Conquérant* (Paris: Librairie Arthème Fayard, 1984); Christopher Brooke, *From Alfred to Henry III, 871–1272* (Edinburgh: Thomas Nelson, 1961); James Chambers, *The Norman Kings* (London: Weidenfeld & Nicolson, 1981); John Chancellor, *The Life and Times of Edward I* (London: Weidenfeld & Nicolson, 1981); R. H. C. Davis, *King Stephen* (London: Longman, 1990); Michael Dolley, *Anglo-Norman Ireland* (Dublin: Gill & Macmillan, 1972); Eleanor Shipley Duckett, *Alfred the Great: The King and His England* (Chicago: University of Chicago Press, Phoenix Books, 1956); Rex Weldon Finn, *The English Heritage* (London: MacDonald, 1948); John Harvey, *The Plantagenets* (New York: John Wiley & Sons, 1967); Victor Head, *Hereward* (Gloucester, England: Alan Sutton, 1995); Michael Holmes, *King Arthur: A Military History* (London: Blandford, 1996); Richard Humble, *The Saxon Kings* (London: Weidenfeld & Nicolson, 1980); Gerald W. Johnson, *Our English Heritage* (Westport, Conn.: Greenwood, 1949); J. R. Lander, *Ancient and Medieval England: Beginnings to 1509* (New York: Harcourt, Brace, Jovanovich, 1973); Sidney Painter, *The Reign of King John* (Baltimore: Johns Hopkins University Press, 1966); John Peddie, *Alfred, the Good Soldier: His Life and Campaigns* (Bath: Millstream Books, 1992); *Seven Old English Poems,* ed. John C. Pope (Indianapolis: Bobbs-Merrill, 1966); Barbara Softly, *The Queens of England* (New York: Stein & Day, 1976); Goldwin Smith, *A History of England* (New York: Charles Scribner's Sons, 1974); and Snorri Sturleson, *King Harald, Saga,* taken from the *Heimskringla* (Harmondsworth, England: Penguin, 1966).

The section on the impact on the Borderlands of these medieval political and legal developments drew in part on the following sources: Donald E. Chipman, *Spanish Texas* (Austin: University of Texas Press, 1992); Dwight L. Clarke, *Stephen Watts Kearny: Soldier of the West* (Norman: University of Oklahoma Press, 1964); *Introduction to Chicano Studies: A Reader,* ed. Livie Isauro Duran and H. Russell Bernard (New York: Macmillan, 1973); Malcolm Ebright, *Land Grants and Lawsuits in Northern New Mexico* (Albuquerque: University of New Mexico Press, 1994); Carlos M. Fernández, *The Hispanic Presence in North America from 1492 to Today,* trans. Alfonso Bertodano Stourton et al. (New York: Facts On File, 1987); Dario Fernández-Florez, *The Spanish Heritage in the United States* (Madrid: Publicaciones Españolas, 1971); George M. Foster, *Culture and Conquest: America, Spanish Heritage* (Chicago: Quadrangle, 1960); L. H. Gann and Peter J. Duignan, *The Hispanics in the United States: A History* (Boulder, Colo.: Westview, 1986); Nancy González, *The*

Spanish-Americans of New Mexico: A Heritage of Pride (Albuquerque: University of New Mexico Press, 1969); Milo Kearney and Anthony Knopp, *Boom and Bust: The Historical Cycles of Matamoros and Brownsville* (Austin: Eakin, 1991); Milo Kearney and Anthony Knopp, *Border Cuates: A History of the U.S.-Mexican Twin Cities* (Austin: Eakin, 1995); Gabriel Marcella, "Spanish-Mexican Contributions to the Southwest," *The Journal of Mexican American History* 1 (fall 1970); *A Documentary History of the Mexican Americans,* ed. Wayne Moguin and Charles Van Doren (New York: Praeger, 1971); James M. Murphy, *The Spanish Legal Heritage in Arizona* (Tucson: Arizona Pioneers' Historical Society, 1966); *Beyond 1848: Readings in the Modern Chicano Historical Experience,* ed. Michael R. Ornelas (Dubuque, Iowa: Kendall, Hunt, 1993); William R. Shepherd, "The Spanish Heritage in America," *Modern Language Journal* 10 (November 1925); Jerry Thompson, *Warm Weather and Bad Whiskey: The 1886 Laredo Election Riot* (El Paso: Texas Western Press, University of Texas at El Paso, 1991); and John Thomas Vance, "The Background of Hispanic-American Law," Ph.D. diss., Catholic University of America, 1937. Many of the above are important sources throughout this book, even though they will not be repeated as sources at the end of each chapter.

Chapter Three: Economic and Social Class Influences

1. These findings are quoted with the permission of Ralph M. Hausman of the University of Texas at Brownsville from his unpublished article "Exploration of Preferred Learning Styles Among Hispanic Post-Secondary Students."

Various new works, in addition to some of those mentioned above, were utilized for preparing this section. Sources tapped for the economic and social developments in Castile in the Late Middle Ages include Leon Ardzrooni, "Commerce and Industry in Spain during Ancient and Mediaeval Times," *Journal of Political Economy* 21, no. 5 (1913); Gonzalo de Berceo, *Milagros de Nuestra Señora, vida de Santo Domingo de Silos, vida de San Millán de la Cogolla, vida de Santa Oria, y Martirio de San Lorenzo,* ed. Amancia Bolano e Isla (México: Porrúa, 1976); P. Boissonade, *Life and Work in Medieval Europe: The Evolution of Medieval Economy from the Fifth to the Fifteenth Centuries* (New York: Harper Torchbooks, 1964); Fortunato Escribano de la Torre, *Peña Fiel: Notas Históricas* (Valladolid, Spain: Gráficas Color, 1977); Mercedes Gaibrois de Ballesteros, *María de Molina: tres veces reina* (Madrid: Espasa-Calpe, 1967); J. N. Hillgarth, *The Spanish Kingdoms: 1250–1516* (Oxford: Clarendon, 1976); Peggy K. Liss, *Isabel the Queen: Life and Times* (New York: Oxford University Press, 1992); Canciller Don Pedro López de Ayala, *Las Muertes del Rey Don Pedro* (Madrid: El Libro de Bolsillo Alianza Editorial, 1971); Juan Manuel, *Libro de los ejemplos del Conde Lucanor y de Patronio* (Buenos Aires: Editorial Losada, 1965); Gregorio Marañón, *Ensayo biológico sobre Enrique IV de Castilla y su tiempo* (Madrid: Espasa-Calpe, 1956); Townsend Miller, *Henry IV of Castile, 1425–1474* (Philadelphia: J. B. Lippincott, 1972); J. María Moreno Echevarría, *Fernando el Católico* (Barcelona: Plaza y Janes, 1981); John Carmi Parsons, *Eleanor of Castile: Queen and Society in Thirteenth-Century England* (New York: St. Martin's Press,

1995); *Poema de Fernán González* (México: Ediciones Oasis, 1963); *Poema del Cid* (México: Espasa-Calpe Mexicana, 1960); Reyna Pastor de Togneri, *Conflictos sociales y estancamiento económico en la España medieval* (Barcelona: Editorial Ariel, 1973); Stanley G. Payne, *A History of Spain and Portugal* (Madison: University of Wisconsin Press, 1973); François Pietri, *Pedro el Cruel,* trans. Renato Otero Vergara (Palencia: Editorial La Olmeda, 1996); *Realidad e imagenes del poder: España a fines de la edad media,* ed. Adeline Rucquoi (Valladolid: Ambito Ediciones, 1988); Nancy Rubin, *Isabella of Spain: The First Renaissance Queen* (New York: St. Martin's Press, 1991); Claudio Sánchez-Albornoz, *España y el Islam* (Burenos Aires: Editorial Sudamericana, 1943); César Silió, *Don Álvaro de Luna* (Buenos Aires: Espasa-Calpe Argentina, 1948); Desmond Stewart,*The Alhambra* (New York: Newsweek Books, 1974); Luis Suárez Fernández and Juan Reglá Campistol, *España Cristiana: Crisis de la Reconquista, luchas civiles* (Madrid: Espasa-Calpe, 1966); Julio Valdeón Baruque, *Enrique II, 1369–1379* (Palencia, Spain: Editorial La Olmeda, 1996); and W. T. Walsh, *Isabel la Cruzada,* trans. Carlos M. Castro Cranwell (Madrid: Espasa-Calpe, 1963).

Among the sources used for the discussion of economic and social developments in late medieval England are Christopher Allmand, *Henry V* (London: Methuen, 1992); H. S. Bennett, *The Pastons and Their England* (Cambridge: Cambridge University Press, 1968); Marie Louise Bruce, *The Usurper King: Henry of Bolingbroke, 1366–99* (London: Rubicon, 1986); *Everyman and Medieval Miracle Plays,* ed. A. C. Cawley (New York: E. P. Dutton, 1959); Anthony Cheetham, *The Life and Times of Richard III* (London: Weidenfeld & Nicolson, 1972); Peter Coss, *The Knight in Medieval England, 1000–1400* (Gloucester, England: Alan Sutton, 1993); Peter Earle, *The Life and Times of Henry V* (London: Weidenfeld & Nicolson, 1972); Gila Falkus, *The Life and Times of Edward IV* (London: Weidenfeld & Nicolson, 1981); Jean Favier, *La Guerre de Cent Ans* (Paris: Librairie Arthème Fayard, 1980); Kenneth Fowler, *The Age of Plantagenet and Valois* (New York: Exeter Books, 1967); Harold F. Hutchinson, *Edward II, 1284–1327* (New York: Barnes & Noble, 1971); J. R. Lander, *The War of the Roses* (Gloucester, England: Alan Sutton, 1992); Marie de France, *French Medieval Romances from the Lays of Marie de France,* trans. Eugene Mason (London: J. M. Dent, 1976); Gervase Mathew, *The Court of Richard II* (New York: Norton, 1968); A. R. Myers, *England in the Late Middle Ages* (Harmondsworth, England: Penguin Books, 1952); A. J. Pollard, *Richard III and the Princes in the Tower* (Gloucester, England: Alan Sutton, 1991); Michael Senior, *The Life and Times of Richard II* (London: Weidenfeld & Nicolson, 1981); Lacey Baldwin Smith, *This Realm of England: 1399 to 1688* (Boston: D. C. Heath, 1966); Anthony Steel, *Richard II* (Cambridge: Cambridge University Press, 1962); *The Owl and the Nightingale, Cleaness and St. Erkenwald,* ed. Brian Stone (Harmondsworth, England: Penguin, 1971); R. L. Storey, *The End of the House of Lancaster* (Gloucester, England: Allan Sutton, 1986); Bruce Webster, *The Wars of the Roses* (London: UCL Press, 1998); Neville Williams, *The Life and Times of Henry VII* (London: Weidenfeld & Nicolson, 1972); and Charles T. Wood, *Joan of Arc and Richard III: Sex, Saints and Government in the Middle Ages* (New York: Oxford University Press, 1988).

The section looking at the results of the late medieval economic and social developments for Borderlands society tapped various sources in addition to many listed earlier, including Armando Alonzo, *Tejano Legacy, Rancheros and Settlers in South Texas, 1734–1900;* Ray August, "Cowboys vs. Rancheros: The Origins of Western America Livestock Law," *Southwestern Historical Quarterly* 96, no. 4 (1993); A. C. Crombie, *Medieval and Early Modern Science* (Garden City, N.Y.: Doubleday Anchor Books, 1959); Alfred W. Crosby Jr., *The Columbian Exchange: Biological and Cultural Consequences of 1492* (Westport, Conn.: Greenwood, 1973); David De Selm, *The Influence of the Foreign Heritage on the American City* (Washington, D.C.: Department of Housing and Urban Development, 1976); J. V. Fifer, *The Master Builders: Structures of Empire in the New World, Spanish Initiatives and United States Invention* (Durham, N.C.: Durham Academic Press, 1996); George M. Foster, *Culture and Conquest: America, Spanish Heritage* (Chicago: Quadrangle, 1960); Terry G. Jordan, *North American Cattle-Ranching Frontiers: Origins, Diffusion, and Differentiation* (Albuquerque: University of New Mexico Press, 1993); Clara M. Love, "The History of Cattle Ranching in the Southwest (I-V)," *Southwestern Historical Quarterly* 19, no. 4 (1916); William McNeill, *Plagues and People* (New York: Cambridge University Press, 1986); Américo Paredes, *Folklore and Culture on the Texas-Mexican Border* (Austin: Center for Mexican American Studies of the University of Texas at Austin, 1993); Carlos G. Vélez-Ibáñez, *Border Visions: Mexican Cultures of the Southwest United States* (Tucson: University of Arizona Press, 1996); James Diego Vigil, *From Indians to Chicanos: The Dynamics of Mexican American Culture* (Prospect Heights, Ill.: Waveland, 1980); David Weber, *The Spanish Frontier in North America* (New Haven, Conn.: Yale University Press, 1992); and Henry Wiencek, "The Spain among Us," *American History,* vol. 1, ed. Robert James (Guilford, Conn.: Dushkin, 1995).

Chapter Four: Religious Influences

Additional sources utilized in preparing this section are listed as follows. Sources on the paganism of early Iberia and Britain include Janet and Colin Bord, *Mysterious Britain* (Garden City, N.Y.: Doubleday, 1973); Louis Charpentier, *Les Géants et le mystère des origines* (Paris: Éditions Robert Laffont, 1969); Louis Charpentier, *Les Jacques et le mystère de Compostele* (Paris: Éditions Robert Laffont, 1971); *The Mabinogion,* trans. Jeffrey Gantz (Harmondsworth, England: Penguin, 1976); Ward Rutherford, *The Druids and Their Heritage* (London: Gordon & Cremonesi, 1978); and Nikolai Tolstoy, *The Quest for Merlin* (Boston: Little, Brown & Co., 1985).

The sections dealing with medieval Christianity in general drew in part on Adrian H. Bredero, *Christendom and Christianity in the Middle Ages: The Relations between Religion, Church, and Society,* trans. Reinder Bruinsma (Grand Rapids, Mich.: William B. Eerdmans, 1989); Euan Cameron, *The European Reformation* (Oxford: Clarendon, 1991); Louis Charpentier, *Les Mystères Templiers* (Paris: Robert Laffont, 1967); Jean-Luc Jamard, "Confrèries religieuses et dichotomie sociale," *Mélanges de la casa de Velázquez,* vol. 8 (Paris: Éditions E. de Boccard, 1972); David Knowles, *The Evolution of Medieval Thought* (New York: Random House, Vintage Books, 1964); *La Quête du Saint Graal* (Lyon: Confluences, 1946); G. Mollat, *The Popes at Avignon: The "Babylonian Captivity" of the Medieval Church* (New York: Thomas Nelson & Sons, 1963); *The Investiture Controversy: Issues, Ideals, and Results,* ed. Karl F. Morrison (New York: Holt, Rinehart & Winston, 1971); Desmond O'Grady, *Caesar, Christ, and Constantine: A History of the Early Church in Rome* (Huntington, Ind.: Our Sunday Visitor, 1991); Graham Phillips, *The Search for the Grail* (London: Century, 1995); Denis de Rougemont, *L'Amour et L'Occident* (Paris: Union Générale d'Éditions, 1939); James C. Russell, *The Germanization of Early Medieval Christianity: A Sociohistorical Approach to Religious Transformation* (Oxford: Oxford University Press, 1994); Kristin E. White, *A Guide to the Saints* (New York: Ivy Books, 1991); and Otto Wimmer, *Die Attribute der Heiligen* (Innsbruck: Tyrolia Verlag, 1966).

The sources most employed for the treatment of Christianity in medieval Castile were Juan G. Atienza, *Guia de leyendas Españolas* (Barcelona: Editorial Ariel, 1985); Christopher Columbus, *Journal of the First Voyage (Diario del Primer Viaja, 1492),* ed. and trans. B. W. Ife (Warminster, England: Aris & Phillips, 1990); Antonio C. Floriano, *El monasterio de Santa María de Guadalupe* (León: Editorial Everest, 1975); Julio Mangas Manjarrés and José María Solana Sáinz, *Romanización y Germanicazión de la meseta norte* (Valladolid, Spain: Ábito Ediciones, 1985); Chaim Pearl, *Rashi* (London: Weidenfeld & Nicolson, 1988); L. Alonso Tejada, *Historias de amor de la historia de España* (Barcelona: Editorial Bruguera, 1975); and M. H. Vicaire, *Saint Dominic and His Times* (New York: McGraw-Hill, 1964).

The consideration of Christianity in medieval England is informed by Bede, *A History of the English Church and People,* trans. Leo Sherley-Price (Baltimore: Penguin, 1955); G. G. Coulton, *Medieval Village, Manor, and Monastery* (New York: Harper Torchbooks, 1960); R. W. Morgan, *Did the Apostle Paul Visit Britain?* (San Francisco: Dolores Press, 1984); and W. A. Pantin, *The English Church in the Fourteenth Century* (Notre Dame, Ind.: University of Notre Dame Press, 1962).

The medieval religious impact on the Borderlands draws on the following sources, among others: Manuel L. Carlos, "Identidad y raíces culturales de los enclaves hispanos de los EE.UU.," *Hispanos en los Estados Unidos,* ed. Rodolfo J. Cortina and Alberto Moncada (Madrid: Ediciones de Cultura Hispánica, 1988); César Chávez, "The Mexican-American and the Church," *Voices: Readings from El Grito* (Berkeley: Quinto Sol Publications, 1973); *The Spanish West,* ed. George G. Daniels (Alexandria, Va: Time-Life Books, 1976); Christina Hole, *English Traditional Customs* (Totowa, N.J.: Rowman & Littlefield, 1975); *Studies in Brownsville History,* ed. Milo Kearney (Brownsville, Tex.: Pan American University at Brownsville, 1986); *More Studies in Brownsville History,* ed. Milo Kearney (Brownsville, Tex.: Pan American University at Brownsville, 1989); Don Lewis, *Curious and Humorous Customs* (London: Mowbrays, 1972); Clifford L. Linedecker's *Hell Ranch: The Nightmare Tale of Voodoo, Drugs, and Death in Matamoros* (Austin: Diamond, 1989); *The Mexican-American Experience,* ed. Rodolfo O. De la Garza, Frank Bean, Charles M.

Bonjean, and Rodolfo Álvarez (Austin: University of Texas Press, 1985); N. J. G. Pounds, *The Culture of the English People: Iron Age to the Industrial Revolution* (Cambridge: Cambridge University Press, 1994); Gary Provost, *Across the Border: The True Story of the Satanic Cult Killings in Matamoros, Mexico* (New York: Pocket Books, 1989); Moises Sandoval, *On the Move: A History of the Hispanic Church in the United States* (Maryknoll, N.Y.: Orbis, 1991); Thomas J. Steele and Rowena A. Rivera, *Penitente Self-Government: Brotherhoods and Councils, 1797–1947* (Santa Fe, N.M.: Ancient City Press, 1985); Marta Weigle, *The Penitentes of the Southwest* (Santa Fe, N.M.: Ancient City Press, 1970); and Antonio N. Zavaleta, "Medieval Antecedents of Border Pseudo-Religious Folk Beliefs," in *The Medieval Roots of the Mexican American Borderlands,* ed. Milo Kearney, *The Borderlands Journal* (special issue), ed. Antonio N. Zavaleta 5, no. 2 (spring 1982).

Chapter Five: Creative Influences

1. The comparisons of medieval and Borderland recipes are heavily indebted to Patricia John's graduate research paper submitted to Milo Kearney entitled "Food Influences on the Borderlands" and are used with her permission.

2. This information was provided to Milo Kearney by Isabel de la Torre of Brownsville and by Lea Salazar of Harlingen and is quoted with their permission.

Works of or about medieval Castilian literature drawn on in this and other chapters include Ángel del Río and Amelia A. de del Río, *Antología General de la Literatura Española* (New York: Holt, Rinehart & Winston, 1960); Stephen Clissold, *In Search of the Cid* (New York: Barnes & Noble, 1994); Richard Fletcher, *The Quest for El Cid* (New York: Oxford University Press, 1989); Jorge Manrique, *Coplas a la muerte de su padre,* ed. Carmen Díaz Castañón (Madrid: Editorial Castalia, 1983); *Poema del Cid* (México: Espasa-Calpe Mexicana, 1960); Ramón Menéndez Pidal, *Cantar de mio Cid: texto, gramática y vocabulario* (Madrid: Espasa-Calpe, 1964); Fernando de Rojas, *La Celestina,* ed. Julio Cejador y Frauca (Madrid: Espasa-Calpe, 1968); and Juan Ruiz, *Libro de Buen Amor,* ed. Jacques Joset (Madrid: Espasa-Calpe, 1974).

Medieval English literature utilized in this and other chapters include *Ballad Book,* ed. Katherine Lee Bates (Freeport, N.Y.: Books for Libraries, 1969); *Beowulf,* trans. Michael Alexander (Harmondsworth, England: Penguin, 1973); Derek Brewer, *Chaucer and His World* (New York: Dodd, Meade & Company, 1978); *Religious Lyrics of the XIVth Century,* ed. Carleton Brown (Oxford: Clarendon, 1924); *The Penguin Book of the Folk Ballads of the English-Speaking World,* ed. Albert B. Friedman (Harmondsworth, England: Penguin, 1977); John Gardner, *The Life and Times of Chaucer* (New York: Knopf, 1977); *Pearl,* ed. E. V. Gordon (Oxford: Clarendon, 1953); John Gower, *Poema quod dicitur vox clamantis, necnon chronica tripartita* (London: E Typographeo Gulielmi Nicol, 1850); Victor Head, *Hereward* (Gloucester, England: Alan Sutton, 1995); J. C. Holt, *Robin Hood* (London: Thames & Hudson, 1983); Maurice Keen, *The Outlaws of Medieval Legend* (London: Routledge & Kegan Paul, 1961); William Langland, *The Vision of William Concerning Piers the*

Plowman, in Three Parallel Texts, together with Richard the Redeless, ed. Walter W. Skeat (London: Oxford University, 1969); *The Works of Geoffrey Chaucer,* ed. F. N. Robinson (Boston: Houghton Mifflin, 1957); and *Fourteenth Century Verse and Prose,* ed. Kenneth Sisam (Oxford: Clarendon, 1921).

The consideration of the impact of medieval literature on the Borderlands was informed in part by J. T. Canales, "Juan Cortina, Bandit or Patriot?" (address to the Lower Rio Grande Valley Historical Society, October 25, 1951); Nash Candelaria, *Memories of the Alhambra: A Novel of the Chicano Heritage Myth and a Man's Search for His Roots* (Tempe, Ariz.: Bilingual Press / Editorial Bilingüe, 1982); Pascal Civici Jr., *The Portable Steinbek* (New York: Penguin, 1971); Rodolfo Gonzales, *I Am Joaquin: An Epic Poem* (Denver: El Gallo Newspaper, 1967); Rolando Hinojosa, *Estampas del valle y otras obras / Sketches of the Valley and Other Works,* trans. Gustavo Valdez and José Reyna (Berkeley: Editorial Justa, 1973); *The Hispanic Heritage Literary Companion,* ed. Nicolás Kanellos (Detroit: Visible Ink, 1997); Mabel Major and T. M. Pearce, *Southwest Heritage* (Albuquerque: University of New Mexico Press, 1972); Bruce Novoa, *Chicano Authors: Inquiry by Interview* (Austin: University of Texas Press, 1980); Miguel Antonio Otero, *The Real Billy the Kid, with New Light on the Lincoln County War* (New York: Rufus Rockwell Wilson, 1936); *Folktales of Mexico,* ed. Américo Paredes (Chicago: University of Chicago Press, 1970); Américo Paredes, *With His Pistol in His Hand* (Austin: University of Texas Press, 1958); Arthur G. Pettit, *Images of the Mexican American in Fiction and Film* (College Station: Texas A & M University Press, 1980); Robert Potter, "The Illegal Immigration of Medieval Drama to California," *Comparative Drama* 25, no. 1 (spring 1993): 140–56; Lawrence Clark Powell, *Southwest Classics* (Los Angeles: Ward Ritchie, 1974); Cecil Robinson, *With the Ears of Strangers* (Tempe: University of Arizona Press, 1963); Salvador Rodríguez del Pino, *La novela chicana escrita en Español: cinco autores comporetidos* (Ypsilanti, Mich.: Editorial Bilingüe, 1982); Kent L. Steckmesser, "Robin Hood and the American Outlaw: A Note on History and Folklore," *Journal of American Folklore* 79, no. 312 (1966): 348–54; Elaine Steinbek and Robert Wallsten, *Steinbeck: A Life in Letters* (Harmondsworth, England: Penguin, 1976); John Steinbeck, *Tortilla Flat* (New York: Grosset & Dunlap, 1935); Stanley T. Williams, *The Spanish Background of American Literature* (Hamden, Conn.: Archon, 1968); and Lyman L. Woodman, *Cortina, The Rogue of the Rio Grande* (San Antonio: Naylor, 1950).

A number of the observations regarding medieval architecture and its impact on the Borderlands derive from Trevor Beeson, *Westminster Abbey* (Barcelona: Escudo de Oro, 1984); Rafael Castejón y Martínez de Arizala, *La mezquita de Córdoba* (Madrid: Editorial Everest, 1984); Rafael Castejón y Martínez de Arizala, *Medina Azahara* (Madrid: Editorial Everest, 1977); A. C. Crombie, *Medieval and Early Modern Science* (Garden City, N.Y.: Doubleday Anchor Books, 1959); Jean-Pierre Foucher, *La Littérature Latine du moyen age* (Paris: Presses Universitaires de France, 1963); Bernard Gagnepain, *La Musique Fraçaise du moyen age et de la Renaissance* (Paris: Presses Universitaires de France, 1961); *Studies in Brownsville and Matamoros History,* ed. Milo Kearney, Anthony Knopp, and Antonio Zavaleta (Brownsville: University of Texas at Brownsville and Texas Southmost College, 1995); José Luis Monteverde, Tomás Borrás, and Ángel Oliveras Guart, *Monasterio de las Huelgas y Palacio de la Isla, de Burgos, y Monasterio de Santa Clara, de Tordesillas (Valladolid)* (Madrid: Editorial Patrimonio Nacional, n.d.); Fernand Niel, *Conaissance des Mégalithes* (Paris: Robert Laffont, 1976); Julián Pérez López, *La Catedral de Burgos* (Burgos: Artes Gráficas Santiago Rodríguez, 1985); Miguel Salcedo Hierro, *El Alcázar de los reyes Cristianos de Córdoba* (León: Editorial Everest, 1975); Luis Seco de Lucena Paredes, *La Alhambra de Granada* (León: Editorial Everest, 1977); and H. Philip Staats, *California Architecture in Santa Barbara* (Stamford, Conn.: Architectural Book Publishing, 1990).

The principal sources utilized for the section on medieval art and its imprint on the borderlands are George Bain, *Celtic Art: The Methods of Construction* (New York: Dover, 1973); Helen Gardner, *Art Through the Ages,* rev. ed. Horst de la Croix and Richard G. Tansey (New York: Harcourt Brace Jovanovich, 1980); Ernest Günther Grimme, *La Peinture médiévale en Europe* (Paris: Petite Bibliothèque Payot, n.d.); Jacinto Quirate, *Mexican-American Artists* (Austin: University of Texas Press, 1973); Willibald Sauerländer, *La Sculpture médiévale* (Paris: Petite Bibliotèque Payot, n.d.); Bradley Smith, *Spain: A History in Art* (Garden City, N.Y.: Doubleday, n.d.); Marilyn Stockstad, *Medieval Art* (New York: Harper & Row, 1986); and Antonio Viñayo, *La colegiata de San Isidoro-León* (Madrid: Editorial Everest, 1979).

The observations on medieval music and its continuing elements in Borderlands sounds are taken in part from *Albricias: colección de 38 himnos para congregaciones de habla Hispana* (New York: National Hispanic Office, 1987); Alfonso el Sabio, *Antología,* ed. Margarita Peña (México: Editorial Porrúa, 1976); Joseph Arbena, Henry Schmidt, and David Vassberg, *Regionalism and the Musical Heritage of Latin America* (Austin: Institute of Latin American Studies of the University of Texas at Austin, 1980); *Aurelii Prudentii Clementis carmina,* in *Corpus scriptorum ecclesiasticorum Latinorum,* vol. 61, ed. Joannes Bergman (Vienna: Hoelder-Pichler-Tempsky, 1926); *Religious Lyrics of the XVth Century,* ed. Carlton Brown (Oxford: Clarendon, 1967); Gilbert Chase, *The Music of Spain* (New York: Dover, 1959); Anwar G. Chejne, *Muslim Spain: Its History and Culture* (Minneapolis: University of Minnesota, 1974); *The Penguin Book of the Folk Ballads of the English-Speaking World,* ed. Albert B. Friedman (Harmondsworth, England, 1977); A. L. Lloyd, *Folk Song in England* (New York: International, 1967); Antonio Martín Moreno, *Historia de la música Andaluza* (Granada: Biblioteca de la Cultura Andaluza, 1985); Vicente T. Mendoza and Virginia R. R. de Mendoza, *Estudio y clasificación de la música tradicional Hispánica de Nuevo México* (México: Universidad Nacional Autónoma de México, 1986); *170 Christmas Songs and Carols,* ed. David C. Olsen (Hialeah, Fla.: Columbia Pictures Publications, 1983); Manuel Peña, *The Texas-Mexican Conjunto* (Austin: University of Texas Press, 1985); and Lota M. Spell, *Music in Texas: A Survey of One Aspect of Cultural Progress* (Austin: n.p., 1936).

The consideration of medieval dance and cooking influences on the Borderlands was informed by the Brownsville Junior Service League, *Beneath the Palms*

(Memphis: Wimmer Companies, 1996); S. Foster Damon, *The History of Square Dancing* (Barre, Mass.: Barre Gazette, 1957); *On the Border by The Sea* (Kansas City, Mo.: North American Press of K.C., 1968); Raymond Sokolov, "Bread and Water, Spanish Style," *Natural History Magazine* 97, no. 6 (June 1988); and *To The King's Taste: Richard II's Book of Feasts and Recipes,* adapted for modern cooking by Lorna J. Sass (New York: Metropolitan Museum of Art, 1975).

Chapter Six: The Development of Anglo-Hispanic Conflict

1. Carey McWilliams, *North from Mexico* (New York: Praeger Publishers, 1990), 98.

2. Ibid.

In addition to books listed previously, discussion of the general situation of Anglo-Castilian relations depended on information from Ernest Barker, *The Character of England* (Oxford: Clarendon, 1947); M. V. Clarke, *The Medieval City State* (Cambridge, England: Speculum Historiale, 1926); François L. Ganshof, *Histoire des relations internationales* (Paris: Hachette, 1953); Vicki León, *Uppity Women of Medieval Times* (New York: MJF Books, 1997); Jofré de Loaysa, *Crónica de los reyes de Castilla* (Murcia: Biblioteca Murciana de Bolsillo, 1982); James Lydon, *Ireland in the Later Middle Ages* (Dublin: Gill & Macmillan, 1973); Seumas MacManus, *The Story of the Irish Race: A Popular History of Ireland* (New York: The Devin-Adair Company, 1944); Armando Marques Guedes, *A Aliança Inglêsa: notas de história diplomática* (Lisboa: Editorial Enciclopedia, 1938); Henri Pirenne, *Economic and Social History of Medieval Europe* (New York: Harcourt, Brace, & World, 1937); N. A. M. Rodger, *The Safeguard of the Sea: A Naval History of Britain* (London: HarperCollins, 1997); and Julio Valdeón, *El reino de Castilla en la edad media* (Bilboa: Ediciones Moreton, 1968).

The consideration of the period down to the mid-fourteenth century found useful additional information in F. R. Cordero Carrete, "De los esponsales de una hija de Guillermo el Conquistador con un rey de Galicia," *Cuadernos de Estudios Gallegos* 7 (1952): 55–78; John Gillingham, *Richard the Lionheart* (London: Weidenfeld & Nicolson, 1978); Atilano González Ruiz-Zorilla, "Sobre la Restauración de la diócesis de Braga en 1070," *Hispania Sacra* 10 (1957): 431–42; Alan Lloyd, *The Maligned Monarch: A Life of King John of England* (Garden City, N.Y.: Doubleday, 1972); Kate Norgate, *Richard the Lion Heart* (New York: Russell & Russell, 1924); John Schlight, *Henry II Plantagenet* (New York: Twayne, 1973); Jean-Paul Trabut-Cussac, "Don Enrique de Castilla en Angleterre 1256–1259," *Mélanges de la casa de Velázquez,* vol. 2 (Paris: Éditions E. de Boccard, 1966).

Additional sources for the late fourteenth century include Barbara Emerson, *The Black Prince* (London: Weidenfeld & Nicolson, 1976); Anthony Goodman, *John of Gaunt: The Exercise of Princely Power in Fourteenth-Century Europe* (Harlow, England: Longman, 1992); John Gower, *Poema quod dicitur vox clamantis* (London: Roxburgh Society, G. Nicol, 1850); John Harvey, *The Black Prince and his Age* (Totowa, N.J.: Rowman & Littlefield, 1976); P. López de Ayala, *Las crónicas* (Zaragoza, Spain: Clásicos Ebro, 1974); Nigel Saul, *Richard II* (New Haven, Conn.: Yale University Press, 1997); Anil de Silva-Vigier, *This Moste Highe Prince John of Gaunt, 1340–1399* (Edinburgh: Pentland, 1992); and Luis Suárez-Fernández, *Juan I, rey de Castilla (1379–1390)* (Madrid: Revista de Occidente, 1955).

Descriptions of the situation in the fifteenth century are informed by S. B. Chrimes, *Henry VII* (London: Eyre Methuen, 1972); Richard Friedenthal, *Jan Hus: Der Ketzer und das Jahrhundert der Revolutionskriege* (Munich: Piper, 1984); Ralph A. Griffiths, *The Reign of King Henry VI: The Exercise of Royal Authority, 1422–1461* (Berkeley: University of California Press, 1981); Paul Murray Kendall, *Warwick: Le Faiseur de rois,* trans. Éric Diacon (Paris: Librairie Arthème Fayard, 1981); Charles Ross, *Edward IV* (London: Eyre Methuen, 1974); and Elaine Sanceau, *The Reign of the Fortunate King, 1495–1521* (Hamden, Conn.: Archon, 1969).

Consideration of Hispanic and Anglo concepts of each other by the end of the Middle Ages used the following additional sources: *Amadís de Gaula* (México: Editora Nacional, 1975); Haldeen Braddy, *Geoffrey Chaucer: Literary and Historical Studies* (Port Washington, N.Y.: Kennikat, 1971); Peter Brown and Andrew Butcher, *The Age of Saturn: Literature and History in the Canterbury Tales* (Cambridge, Mass.: Basil Blackwell, 1991); Thomas Malory, *The Works of Thomas Malory,* ed. Eugene Vinaver (Oxford: Clarendon, 1967); and Patricia Shaw, "The Presence of Spain in Middle English Literature," *Archiv für das Studium der Neueren Sprachen und Literaturen* 229 (1992): 50–53.

Discussion of transmission and reworking of the negative stereotypes and hostilities used the following sources in addition to those listed previously: Rodolfo Anaya, "Walt Whitman Strides the Llano of New Mexico," *The Anaya Reader* (New York: Warner Books, 1995); Gloria Anzaldua, *Borderlands / La Frontera* (San Francisco: Spinsters/Aunt Lute, 1987); *Audubon's Western Journals, 1849–1850: Being the M.S. Record of a Trip from New York to Texas and an Overland Journey through New Mexico and Arizona to the Gold Fields of California* (Cleveland: Arthur H. Clark, 1906); *Literatura Chicana,* ed. Antonio Castañeda Shuler, Tomás Ybarra-Frauto, and Joseph Sommers (Englewood Cliffs, N.J.: Prentice-Hall, 1972); Dwight L. Clarke, *Stephen Watts Kearny: Soldier of the West* (Norman: University of Oklahoma Press, 1961); Richard H. Dana, Jr., *Two Years Before the Mast,* ed. Thomas Philbrick (1840; reprint, Harmondsworth, England: Penguin American Library, 1981); Arnoldo de Leon, *Mexican-Americans in Texas, A Brief History* (Arlington Heights, Ill.: Harlan Davidson, 1993); Thomas Jefferson Farnham, *Life, Adventures and Travels in California* (New York, 1849); *The Personal Narrative of James O. Pattie of Kentucky,* ed. Timothy Flint (San Francisco: A. Roman, 1906); Sam S. Hall, *Big Foot Wallace: The King of the Lariat* (New York, 1882); Rolando Hinojosa, *Claros varones de belken / Fair Gentlemen of Belken County* (Tempe, Ariz.: Bilingual Press/Editorial Bilingüe, 1986); Howard Roberts Lamar, *The Far Southwest, 1846–1912: A Territorial History* (New Haven, Conn.: Yale University Press, 1966); *Bernard Lile* (Philadelphia: J. B. Lippencott, 1856); Matts S. Meier and Feliciano Ribera, *Mexican Americans / American Mexicans* (New York: Hill & Wang, 1993); H. L. Mencken, *The American Language, Supplement I* (New York: Knopf, 1948); David Montejano, *An-*

glos and Mexicans in the Making of Texas, 1836–1986 (Austin: University of Texas Press, 1987); *Narrative of the Texan Santa Fe Expedition* (London: Henry Washbourne, 1847); *Between the Conquests: Readings in the Early Chicano Experience,* ed. Michael Ornelas (Dubuque, Iowa: Kendall-Hunt, 1996); Américo Paredes, *George Washington Gómez* (Houston: Arte Público, 1991); Raymund Arthur Paredes, "The Image of the Mexican in American Literature," Ph.D. diss., University of Texas at Austin, 1973; *Piney Woods Tavern, or Sam Slick in Texas* (Philadelphia: T. B. Peterson & Brothers, 1858); W. T. Pritchard, "In the Backwoods of Mexico," *The Overland Monthly* 2 (June, 1869); Jerry D. Thompson, *Juan Cortina and the Texas-Mexican Frontier* (El Paso: Texas Western Press, University of Texas at El Paso, 1994); Saline R. Ulibarri, "The Stuffing of the Lord," *Tierra Amarilla* (Albuquerque: University of New Mexico Press, 1971); and *Corridos Mexicanos,* ed. Gilberto Vélez (México: Editores Mexicanos Unidos, 1982).

Conclusion

1. Translation from the written Anglo-Saxon original text by Mimosa Stephenson, taken from Milo Kearney and Ken Hogan, *The Historical Roots of Medieval Literature* (Lewiston, N.Y.: Edwin Mellen, 1992), 194.

The few additional books hitherto unquoted but used for the conclusion were *Bright's Anglo-Saxon Reader,* rev. ed. James R. Hulbert (New York: Holt, Rinehart, & Winston, 1961); *Las 323 adivinanzas mas famosas del idioma Castellano* (Madrid: Susaeta Ediciones, 1986); Logan Pearsall Smith, *Words and Idioms: Studies in the English Language* (Ann Arbor, Mich.: Gryphon, 1971); and Lewis Spence, *The History of Atlantis* (New York: Bell, 1968).

INDEX

ISBN 1-58544-132-5
90000
9 781585 441327